WOMEN IN A MEDIEVAL HERETICAL SECT

AGNES AND HUGUETTE THE WALDENSIANS

WOMEN IN A MEDIEVAL HERETICAL SECT

AGNES AND HUGUETTE THE WALDENSIANS

SHULAMITH SHAHAR

Translated by
YAEL LOTAN

THE BOYDELL PRESS

First published 2001

Published by The Boydell Press
an imprint of Boydell & Brewer Ltd
PO Box 9, Woodbridge, Suffolk IP12 3DF, UK
and of Boydell & Brewer Inc.
PO Box 41026, Rochester, NY 14604–4126, USA
website: http://www.boydell.co.uk

ISBN 0 85115 815 3

A catalogue record for this book is available
from the British Library

Library of Congress Cataloging-in-Publication Data
Shahar, Shulamith.
    Women in a medieval heretical sect : Agnes and Huguette
the Waldensians / Shulamith Shahar ; translated by Yael Lotan.
        p. cm.
    Includes bibliographical references and index.
    ISBN 0–85115–815–3 (alk. paper)
        1. Waldenses.   2. Franco, Agnes, d. 1320.   3. La Cote,
Huguette de, d. 1321.   4. Women in Christianity – France,
Southern – History – Middle Ages, 600–1500.   I. Title.
BX4881.3.S53 2001
272'.3'0922 – dc21   00–051861

This publication is printed on acid-free paper

Printed in Great Britain by
St Edmundsbury Press Ltd, Bury St Edmunds, Suffolk

Contents

'. . . if one asks, with whom the adherents of historicism actually empathize, the answer is inevitable: with the victor. And all rulers are the heirs of those who conquered before them. Hence, empathy with the victor invariably benefits the rulers . . . According to traditional practice, the spoils are carried along in the procession. They are called "cultural treasures" . . .'

Walter Benjamin, 'Theses on the Philosophy of History', VII

'Happy are they who sow and do not reap
for they shall wonder far afield.'

Avraham ben Yitzhak, 'Happy are They'

Introduction

In August 1319, during Bishop Jacques Fournier's first year as Inquisitor in Pamiers, in the County of Foix,[1] four of The Poor of Lyons (also known as Waldensians)[2] were arrested and jailed – two men and two women. Southern France had been since the last decades of the twelfth century one of the central locations of the expansion of The Poor of Lyons, but since their persecution by the Inquisition during the latter half of the thirteenth century their numbers in the region had been dwindling. Those who were not executed or imprisoned had migrated to other parts. In 1319 they were a mere smattering in the County of Foix, and not many in

---

1   The Papal Inquisition began to function in this region in the early 1240s, but not until Jacques Fournier's appointment as bishop did bishops act as Inquisitors. Following the Bull published by Pope Clement V (*Multorum querela*, 1312), which permitted bishops to act as Inquisitors, Jacques Fournier began to function as one, in cooperation with one or more representatives of the Inquisition court of Carcassonne. The court he established in Pamiers continued to function after he left, following his appointment as bishop of Mirepoix. But its activity became lukewarm. Pamiers was the centre of the diocese and the seat of the bishop. Some of the interrogations of the Inquisition during Jacques Fournier's tenure took place at the bishop's palace at Pamiers, which also contained a jail for short detentions.

2   The name Waldensians (Vaudois, Valdenses) was given by the Catholics, after the founder of the sect Valdés, or Vaudés, who began his activity in Lyons. The members of the sect called themselves the Poor of Lyons (*Pauperes de Lugduno*), or the Poor of Christ (*Pauperes Christi*). The Catholics also dubbed them the 'sandalled ones' (*Insabbatatorum, Sandaliati, Ensates*), because their spiritual leaders in the thirteenth century wore sandals. Later they wore shoes whose uppers were cut in the shape of sandals, or were marked with a sign like a shield. As their persecution intensified they avoided external marks. Hereafter the terms Waldensians and Poor of Lyons will be used interchangeably.

the south of France as a whole. The two men and two women who were arrested that year belonged to a tiny group, consisting of about a dozen men and women who gathered in Pamiers.[3]

Jacques Fournier did not send many condemned people to the stake. In the one extant volume of his register, five individuals are recorded as burnt at the stake. Like other Inquisitors, he sentenced people to prison; some of these were condemned to a 'narrow cell', a kind of cubicle in which the prisoner's legs were fettered and sometimes chained to the wall; others were given a 'wide cell', in which the prisoner could move about.[4] He ordered some to wear a yellow cross sewn onto their garment ('ordinary' – sewn on the back only, or 'double' – both front and back),[5] and many others were ordered to atone for their sins with fasts, prayers, pilgrimages to the shrines of saints, or alms to churches, monasteries and the poor.[6] Four of the people he condemned to

---

[3] Waldensians returned to Foix in 1344, when they were forced to flee from Toulouse. They scattered through Foix, Bearn and Aragon.

[4] Examples of the imposition of this penalty by Jacques Fournier may be found in *Liber sententiarum inquisitionis Tholosanae*, in *Historia inquisitionis*, ed. Ph. Van Limborch, Amsterdam, 1962, p. 287 (145b).

[5] For a description of the yellow crosses: *ibid.*, p. 286 (145). A woman of Narbonne sentenced to wear the yellow cross was forbidden to wear a dress of that color: *Quellen zur Geschichte der Waldenser*, eds A. Patschovsky and K.V. Selge, Göttingen, 1973, p. 64.

[6] Jacques Fournier's register held three volumes, of which only one remains extant. Of the eighty-nine condemned mentioned in this volume, five were burnt at the stake, fourteen were sentenced to life imprisonment, thirty-two spent one to five years in prison, after which their sentence was commuted to the obligation to wear the yellow cross; seven were ordered to wear it directly. The remainder were ordered to atone with pilgrimages, prayers and the like. A similar ratio between the number of those handed over to the 'secular arm' – i.e. sentenced to be burnt at the stake – and those given other punishments, is typical of the sentences meted out by most of the other Inquisitors in the South of France. Being a Church court, the Inquisition was not empowered to sentence people to death. Therefore when a condemned person was turned over to the 'secular arm', a formal appeal was attached to spare his life and limbs that the Inquisitors were constrained by canon law to include. All other penalties, including life imprisonment, were considered not punishments

the stake were the Waldensians arrested in 1319.[7] Two of them, Raymond de la Côte and Agnes Franco, were burnt at the stake on May 1, 1320, after some nine months of imprisonment and interrogation. The other two, Huguette de la Côte and her husband Jean of Vienne, were burnt at the stake after two years of imprisonment and interrogation, on August 2, 1321.

The reaction to the burning of Raymond and Agnes may be deduced from the records of Jacques Fournier's court, where two people were tried for things they said following the execution. The event was a subject of talk at the inn in Pamiers and under the elm tree in the square at Ornolac. Witnesses reported that a customer at the inn related that when Raymond was at the stake and the ropes binding his arms had burned away, he folded his hands together, raised them to heaven as if in prayer and entrusted his soul to God. According to the witness, when the accused heard this he said that it was not possible that a man who called on God and the Holy Virgin and prayed while being burnt at the stake could be a heretic. If he entrusted his soul to God,

but ways of atonement, with this distinction, that it was imposed by judicial sanction. Dossat's research has shown that in the region of Lauragais seven percent of 306 individuals on trial were sent to the stake, two percent lapsed and were also burnt, the remainder were sentenced to imprisonment or other forms of atonement: Y. Dossat, *Les crises de l'inquisition toulousaine au XIIIe siècle (1233–1273)*, Bordaux, 1959, pp. 265–267. Bernard Gui sent to the stake, between 1308 and 1323, forty-two out of 930 condemned. Three more were supposed to be burnt but managed to escape: *Heresies of the High Middle Ages*, ed. and trans. W.L. Wakefield and A.P. Evans, New York, 1969, p. 374 and note 3; A. Pales Gobillard, 'Bernard Gui, inquisiteur et auteur de la Practica', in *Bernard Gui et son monde. Cahiers de Fanjeaux* 16 (1981), pp. 262–263. Some of those sentenced to be imprisoned, mainly to the 'narrow cell', died while incarcerated, but many had their term shortened, another form of atonement imposed, and generally had some of the confiscated property restored to them: B. Hamilton, *The Medieval Inquisition*, London, 1981, p. 57.

7 The fifth was a Cathar from Montaillou who recanted, but relapsed and was then burnt at the stake: *Le registre de l'inquisition de Jacques Fournier, évêque de Pamiers (1318–1325)*, ed. J. Duvernoy, Toulouse, 1965, Vol. I, pp. 442–454, hereafter *Le registre*; *Liber sententiarum*, pp. 289–291 (146b–147b).

God must have accepted and treasured it. The witnesses further reported that when the accused heard a customer stating that Jacques Fournier was a good bishop, who wept and mourned when Raymond refused to recant, he rejected this statement out of hand and said that Raymond and Agnes had been good Christians, which was why they were burnt at the stake. The other accused also said, according to the witnesses, that Raymond had been a good Christian, and that it was a great injustice to send him to the stake. Even more explicitly than the former accused, he expressed sympathy with some of the beliefs attributed to Raymond, and referred to Jacques Fournier in even harsher terms. The witnesses reported him saying that rather than Raymond and Agnes, it would have been more appropriate to burn him, who collected tithes not only from field crops, but even from the locally bred cattle (in violation of local customs).[8] At their trial the two accused recanted some of their statements and even denied some of the charges. The first accused was sentenced to imprisonment and was jailed for over a year, and when he was released, was made to wear the yellow cross.[9] This was a mark of humiliation and exposed the branded person to provocations and to possible ostracism by the Catholic faithful, or even by the less faithful who feared the long arm of the Inquisition. The other accused, who also denounced the tithes and was charged with holding Cathar beliefs, was sentenced to a long period in prison, and served nine years. He too, upon his release, was obliged to wear the yellow cross.[10] According to the witnesses, the two men had also referred to the execution of Agnes, but spoke mainly about Raymond. There may have been men and women who voiced regret about the execution of Huguette and her husband Jean, or sympathy for them, but they were more cautious, and

8 In 1323 Jacques Fournier concluded an agreement with the inhabitants of the Savartès regarding the tithes they would have to pay on locally bred cattle and on wool shearing: J.F. Lemarignier, J. Gaudemet and G. Mollat, *Institutions ecclésiastiques*, in F. Lot and R. Fawtier eds, *Histoire des institutions françaises au moyen-âge*, Vol. III, Paris, 1962, pp. 374–375.
9 The trial of Berenger Escoulan: *Le registre*, Vol. I, pp. 169–176.
10 The trial of Guillaume Austatz: *Le registre*, Vol. I, pp. 191–213.

whatever did not reach the Inquisitor's ears has not come down to us.

Raymond de la Côte's testimony was already used by a contemporary. In his manual for Inquisitors, Bernard Gui used the testimonies taken by him and other Inquisitors,[11] and his description of the clerical hierarchy among The Poor of Lyons was based on the testimony of Raymond.[12] But that testimony has been used mainly by modern historians of The Poor of Lyons. Since the late nineteenth century historians have referred to it, used it to describe and analyse the sect's beliefs and rituals, published portions of it (before the publication of the register), and translated some of it.[13] It is not surprising. Raymond de la Côte was an

---

[11] For the Inquisitors' manuals and their various sources (in addition to the testimonies given by accused persons), e.g. decisions of Church Councils, jurists opinions, papal decrees etc.: A. Dondaine O.P., 'Le manuel de l'inquisiteur (1230–1330)', *Archivum Fratrum Praedicatorum* 17 (1947), pp. 85–194.

[12] Bernard Gui, *Manuel de l'Inquisiteur*, ed. and trans. G. Mollat, Paris, 1964, Vol. I, pp. XVII, 46, 148–152. Bernard Gui was a theologian, jurist, historian and Inquisitor. Between 1308 and 1324 he was Inquisitor of Toulouse, and in the years 1316–1323 he especially hounded the Waldensians. It was he who managed to uproot their communities from Toulouse and the regions of Rouergue and Astrac, which had been formed mainly in 1273–1275 by immigrants from the Franche-Comté and Burgundy. The title of his manual was *Practica officii Inquisitionis pravitatis*. It is based on testimonies obtained by himself and other Inquisitors, as well as other sources (see Note 11). This manual reveals what the Inquisitors knew about the various heretical movements, and what they considered the most efficient way of interrogating people suspected of belonging to them. He finished writing the manual in 1323–1324, that is several years after Raymond and the other three Waldensians were burnt at the stake.

[13] J.J. Ign. von Döllinger, ed., *Beiträge zur Sektengeschichte des Mittelalters*, Munich, 1890, Vol. II, pp. 97–143; Mgr. Douais, ed., *Documents pour servir à l'histoire de l'inquisition dans le Languedoc*, Paris, 1900, Vol. I, pp. CVI–CVII; J.M. Vidal, *Le tribunal d'Inquisition à Pamiers*, Toulouse, 1906, pp. 129–135; J. Duvernoy, ed. and trans., *L'Inquisition de Pamiers*, Toulouse, 1966, pp. 19–31; *Quellen zur Geschichte der Waldenser*, eds Patschovsky and K.V. Selge, Göttingen, 1973, pp. 104–106; J. Gonnet and A. Molnar, *Les Vaudois au moyen âge*, Turin, 1974, pp. 191, 205, 422; G.G. Merlo, 'Sul Valdismo "colto" tra il XIII e il XIV secolo', in

educated Waldensian deacon, who had acquired at his first school the elements of Latin philology as part of the *trivium*, and later studied at the Franciscan school of theology in Montpellier. He was taken from prison for questioning no less than twenty-four times, and there is no question that the record of his interrogation, spreading over eighty-one pages in the printed register,[14] is a major source for The Poor of Lyons in the second decade of the fourteenth century in the south of France. By contrast, there has been scarcely any reference to the testimonies of the other three Waldensians.[15] This, despite the fact that there are very few

I Valdesi e l'Europa, Collana della Società di Studi Valdesi 9, Torre Pellice, 1982, pp. 69–98; P. Segl, *Ketzer in Österreich. Untersuchungen über Häresie und Inquisition im Herzogtum Österreich im 13 und beginnen den 14 Jahrhundert*, Paderborn, 1984, p. 322 and note 244; G. Audisio, *Les 'Vaudois'. Naissance, vie et mort d'une dissidence (XIIe–XVIe siècles)*, Turin, 1989, pp. 52–53, 120, 127, 158, 167; A. Patschovsky, 'The Literacy of Waldensianism from Valdes to c. 1400', in *Heresy and Literacy 1000–1350*, eds P. Biller and A. Hudson, Cambridge, 1994, pp. 112–136.

[14] La registre, Vol. I, pp. 40–122; about his education: *ibid.*, pp. 99, 102.

[15] Döllinger, who published almost the whole of Raymond's interrogation, published only a very small excerpt from the interrogation of Jean of Vienne, and an even smaller one from that of Huguette: J.J. Ign. von Döllinger, *op. cit.*, Vol. I, pp. 143–144. Vidal states that all four testimonies are highly detailed and lively, but his analysis refers almost exclusively to that of Raymond: J.M. Vidal, *op. cit.* To the best of my knowledge, of present-day historians only Peter Biller has made use of the women's testimonies in certain matters: P. Biller, 'Medieval Waldensian Abhorrence of Killing pre c. 1400', in *The Church and War*, ed. W.J. Sheils, *Studies in Church History* 20 (1983), p. 133, note 23, p. 140; P. Biller, ' "Thesaurus Absconditus": The Hidden Treasure of the Waldensians', in *The Church and Wealth*, eds W.J. Sheils and D. Wood, *Studies in Church History* 24 (1987), p. 148; P. Biller, 'The Preaching of the Waldensian Sisters', manuscript to appear in *La prédication sur un mode dissident: laics femmes, hérétiques (XIe–XIVe siècles)*, Actes de la 9e session d'histoire mediévale organisée par le C.N.E.C./R. Nelli, 26–30 août 1966, ed. M.B. Kienzle, Carcassonne, forthcoming, notes 24, 68; Paravy refers briefly to the testimonies of Agnes and Huguette in her study of the trial of the four Waldensians, but mainly to the testimony of Raymond: P. Paravy, *De la chrétienité romaine à la Réforme en Dauphiné*, Rome, 1993, Vol. II, pp. 922–926.

sources relating to the female Poor of Lyons, and that the quality and relatively detailed testimonies of the two women make possible even partial biographies, and add up to a rare source about two individual women as part of the history of the sect, and could help clarify the position and status of women in the sect as a whole. The testimony of the other man, Jean of Vienne, Huguette's husband, makes it possible to compare the ways of inculcating the beliefs, their absorption and the commitment to them by husband and wife of similar social background, who had to contend with the same existential problems as a couple, and later with imprisonment and Inquisitorial questioning. The transcript of the interrogation of the two women, a translation of which is given in the appendix, served as my point of departure for the present book.

This study seeks to examine the position of women in The Poor of Lyons sect, a persecuted minority whose female members – being marginalized in the general society – were thus doubly marginalized as women and as heretics (the world heretic takes a female form – *heretica*). I shall also explore the manner in which they were regarded and treated by the Inquisition. I have tried to examine the attitude, in theory and in practice, of The Poor of Lyons towards the women who joined the sect in its early days, a period in which researchers believed that women enjoyed equality with men within the sect (until the publication of G. Merlo's article in 1991[16]); the position of 'sisters' as compared to that of the 'brothers' after the division, towards the end of the second decade of the thirteenth century, between 'brothers' and 'sisters' and 'believers' (male and female); the position and roles of the female 'believers' versus those of the male ones, and the suspension of the gender identification of individuals charged with heresy by the Inquisitors. I have also attempted to answer the question of whether the women who joined the sect developed a distinctive self-identity.

In light of the above, this is clearly a book about the women

---

[16] G.G. Merlo, 'Sulle "misere donnicciuole" che predicavano', *Identita Valdesi nella storia e nella storiografia, Valdesi e Valdismi medievali II*, Turin, 1991, pp. 92–112.

Waldensians. Had women been included in the leading narratives about The Poor of Lyons there would have been no justification for it. The question of the position of women in ideology and reality – whether The Poor of Lyons regarded the equality of the sexes as a tenet, as did certain other sects, whether at some stage in the sect's history women enjoyed equality with the men, or if there was merely some softening of the polarization between their respective positions, and similar questions discussed in the book – would have been readily answered if they had been included in the narrative. Peter Biller, the historian whose articles dealt with specific issues concerning the sect, including the women in his analyses, and who also devoted articles to the 'sisters', has already noted that as a rule women are discussed in a few lines, when not confined to footnotes.[17] The inclusion of women as an integral part of the narrative would not just have contributed to the history of women in one of the main sects in the Middle Ages and the gender relations within it. Today it is widely accepted that it is impossible to discuss the history of the economy and of labour in medieval society, when many lived on the edge of subsistence and could hardly forgo the labour force of half its members, namely the women, without discussing their role in production and economic life. In the same way, it is impossible to discuss a sect whose membership was voluntary, whose existence was secret and depended on the women's cooperation for its survival, without reference to the role women played in its history. Incorporating them might not have created an antithesis to the hegemonic historical narrative, but would have revealed an important element in the sect's way of life, its identity and experience. However, there are in existence scholarly syntheses concerning The Poor of Lyons, and I have made no attempt to add a new synthesis. I have concentrated on the history of women in the sect, and references to the men, including the testimonies of Raymond

---

17 P. Biller, 'The Oral and the Written: The case of the Alpine Waldensians', *Bulletin for the Society for Renaissance Studies* 4 (1986), p. 28 and note 14. Other articles by Biller and some by other historians on the subject of women are mentioned in the notes to the following chapters and in the bibliography.

de la Côte and Jean of Vienne, are brought in mainly to clarify matters affecting the women. Thus the first chapter, devoted to a brief summary of the history of The Poor of Lyons, is meant to serve as the basis and background for their position in the community and to place it in its historical context.

Like all historical sources, the records of the courts of the Inquisition are not without their particular limitations and problems. Historians have already noted these, as well as the distinctive methods of interrogation that Jacques Fournier applied to the persons brought before him. These aspects should be briefly dealt with, seeing that the records of the Inquisition are among the principal sources for The Poor of Lyons, in general, and the four who were arrested were interrogated by Jacques Fournier. Historians agree that no speech truly reflects the speaking 'I', even when it is an 'authentic' voice, and the voices of the individuals interrogated by the Inquisition are certainly not 'authentic'. They reach us via the notary or the court clerk. The accused spoke in the vernacular of their region (in the South of France this was the Occitan tongue or one of its dialects), and the notary or clerk took it down in Latin. Evidently they often wrote down only those of the questions and answers which seemed to them central and significant. The transcript was not written in the form of first-person questions and answers, but in the third-person, which also distorts the original expression. No doubt some of the translators and recorders also put in the mouths of men and women being questioned theological terms which they did not use.[18] Not only did they translate their statements into Latin, they also translated terms taken from the vocabulary of the community to which the questioned person belonged into terms from the Catholic vocabulary; and when they used a term employed by the Catholic clergy, it could have had a different meaning in the textual community to which the accused person belonged. The leading questions put by the Inquisitors, relying on the manuals that were based on the *topos* of the heretic of that sect, in its formulaic version, sometimes

---

[18] L.E. Boyle O.P., 'Montaillou Revisited: *Mentalité* and Methodology', in *Pathways to Medieval Peasants*, ed. J.A. Raftis, Papers in Medieval Studies 2, Toronto, 1981, pp. 119–140.

INTRODUCTION

led to the accused confessing to things they did not believe in, and
to similar responses which might give the impression of more
uniform and consistent faith and custom than they were in reality.
Finally, the exchange between the Inquisitor and the person being
questioned was scarcely a free dialogue. The power was in the
hands of the interrogator, especially if the person before him was
already jailed and was brought repeatedly from prison.[19] On the
other hand, the court records do not suffer from the limitations
and problems, which characterize polemical writings, chronicles
and literary sources.[20] The text of the records is not only the story
or the whole story of the persons questioned. It is certainly not
the whole 'truth' about them, but only such 'truth' as was uncov-
ered in process of the interrogation, whose relationship to the
'truth' about them was uneven, due to the various methods used
by the Inquisitors, and the personal differences among the individuals questioned. Yet the written record is dry and matter-of-
fact, free from stylistic devices and rhetorical strategies, its
purpose being pragmatic and for internal use, rather than didactic
or propagandistic. Let us move on to Jacques Fournier.

Jacques Fournier was born in the region in which he would
serve as an Inquisitor. He was born in Saverdun in northern Foix.
Therefore, unlike most of the other Inquisitors who were sent to
the region, he knew the Occitan language. He maintained good
terms with the Count of Foix and the King of France, which
enabled him to function without hindrance. His interrogations
were conducted in strict observance of the legal process in accordance with canon law and the accepted forms. He conducted most
of the interrogations himself, and unlike some other Inquisitors,
did not allow his notaries to conduct them on his behalf. He was
no respecter of persons and did not take bribes, and apparently
resorted to torture only once. The questions he put to the four

19 R. Rosaldo, 'From the Door of his Tent: The Fieldworker and the
Inquisitor', in *Writing Culture. The Poetics and Politics of Ethnography*, eds
J. Clifford and G.E. Marcus, Berkeley, 1984, pp. 77–97, mainly pp.
78–82.
20 For an analysis of distortion in the chronicles and its causes, see: P.
Strohm, ' "A Revelle!" Chronicle Evidence and the Rebel Voice', in
Hochon's Arrow, Princeton, 1992, pp. 33–56.

Poor of Lyons regarding the beliefs, rituals and hierarchy of their sect, as much as the questions concerning the individuals them-selves – when he or she joined the sect, who brought them to it, who were their fellow sectarians – were the kind that any Inquisitor was bound to put to persons suspected of belonging to that sect in accordance with the manuals, such as that of Bernard Gui,[21] Fournier's contemporary, and to match the list of questions composed by Peter Zwicker, who served as Inquisitor in Stettin, Austria and Hungary some seventy years later.[22] He was deter-mined to obtain answers to his questions. If the answers he got in one session did not satisfy him, because he thought they were untruthful, contradictory or partial, he repeated them in subse-quent sessions. Sometimes when he seemed to have obtained a full and truthful answer to his question, he nevertheless put it again in the next session in order to verify that the accused had indeed answered truthfully and fully. But although the questions in the manuals were based on information about The Poor of Lyons already gathered by the Inquisitors, he sometimes asked additional questions that did not appear in the manuals. These, as well as his sharp perception, enabled him to discover the extent of the accused person's knowledge, at what level the investigation might be conducted (to Raymond he quoted at length from the Scriptures and the Church Fathers in the original Latin to show him his errors),[23] how strong was his or her commitment to the sect, and even to understand the individual's personality.[24] Some

21 See note 12.
22 Peter Zwicker was a Celestine monk from Bohemia. He served as Inquisitor in Stettin, on the Baltic coast, and was later sent to serve in Austria and Hungary. He functioned as Inquisitor for at least thirteen years (1391–1404), and was familiar with the Poor of Lyons. His list of questions: *Quellen zur Ketzergeschichte Brandenburgs und Pommerns*, ed. D. Kurze, Berlin, 1975, pp. 73–75. He also wrote a polemic against them, entitled *Cum dormirent homines*.
23 *Le registre*, Vol. I, p. 112; 'in originali . . .'
24 About Jacques Fournier the Inquisitor and the rest of his career as bishop of Mirepoix, cardinal and later as Pope Benedict XII, see: J.M. Vidal, *Histoire des évêques de Pamiers II. Quatorzième et quinzième siècles (1312–1467)*, Castillon (Ariège), 1932, pp. 19–46; *Le registre*, Vol. I, pp. 18–20; E. Le Roy Ladurie, *Montaillou. Village occitan de 1294 à 1324*,

historians explain Jacques Fournier's method by suggesting that, more than other Inquisitors, he sought to bring the accused to recant. Comparing Jacques Fournier and Bernard Gui, Raoul Manselli states that whereas the latter was interested only in the judicial aspect of his role, that is to say, to discover if the person being interrogated was guilty or not, and to punish the guilty, the former sought above all to bring the accused to recant, thereby to save their souls.[25] (We have seen that one of the customers at the inn who talked about the execution of Raymond and Agnes said that Jacques Fournier was sorrowful about Raymond's refusal to recant.) For this reason he attempted to discover the source of the accused person's 'error', to find out in what circumstances and for what reasons he or she adopted heretical beliefs, to understand their thinking and the psychological context in which they formed their religious worldview. It is of course possible that his unusually strong desire to cause the accused to recant was the reason for Jacques Fournier's method of interrogation, but it is not certain. Without doubt, he repeatedly urged his accused to recant, but it is also possible that he was impelled by greater curiosity than other Inquisitors, and was more interested in human nature and the formation of beliefs. (This might be so, despite Michel Foucault's argument that prior to the nineteenth century judges took no interest in the offender's personality, and that the question was a modern innovation.[26]) Whatever the reason, he certainly put questions that other Inquisitors did not, and therefore the

Paris, 1975, pp. 10–19. After Jacques Fournier left Pamiers in 1326, the court in that town did not exhibit the same diligence it had in his time. But he himself continued to engage in the work of the Inquisition in later years, as bishop of Mirepoix, as cardinal and as pope. He was especially active in the persecution of the Waldensians in the Dauphiné region: P. Paravy, op. cit., Vol. II, p. 947.

25 R. Manselli, 'Bernard Gui face aux Spirituels et aux Apostoliques', in Bernard Gui et son monde. Cahiers de Fanjeaux 16 (1981), pp. 265–267; such is also the opinion of M. Benad, Domus und Religion in Montaillou, Spätmittelalter und Reformation Neue Reihe 1, Tübingen, 1990, p. 12.

26 M. Foucault, 'Prison Talk', in M. Foucault, Power and Knowledge. Selected Interviews and Other Writings, ed. C. Gordon, trans. C. Gordon and others, New York, 1980, p. 49.

answers he obtained serve as a source not only for their religious beliefs and customs, but also for their social background, ways of thinking, self-image and sometimes even their existential experiences.

It is a sad irony that the records of the Inquisition, the body which caused so much suffering in its time, should be such a valuable source for the historian that every new discovery of such material should be a cause for rejoicing. During the centuries of its activity it caused immense suffering by sending people to the stake (though in smaller numbers than past historians credited), imprisoning them in the 'narrow cell' or even the 'wide cell', confiscations of property, the imposition of the yellow cross, the atmosphere of fear and suspicion it created, and the way it exploited and intensified the existing political, social and familial tensions.[27] Yet for the historian its records are an extraordinary source in which may be heard, if limited and distorted, the voices of the lower levels of society, speaking also about aspects of life which other sources do not reveal, including those in which the people themselves speak (such as the records of secular or Church courts in which ordinary people sued or were prosecuted). It is also unquestionably the main source for the women members of The Poor of Lyons, and the sole one for individual women identified by name.

The Poor of Lyons, the only sect which survived until the Reformation, when it united with the Calvinists, have been a subject of research for some time. Additional sources have been published in recent decades, as well as an impressive series of studies which served to modify certain notions concerning that sect. Only the women of the sect have not yet been given their proper place. The first chapter, as stated before, is a brief summary, and inevitably somewhat schematic, chiefly about the period up to and including the fourteenth century, without going into the differences that arose between the communities in various regions.

[27] J.B. Given, 'Social Stress, Social Strain and the Inquisitors of Medieval Languedoc', in *Christendom and its Discontents. Exclusion, Persecution and Rebellion 1000–1500*, eds S.L. Waugh and P.D. Diehl, Cambridge, 1996, pp. 67–85.

1

The Poor of Lyons

The beginnings of The Poor of Lyons (or Waldensians)[1] lie in the late 1170s, when a man by name of Waldes (to whom in the fourteenth century would be added the Christian name Peter), a wealthy burgher of Lyons, who had made his fortune in commerce and finance, experienced a religious conversion, distributed his property to the poor as commanded by the Gospels, and began to preach voluntary poverty, a life in the spirit of the Gospels and penitence. Neither Waldes nor his first disciples launched a new theology or sought to leave the Catholic Church. All they wanted was to live in poverty, to wander and preach the Gospel. Right from the start, Waldes commissioned a translation of the New Testament, some parts of the Old Testament and portions from the writings of the Church Fathers,[2] to

---

1 See note 2, Introduction.
2 This was a French translation; later The Poor of Lyons had the texts translated into German and other languages. For the first translation, see: Etienne de Bourbon, *Tractatus de diversis materiis praedicabilis*, in *Anecdotes historiques, légendes et apologues tirés du recueil inédit d'Etienne de Bourbon*, ed. A. Lecoy de la Marche, Paris, 1877, pp. 290–291; the chronicler Aubri of Trois-Fontaines described the burning of translations from Latin into Waldensians' Romance language, and expressed the hope that thereby the sect would be utterly devastated: *Chronica Albrici monachi Trium Fontium*, in *M.G.H. Scriptores*, Vol. 23, ed. G.H. Pertz, Hanover, 1874, p. 878. A translation of the Scriptures for the use of a highly placed individual aroused no objections, but the Church categorically objected to the dissemination of such translations among the laity.

make them accessible to every Christian who wished to know the will of God. Thus he and his disciples could read these texts aloud in a language understood by their audience, and to preach accordingly in the vernacular. The Church failed to adopt The Poor of Lyons and use them to its purpose, as it would later do with the Franciscans. At the Third Lateran Council (1179), Pope Alexander III praised Waldes for his voluntary adoption of poverty, but refused to allow him to preach without the permission of the bishop of his diocese. This permission was not given. Waldes and his disciples continued to preach without permission, and in 1182 they were expelled from Lyons. The duty to preach was a central tenet of the faith and the consciousness of their mission for The Poor of Lyons, as spelled out in the Epistle of St James, 4:17: 'Therefore to him that knoweth to do good and doeth it not, to him it is sin.' Just as they could not renounce the ideal of voluntary and complete poverty (which the Church interpreted as advice to those wishing to live the perfect life, rather than a commandment), so they could not forgo preaching.[3] At the Church Council of Verona (1184) they were denounced as disobedient and were excommunicated, and at the Fourth Lateran Council (1215) they were condemned as heretics and irreversibly excommunicated.

But they were not yet persecuted. Until the second crusade against the Cathars (1229), the Church regarded the latter as its main enemies and most immediate danger, rather than The Poor of Lyons, for all their disobedience and defiance of the clergy's monopoly over the written and spoken word. Moreover, The Poor of Lyons rejected the Cathars' beliefs and rites no less than did the Catholic Church.[4] They preached against the Cathars, disputed with them in public, and one of them, Durand Osca,

---

[3] Regarding the question, what was Waldes' primary motive – the adoption of the principle of voluntary poverty or preaching – see: G. Gonnet, 'I primi Valdesi erano veramente eretici?' Bolletino della Società di Studi Valdesi 122 (1968), pp. 7–17.

[4] In his testimony at the end of the 1310s, Raymond de la Côte still expressed enmity for the Cathars, and supported their persecution by the Church: Le registre, Vol. I, pp. 73, 103.

even composed a religious work containing a strong polemic against the Cathars.[5] In some towns in the South of France they openly maintained their own hospitals, schools and cemeteries until the end of the 1230s,[6] and occasionally still preached in public. Then came the change – The Poor of Lyons became themselves an object of persecution by the Inquisition as it began to strike root in the region. Preaching in the town squares and public disputes were at an end. The Poor of Lyons moved underground and from that time until the Reformation conducted their communal life in secret in the homes of the faithful. Having been put outside the camp, they gradually organized into a separate church, set up their own clerical hierarchy, and, powered by the dynamic of a dissenting movement and ideas adopted from other heretical groups, they gradually deviated from the Catholic ritual and some of the Catholic beliefs. But even then they did not develop a new, systematic theology. They acknowledged the seven principles of the Catholic faith and the seven sacraments, and as we shall see, did not cut themselves off completely from the

---

5 Durand Osca, *Liber antiheresis*, in *Die Ersten Waldenser*, ed. K.V. Selge, Berlin, 1967, Vol. 2. Durand, a disciple of Waldes, wrote the book between 1190 and 1194, when he was still a Waldensian. In it he attacks the Cathars and offers an apologia for The Poor of Lyons, who believe in the universal right to preach, and do not work but subsist on alms. He also criticized the priests inter alia for disregarding the duty of preaching. Theologically speaking, this is a purely orthodox document, except for its negation of the belief in predestination: *ibid.*, pp. 83–93. In 1208 Durand reverted to Catholicism together with some of his companions, and thereafter disputed with the Cathars as a Catholic. He even put together a number of 'distinctions' for popular sermons against heretics. See: M.A. Rouse and R.H. Rouse, 'The Schools and the Waldensians: A New Work by Durand of Huesca', in *Christendom and its Discontents. Exclusion, Persecution and Rebellion 1000–1500*, eds S.L. Waugh and P.D. Diehl, Cambridge 1996, pp. 86–111.

6 So it was in the years 1241–1242 in Montauban, Gourdon, Moissac, Beaucaire and Castelnau. See: H.Ch. Lea, *A History of the Inquisition of the Middle Ages*, New York, 1906, Vol. II, Appendix X, pp. 579–582; J. Duvernoy, 'À l'époque l'eglise ne poursuivait pas les Vaudois', in *I Valdesi e l'Europa*, Collana de la Società di Studi Valdesi 9, Torre Pellice, 1982, pp. 27–38.

Catholic Church, and their attitude towards it remained ambiva-
lent. But the Church, which had felt under threat since the late
twelfth century and sought to define clear boundaries and to
expel the various deviates from the camp of the orthodox 'us', put
them also beyond the pale of legitimacy.

The Poor of Lyons spread over a considerable area. After the
expulsion from Lyons they moved south to the Dauphiné and
Provence, and thence to Languedoc, Gascony and Catalonia. At
the same time they spread north along the river Saône to Alsace
and Lotharingia, and thence eastward to other parts of Germany,
to Austria, Bohemia and Moravia, and as far north as the Baltic. In
Italy they spread to Lombardy, the south and Sicily, and especially
in the Alpine valleys of Piedmont (whence demographic pressure
pushed many of them in 1470–1510 to the Luberon valley in
Provence). This expansion halted about 1300. The existence of
such far-flung communities speaking different languages, living in
secrecy and without an overall central organization, impeded the
contacts between them. Though they held annual conferences of
communal representatives, only some of the regions were able to
send delegates. Thus there is no doubt that in the course of the
years certain differences of custom and ritual arose between the
diverse communities, differences which stemmed from the
sermons and instruction of the leadership, which were not identical in every aspect, due to the influence of contemporary local
sects as well as popular local beliefs. By the fourteenth century the
sect was certainly no longer homogeneous, though the basic
tenets and principal moral precepts were common to all. During
the fifteenth century, the short-lived triumph of the Hussites in
Bohemia revived the hopes of The Poor of Lyons, which had been
at a low ebb since their descent underground, to spread the
universal tidings. They moved freely in Bohemia, collaborated
with the Hussites, whom they influenced (particularly the
Taborite element), and were influenced by them in turn. But the
suppression of the Hussites put an end to their hopes.[7] Being an

---

[7] Regarding the Waldensians in Bohemia in the time of the Hussites,
see: G. Gonnet and A. Molnar, *Les Vaudois au Moyen Age*, Turin, 1974,
ch. 5.

underground movement inevitably restricted the missionary work of The Poor of Lyons. Waldensian men married Waldensian women, and membership of the sect passed chiefly in families, from parents to offspring. Nevertheless, a certain number of men and women whose parents had not been Waldensians continued to join the sect.

The persecution and the transformation to underground conditions also caused a gradual change in the social makeup of the faithful. Before the mid-thirteenth century The Poor of Lyons functioned chiefly in the cities among more-or-less prosperous burghers as well as the petty artisans. The ideal of voluntary poverty promoted by Waldes and his disciples spread in the cities with their money economy, with their conspicuous new wealth and obvious contrast between rich and poor. It was no accident that the cities were also the centres of activity of the new thirteenth-century orders, the Franciscans and the Dominicans. When the Inquisition stepped up the persecution, when it was no longer possible to preach before large crowds in the city square, the Waldensians began to transfer their main activity to the small towns and villages, and thereafter most of their followers were artisans – tailors, weavers, carpenters, smiths, barbers, various journeymen, and above all farmers, among them prosperous ones who supported them financially. An anonymous writer of the late thirteenth century wrote that the Brothers (i.e. the spiritual leaders) visit the homes of the faithful in order to preach to them and hear their confessions, especially in winter, since as peasants they have more leisure in that season.[8] But in some regions, even in the fourteenth century, occasionally royal or seniorial officers, lower-echelon clerics, but mainly prosperous merchants, joined the sect. The Dominican Inquisitor known as the Anonymous of Passau wrote in the 1260s that though their *doctores* are weavers and cobblers, they do manage to attract successful merchants. In Strasbourg and Augsburg, as well as in other German cities, there were in the thirteenth and fourteenth centuries prosperous

8 *De vita et actibus*, in *Beiträge zur Sektengeschichte des Mittelalters*, ed. J.J. Ign von Döllinger, Munich 1890, Vol. II, p. 97.

leather and cloth merchants who belonged to the sect, and in Berne and Fribourg at the end of the fourteenth century, alongside the well-off merchants, there were also some highly placed municipal officers.[9] A Waldensian man who recanted was ordered to give to charity the same amount he had formerly donated to the Brothers.[10]

I have said that The Poor of Lyons did not develop their own systematic theology. It was the ecclesiastical bureaucrats who exaggerated the threat represented by the sect and ascribed to it a doctrine that was more structured, consistent and shared by all the communities than it was in reality.[11] Their own scanty writings presented their doctrine piecemeal and sometimes indirectly. Which of their deviations from Catholicism may be deduced from Catholic sources, from their own sources or their testimonies before the courts of the Inquisition? As a general principle, they rejected some of the beliefs that did not derive from the Scriptures, and took the moral precepts of the New Testament literally, rejecting their Catholic interpretations. In effect, their rejection of beliefs and rites which were not directly based on the Scriptures, and of the Catholic interpretation, amounted to challenging the standing of the Church with the papacy at its head as the heirs of

9   The Anonymous of Passau, *Auszuge aus dem Sammelwerk des Passauer Anonymus*, in *Quellen zur Geschichte der Waldenser*, eds A. Patschovsky and K.V. Selge, Göttingen, 1973, pp. 74–75. A priest who joined the Waldensians was tried in Toulouse: *Liber sententiarum inquisitionis Tholosanae*, in *Historia inquisitionis*, ed. Ph. van Limborch, Amsterdam, 1692, pp. 274–275 (136b–137). Regarding the merchants and officials in the cities of Germany and Switzerland, see: M. Lambert, *Medieval Heresy. Popular Movement from the Gregorian Reform to the Reformation*, Oxford, 1992, p. 149; R. Kieckhefer, *Repression of Heresy in Medieval Germany*, University of Pennsylvania 1979, pp. 71 ff.; J. Gonnet and A. Molnar, *op. cit.*, pp. 252–253; Barnes G. Fiertz, 'An Unusual Trial under the Inquisition at Fribourg, Switzerland, in 1399', *Speculum* 18 (1943), pp. 340–357.

10 A. Dondaine O.P., 'Le manuel de l'Inquisiteur', *Archivum Fratrum Praedicatorum* 17 (1947), p. 92, note 19.

11 R.I. Moore, *The Formation of a Persecuting Society*, Oxford, 1987, mainly pp. 90, 151.

the Apostles with St Peter at their head. The Poor of Lyons rejected the belief in Purgatory, a theological innovation adopted in the thirteenth century, which entailed a re-mapping of the cosmos and revisions in the theology of penitence and atonement. In consequence, they also disbelieved the ability of the living to help the dead pass from Purgatory to Paradise by means of prayers, masses and charity for their souls.[12] They did not believe in the power of excommunication, repudiated the belief in the remissive power of the papal indulgences, which they regarded as an expression of the Church's greed, as well as its right to collect tithes. They wanted the rites and ceremonies to be reduced and simplified, rejected the decoration of churches with paintings and statues and the use of certain ritual objects, as well as some of the prayers and chants, and music in church. They were not concerned about burial in consecrated ground, and rejected some of the Catholic feasts and fasts. They cast doubt on the institutionalized sanctity of those who were canonized as well as on the will and ability of the saints to help people, and did not support their veneration.

[12] Belief in Purgatory became established in the thirteenth century, but it was only at the Church Council of Florence in 1483 that the belief in the possibility of purification of sins after death became part of the dogma. Raymond de la Côte justified the negation of the belief in Purgatory by arguing that there is no mention of it in the Scriptures, and added that Jesus said to the thief who was crucified beside Him: 'Verily I say unto thee: Today thou shalt be with me in paradise' (Luke 23:43) – i.e. not in Purgatory. He justified the rejection of prayers, masses and aims for the dead with the objection to the Second Book of Maccabees, 12:43–45, a book which was rejected by other Waldensian groups elsewhere: Le registre, Vol. I, pp. 42, 102–103. In rejecting belief in Purgatory the Waldensians also referred to I Corinthians 3:11–13, as symbolizing the tribulations and vanities of this world, whereas in their rejection of the efforts on behalf of the dead they also referred to II Corinthians 5:10 and Revelation 14:13. The Inquisitor Matthew of Cracow discussed this matter in his sermon of 1384, based on the testimony of four Waldensians who had been interrogated in Prague: Quellen zur Böhmischen Inquisition im 14 Jahrhundert, ed. A. Patschovsky, Weimar, 1979, p. 321.

In 1205, shortly after Waldes' death, a split occurred between The Poor of Lyons and The Poor of Lombardy. A letter that was sent after a conference held in Bergamo in 1218, with the aim of reconciling the Lombards with their 'ultramontane' brothers (i.e. The Poor of Lyons), reveals the issues on which they were divided. The two main issues about which they could not agree, and which made the controversy intractable, were the right to work and the validity of a sacrament administered by a sinful priest. The Poor of Lombary argued that despite the ideal of poverty and the renunciation of private property, people should work for their living as the Apostles had done, whereas The Poor of Lyons, faithful to Waldes' teaching, argued that they ought to devote themselves totally to wandering and preaching and to subsist on alms. With regard to the sacrament of the Eucharist, the two groups agreed that the miracle of transubstantiation was performed by Christ Himself, but the Lombards argued that the sacrament was valid only if given by a sinless priest, or even a virtuous layman. The Poor of Lyons, however, accepted the Catholic belief in the objective action of the sacrament (*ex opero operato*), meaning, that it was valid provided it was administered by an ordained priest, whether or not free of sin, so long as he was not excommunicated.[13] The position of the Lombards was known as Donatism, after the fourth-century Donatus, who denied the validity of a sacrament administered by a sinful priest, and whose position was rejected by the Church councils in his time,[14] but was adopted by various heretical movements during the High Middle Ages. Some of the Catholic writers on the subject of the Waldensians in the thirteenth century attributed this denial of the validity of a sacrament administered by a sinful priest to the

---

13 *Rescriptum heresiarchum Lombardiae ad Pauperes de Lugduno*, in *Enchiridion fontium Valdensium*, ed. G. Gonnet, Torre Pellice, 1958, pp. 169–183. For an analysis of the entire letter, see: G. Gonnet and A. Molnar, *op. cit.*, pp. 85–103.

14 Donatus' position was rejected and denounced at the Councils of Arles (314) and Carthage (411). Augustine of Hippo disputed with him in *De baptismo contra Donatistas*, and strongly defended the persecution of his followers.

Lombards alone,[15] but it seems that it was gradually adopted by at least some communities of The Poor of Lyons, though it is not certain which of them upheld this denial and for how long.[16] This disbelief in the validity of a sacrament administered by a sinful priest (and, according to some Inquisitors, the Waldensians regarded all Catholic priests as sinful) justified the administering of sacraments by a virtuous layman, namely, by one of The Poor of Lyons who was not ordained in the Catholic church. As the Anonymous of Passau wrote: 'They believe that a sinful priest cannot accomplish the sacrifice of the mass. A layman who is virtuous, and even a woman who knows the words [that must be

---

15 The Dominican Moneta of Cremona, who finished the work in 1241, ascribed the rejection of sacraments given by a sinful priest only to The Poor of Lombardy, and so did Anselm of Alessandria: Moneta of Cremona, *Adversus Catharos et Valdenses, libri quinque*, ed. T. Ricchini, Rome, 1743, L.V.C. 5, pp. 434–435; Anselm of Alessandria, *Tractatus de hereticis*, in A. Dondaine O.P., ed., 'La hierarchie cathare en Italie: le tractatus de hereticis d'Anselme d'Alexandrie O.P.', *Archivum Fratrum Praedicatorum* 20 (1950), p. 318. Similarly, a *summa* from the 1230s attributed to Peter Martyr maintains that this belief was held only by The Poor of Lombardy: Petrus Martyr, *Summa contra hereticos*, in T. Käppeli, 'Une somme contre les hérétiques de Pierre Martyr?' *Archivum fratrum Pradicatorum* 17 (1947), pp. 334–335.

16 The learned Cistercian Alain of Lille, writing before 1205 – i.e. before the split – ascribed this rejection to all Waldensians, and so did the Dominican Etienne de Bourbon in the middle of the thirteenth century, and the Franciscan David of Augsburg at the end of the century: Alain of Lille, *De fide catholica*, PL 210, col. 298; David of Augsburg, *Tractatus de inquisicione hereticorum*, ed. W. Preger, Munich, 1878, p. 27 (207). Bernard Gui went further and stated that they regarded every Catholic priest as sinful and his sacrament as invalid: Bernard Gui, *Manuel de l'inquisiteur*, ed. and trans. G. Mollat, Paris, 1964, Vol. I, p. 42. This is sustained by the testimony of some Waldensians who were interrogated in the courts of Inquisition: J.J. Ign von Döllinger, *op. cit.*, Vol. II, p. 366; *Quellen zur Böhmischen Inquisition im 14 Jahrhundert*, p. 242. Yet according to Raymond de la Côte, any sacrament given by a properly ordained priest was valid: *Le registre*, Vol. I, pp. 63, 70, 94. Regarding the problem of determining which communities upheld this rejection and when, see: G. Gonnet and A. Molnar, *op. cit.*, pp. 437–441.

said in the rite] can administer the sacrament'; also: 'a priest in a state of mortal sin cannot grant absolution for sin [after confession]. Rather let a virtuous layman do this.'[17]

The Catholic polemicists denounced The Poor of Lyons, among other things, for being a new sect that presumed to succeed the Apostles.[18] In response, The Poor of Lyons constructed their own historical narrative to enable them to claim that the apostolate had been transferred from the Church of Rome to them. According to this history, which was probably composed in the early fourteenth century, their origins lay not with Waldes in the late twelfth century, but under Pope Sylvester I, who received the 'Donation of Constantine' – after which the Church lost its primacy which was given to the opponents of the 'Donation of Constantine', of whom The Poor of Lyons were the successors. Waldes was no longer represented as the founder of the sect but as the person who revived it. This argument not only provided The Poor of Lyons with a rebuttal to their opponents; it also answered their own questions about their origins, justified their chosen way, while its vision of the End of Days offered hope and comfort.[19]

---

17 Anonymous of Passau, op. cit., pp. 82, 86.
18 One person who accused them of this was Salvo Burci, a noble of Piacenza, in a polemic he wrote in 1235: Salvo Burci, Liber supra stella, in J.J. Ign von Döllinger, op. cit., Vol. II, pp. 64–65.
19 The document known as the Donation of Constantine was a letter supposedly sent by the Emperor Constantine in 315 to Pope Sylvester, in which he declared that the Vicar of Rome was chief of all the Patriarchs and head of the Christian Church, and moreover granted him Italy and all the provinces of the West. During the Middle Ages no one questioned the authenticity of the document, and the supporters of the Pope and the Emperor argued only about its import. Only in the fifteenth century was the document proved to be fabricated. (It was probably forged in the eighth century by papal supporters.) Many of the heretical movements regarded the Donation of Constantine as a turning-point in the history of the Church, which thereafter became a materialistic organization motivated by greed and power-seeking (and therefore the Apostolate was transferred to their sects). This legendary history was included, inter alia, in a letter sent in 1368 by Italian Waldensians to their comrades in Austria who

To return to Waldensians' literal reading of the moral precepts of the New Testament – they rejected private property and upheld voluntary poverty (Matthew 6:28, 34; 19:21); they rejected tyrannical authority (Luke 22:25), and defied the authority of the ruling powers to try people at all, particularly to sentence a criminal to death or to mutilation; they opposed war and all forms of violence (Matthew 7:1; 5:21; Luke 6:37), including crusades against the infidels, and forbade the taking of oaths, even on the truth, in court and in all agreements and commitments between people (Matthew 5:34–37; Epistle of St James 5:12).

In their early days, The Poor of Lyons renounced all their properties and dedicated themselves to wandering and preaching. According to some of the Catholic writers, they could all not only preach but also hear confessions and administer the sacrament of the Eucharist. It is uncertain if that was indeed so, or when they began to administer the sacraments, because the information is patchy and contradictory. (We shall return to this issue in connection with the women.) It is, however, certain that from the second decade of the thirteenth century they no longer upheld universal priesthood, and put an end to general equality. A distinction was drawn between the Believers (*credentes*), as they were dubbed by the Inquisitors, or 'friends' (*amici*), as The Poor of Lyons called themselves – i.e. most of the members of the sect – and their spiritual leaders. The Inquisitors called the leaders the 'Perfects', as they had called the leaders of the Cathars (although among the latter the division between these and the mass of Believers had a different and more profound significance). The Poor of Lyons, for their part, called their leaders Brothers (*fratres*) or Teachers (*magistri*) – a term which the Inquisitors also used sometimes, and in the German-speaking regions they were also called Preachers (*Prediger*) or Confessors (*Beichtiger*). The Brothers vowed to observe celibacy, live a life of asceticism, renounce private property and obey Brothers who were higher in rank. They were

had reverted to Catholicism: P. Biller, 'Medieval Waldensian Construction of the Past', *Proceedings of the Huguenot Society* 25 (1989), pp. 39–54.

expected to devote many hours a day to prayer, and to dedicate themselves to the spiritual guidance of the Believers, and consequently not to work for their living but subsist of the alms of the Believers. A person would usually choose to become a Brother early in life, and if accepted, had to undergo a long period of preparation lasting six years and more.[20]

The spiritual leadership was chosen from among the Brothers. The Dominican Moneta of Cremona, whose work on the subject was completed in 1241, already reported that the spiritual leaders of The Poor of Lyons had a three-stage hierarchy: deacon, presbyter and bishop.[21] In his testimony, Raymond de la Côte confirmed the existence of this hierarchy (only he called the highest rank *majoral*), and described in detail how they were ordained and the prerogatives of each rank. According to him, a man became one of the Brothers only when he was made deacon, and reached the 'first level of perfection' (*primus gradus perfectionis*).[22] This hierarchy persisted until the early fifteenth century, and came to an end in the course of that century. Thereafter, the spiritual leaders formed a single level, which in Romance-language regions was called the 'elders' (*barbes*), and in the German-speaking regions 'teachers' (*meister*). But although there was no formal hierarchy among them, the older and more experienced ones enjoyed a status of seniority. The Brothers generally worked in pairs, and usually a young Brother was paired off with an older, more experienced one, who was familiar with the network of Believers and their locations and knew where to go. Their joint activity served as an additional stage in the training of a young Brother. This wandering in pairs also followed Jesus' injuction to his Apostles (Mark 6:7), to go forth by two and two. Ironically, the Inquisitors also worked in pairs, and called the Waldensian pairs *socii* – the same term they used for their own partners.

The spiritual leaders preached to the Believers, heard confes-

---

[20] De vita et actibus, in J.J. Ign von Döllinger, *op. cit.*, Vol. II, pp. 92–96.
[21] Moneta Cremona, *op. cit.*, L.V.C. 1, p. 402.
[22] *Le registre*, Vol. I, pp. 71, 56–64, 66–67, 73.

sions and gave absolution. As for the holy communion – just as we do not know which communities denied the validity of this sacrament when given by a sinful priest, so we cannot tell in which it was administered by one of the Brothers. It is more certain that once a year, on Maundy Thursday, they held a ceremony, which Raymond de la Côte described in detail, in which they drank wine and ate bread and fish, in memory of the last supper of Christ. According to Raymond, they did not believe that the bread and wine underwent transubstantiation, did not regard the ceremony as a sacrament, and its significance was purely commemorative. He added that it was held for the Brothers alone, and the Believers were not even supposed to know about it.[23] Nonetheless, Bernard Gui and other Inquisitors claimed that this ceremony was in fact regarded as a sacrament, and that the Brothers believed that transubstantiation took place in the bread and wine. But they too stated that the majorals gave this sacrament on very rare occasions, and that only they who were at the top of the hierarchy of Brothers were allowed to administer it.[24]

More is known about confession, to which both the Brothers and the Believers attached great value. Whenever Brothers visited their community, the Believers would make their confession to them. The Brothers laid stress on contrition, profound remorse and a deep personal sense of sin, and the Believers did not doubt that the Brothers had the power to give them absolution. But whereas the Catholic priest would say, 'I absolve thee,' the Brothers said, 'God will absolve thee and I impose upon thee contrition and penitence.'[25] According to the Anonymous of

---

[23] Raymond also stated that the majoral was empowered to administer the sacrament of the Eucharist, and had heard that he had done so, but did not himself witness the act: *ibid.*, pp. 60–61, 67–68.

[24] Anselme of Alessandria, *op. cit.*, pp. 320–321; Bernard Gui, *op. cit.*, Vol. I, p. 44. The author of the work entitled *De vita et actibus*, written at the end of the thirteenth century or beginning of the fourteenth in Languedoc, stated that only those at the top of the hierarchy were empowered to give this sacrament. He called them *Sandaliati*, and said they were the *sacerdotes, magistri, rectores* of the sect: *De vita et actibus*, in J.J. Ign von Döllinger, *op. cit.*, Vol. II, p. 95.

[25] A testimony to this effect: J.J. Ign von Döllinger, *op. cit.*, Vol. II, p. 600.

Passau, the Brothers did not usually impose penance, but would repeat the words of Jesus to the woman taken in adultery: '. . . go, and sin no more' (John 8:11).[26] Raymond de la Côte also testified that this was the Scriptural verse said by the confessor, nor did he mention any penance imposed by the confessor, but noted that he would demand that the person who made the confession repent wholeheartedly of his or her sin until their dying day. But there is some conflicting evidence too. A woman who committed adultery testified that she confessed before the Brother, who imposed upon her fasts and an obligation to say 'Our Father' numerous times. The same penance was also testified to by men who committed different sins. The polemic written at the end of the fourteenth century by the Inquisitor Peter Zwicker, who was familiar with The Poor of Lyons, implies that the Brothers imposed even harsher penances than did the Catholic priests.[27]

Testimonies taken in Bohemia between 1335 and 1353 show that Brothers sometimes administered Extreme Unction to the dying, and marriage ceremonies were sometimes conducted in their presence and with their blessing.[28] But it seems that in most regions the Brothers only administered the sacrament of confession, ordination and possibly sometimes the Eucharist. According to Raymond de la Côte, the majoral did not administer the sacrament of baptism or confirmation, nor that of extreme unction, and did not preside over or bless the marriage ceremony.[29] It would appear that in most regions the Believers received these

---

26 Anonymous of Passau, op. cit., p. 77.

27 Le registre, Vol. I, pp. 61, 64; J.J. Ign von Döllinger, op. cit., Vol. II, p. 365; Quellen zur Ketzergeschichte Brandenburgs und Pommerns, ed. D. Kurze, Berlin, 1975, pp. 79–80, 82, 113, 119, 176; see also P. Paravy, De la chrétienté romaine à la Réforme en Dauphiné, Rome, 1993, Vol. II, p. 1076. Zwicker's polemical work was entitled Cum dormirent homines. See: P. Biller, 'Les Vaudois dans les territoires de langue allemande vers la fin du XIVe siècle: le regard d'un inquisiteur', Heresis 13–14 (1989), pp. 221, 226.

28 Quellen zur Böhmischen inquisition im 14. Jahrhundert, pp. 191–192.

29 Le registre, Vol. I, pp. 61–62, 74, 76–77. With regard to marriage, it should be noted that not all Catholics married in church, and there were many private marriages. When the marriage was held in church,

sacraments, probably including holy communion, in the Catholic church. The Brothers encouraged the Believers to attend church – which the Catholic polemicists regarded as hypocrisy, maintaining that they did so only to hide their membership of the sect. The Franciscan David of Augsburg wrote at the end of the thirteenth century that, while they attend church like the Catholics, receive the sacraments and the priestly blessing with their heads bowed, and observe the fasts and feasts, in their heart of hearts they despise all these things and hold them in contempt. They are, he said, like a wolf in sheep's clothing.[30] However, though Raymond de la Côte stated that the majoral was empowered to consecrate the body of Christ in the sacrament, he also testified that the Brothers encouraged the Believers to attend church for the good of their souls, for there they would hear the prayers and passages read from the Scriptures, see the body of Christ in the eucharist and receive the priest's blessing in the name of the Holy Trinity. Furthermore, it is easier for a person to concentrate on prayers in church than at home, where one is distracted by the daily preoccupations. He added that although the Believers knew no Latin, it would do them good to listen, since these were the words of the Holy Spirit, and in time they would learn the prayers by heart. He also stated that they encouraged the Believers to make their deathbed confession to a Catholic priest and receive from him the extreme unction.[31] And just as the Brothers in the South of France in the early decades of the fourteenth century

the couple gave each other the sacrament in the presence of the priest and with his blessing. It is possible that here and there the Waldensians also administered the sacrament of confirmation, though not with the holy oil, but with the laying on of hands. Some testified that they had never received this sacrament and others said that they set no value upon it: J.J. Ign von Döllinger, *op. cit.*, Vol. II, pp. 307, 339. Many Catholics also did not receive this sacrament, certainly not in childhood as expected, since only a bishop was authorized to administer it, and he did not reach every part of his diocese to do so.

30 David of Augsburg, *op. cit.*, p. 32 (212).
31 *Le registre*, Vol. I, pp. 60–61, 81.

encouraged the Believers to attend Catholic churches, so did the Brothers in other regions and in later times.[32]

Once a year the Brothers held a general council (*capitulum vel concilium generale*) of community delegates in a big city, in a house rented for the purpose. (According to the Inquisitors, they would come disguised as merchants.) These councils were attended by the leading Brothers who headed 'hospices'. They discussed the admission of new Brothers and where they would be trained, cases of disobedience and their appropriate treatment, assigned missions to Brothers and distributed the funds to the hospices. These last were the sect's centres, whose numbers fluctuated over time. Each hospice was headed by a Brother (known as *gubernator*), maintained by several Brothers and Sisters, and served as a centre of study, prayers and ceremonies. The council heard reports about donations and decided on their distribution to the hospices, and the division of the remainder among needy Believers. David of Augsburg admits that the donations collected by the Brothers were destined for the sustenance of the poorer Believers, but adds, 'and to tempt the greedy to join their sect'.[33] The Catholic author from Languedoc, writing at the end of the thirteenth century or the beginning of the fourteenth, described these councils extensively, and stated that when held in Lombardy and Provence they were also attended by Brothers from Germany, accompanied by an interpreter.[34] But the evidence suggests that due to the persecution, the links between the communities in the Romance-language regions and those in the German-speaking regions became attenuated, and the councils gradually became confined to the former.

Despite their attendance at Catholic churches, and acceptance of at least some of the sacraments, there is no doubt that the Waldensian Believers placed their trust and their faith in the

---

[32] Thus, for example, in the testimony of a Waldensian from the French Alpine valleys in 1506: J.J. Ign von Döllinger, *op. cit.*, Vol. II, pp. 365–366.

[33] David of Augsburg, *op. cit.*, p. 30 (210)

[34] *De vita et actibus*, in J.J. Ign von Döllinger, *op. cit.*, Vol. II, pp. 95–96; see also: *ibid.*, p. 368; Bernard Gui, *op. cit.*, Vol. I, pp. 50–52.

Brothers and their sect. Once the sect became clandestine, the
Brothers would arrive, usually after dark, at the house of a
Believer, and from the fourteenth century often carrying a small
book hidden about their person, which in addition to translations
from the Scriptures contained homilies, a history of the sect and
verses.[35] One of the four Waldensians arrested by Jacques Fournier in 1319, Jean of Vienne, husband of the younger woman,
described how when he was admitted into the sect, the Brother
who received him held a volume from which he read 'of the
gospels'.[36] The Believers would inform their fellow sectarians in
the neighbourhood of the forthcoming visit by Brothers, and they
would all gather in the same house. There they made their confessions to the Brothers, and listened to them reading from the Scriptures and to their sermons, all in the vernacular. Listening to the
Scriptures and homilies and, chiefly from the latter half of the
fourteenth century, also to moral literature and poems that
promoted withdrawal from the vanities of the world, for inner
purification and penitence, in a language that the hearers could
understand, gave rise to what Brian Stock has called a 'textual
community', one in which texts form the cohesive force of a
community, which fashions its self-image and its image in the eyes
of its opponents[37] – although the spoken rather than the written
word predominated in the study. Most of the Believers did not
read but listened to the Brothers who relied on the texts. The
Brothers placed a high value on the teaching, which they gave to
men, women and children, and before the great persecutions they
maintained special schools for the Believers. The Anonymous of
Passau, writing in the 1260s, states that in the diocese of Passau
alone there were forty-one such schools. Teaching was a central

35 T.W. Röhrich, ed., *Factum hereticorum Mitteilungen aus der Geschichte der
evangelischen Kirche des Elsasses*, Paris–Strasbourg, 1855, Vol. I, p. 49;
see also P. Biller, 'The Oral and the Written: The case of the Alpine
Waldensians', *Bulletin for the Society of Renaissance Studies* 4 (1986), pp.
19–28.
36 *Le registre*, Vol. I, p. 512.
37 B. Stock, *The Implications of Literacy. Written Language and Models of
Interpretation in the Eleventh and Twelfth Centuries*, Princeton, 1983.

component in their mission – it meant taking responsibility for another person's soul. Indeed, their devotion to teaching, as well as the willingness of the Believers to study, aroused both envy and anxiety in the minds of the Inquisitors and the Catholic writers, who referred to it with venom and contempt and sometimes unwittingly revealed their envy.[38] Those Believers who could not read and write (who were the majority) learned by listening to the Brothers and repeating by rote, and the literate ones also read the Scriptures in translation.

Some of the Brothers (e.g., Durand Osca and Raymond de la Côte) had had a proper Latin education, others were less scholarly but could read Latin. The Inquisitors were aware that not all The Poor of Lyons were illiterate,[39] as many of the Catholic polemicists tended to depict them, at least in the early years. However, it is clear that most of the Brothers did not know Latin. In Stettin in 1392, a person being interrogated was asked what kind of people were the Brothers; he replied that not only were they good and virtuous men, but they were *litterati*. A woman testifying before the same court showed greater discrimination. She stated that they were all good and honest men, but some were cobblers and some *litterati*. A third witness testified only that they knew the Scriptures.[40] It is not clear if the woman and the first male witness had indeed met Brothers who were *litterati* in the common meaning of the word, that is to say, familiar with classical Latin literature and the Christian theological writings, and capable of

---

[38] Alain of Lille wrote about it with venom and contempt: Alain of Lille, *op. cit.*, L.II, C. 1, col. 380; while the Anonymous of Passau and Etienne de Bourbon failed to disguise their envy: Anonymous of Passau, pp. 70–73, Etienne de Bourbon, *op. cit.*, pp. 308–309. The testimonies of Waldensians who reverted to Catholicism matched the two Inquisitors' evaluations: *Hec sunt manifesta per conversos de secta Waldensium*, in A. Dondaine O.P., 'Durand Huesca et la Polémique anti-cathare', *Archivum Fratrum Praedicatorum* 29 (1959), Appendix IV, pp. 274–275.

[39] Bernard Gui, *op. cit.*, Vol. I, p. 62; J.J. Ign von Döllinger, *op. cit.*, Vol. I, p. 13.

[40] *Quellen zur Ketzergeschichte Brandenburgs und Pommerns*, pp. 102, 107, 164.

speaking and writing in Latin. Be that as it may, most of the Brothers did not know Latin, and were unfamiliar with either the classical literature or scholastic theology. Until the latter half of the fourteenth century, the writings of The Poor of Lyons (except the composition of Durand Osca) consisted only of translations, chiefly of the Scriptures. Nor did their writings after the middle of the fourteenth century match those of the Catholic theologians for literary quality or intellectual level of discussion.[41] This was due not only to the social stratum from which most of them came, and to the limited means of acquiring better education when they had to hide their affiliation, but also to their conscious rejection of the method and style of contemporary scholastic theology, and their desire to approach the Scriptures with a literal interpretation. Sometimes they even idealized the lack of education, since St Paul had warned against knowledge that causes pride (I Corinthians 8:1–3), and of the Apostles it was said that they were 'unlearned and ignorant men' (Acts 4:13). Raymond de la Côte testified that education (meaning, no doubt, Latin education) was not a condition of ordination as deacon, presbyter or even majoral. A man had to be virtuous and knowledgeable in the Scriptures.[42] Likewise, a young man's abilities and capacity to learn (i.e. the Scriptures) were taken into consideration in his acceptance as a Brother.

The Believers revered the Brothers, believed in their spiritual power and ability to absolve sin, and regarded loyalty to them, attention to their preaching and its absorption as conditions for salvation. Under interrogation they testified to the great piety of the Brothers, and indicated that they regarded them as priests in every sense, who were actually better at giving absolution than the Catholic priests.[43] The Believers supported the Brothers finan-

---

[41] See: A. Patschovsky, 'The Literacy of Waldensianism from Valdes to c. 1400', in *Heresy and Literacy 1000–1350*, eds P. Biller and A. Hudson, Cambridge, 1994, pp. 112–136.

[42] *Le registre*, Vol. I, pp. 56–57, 59.

[43] Thus, for example, in a testimony given in Stettin at the end of the fourteenth century: *Quellen zur Ketzergeschichte Brandenburgs und Pommerns*, p. 219.

cially, received them in their homes, provided them with food for the journey when they set out again, and often drove them or accompanied them on foot to their next destination. It was the duty of the Brothers to dedicate themselves totally to their spiritual role and to subsist on the donations of the Believers. In wandering from place to place they would sometimes disguise themselves as artisans or pedlars (chiefly as makers and sellers of needles and other petty merchandise). One trade which it is known that they certainly practised was medicine. Testimonies given in the South of France in the years 1241–1242 described them as visiting the sick and treating them, whether they were of their own sect, Cathars or Catholics, and that they even maintained their own hospitals. Later, when they retreated into the Alpine valleys, they continued to care for the sick without payment. They only accepted some food by way of recompense and token of appreciation. In caring for the sick they were following the Scriptural precept (Matthew 10:8). Most of them were healers and surgeons, but it is possible that, at least in the thirteenth century, there were some academic physicians among them.[44]

By rejecting oath-taking, trials, killing, war and crusades, and by promoting voluntary poverty, The Poor of Lyons were undermining the foundations of feudal society and defying the Catholic Church, with its vast possessions and its collaboration with the secular powers which enforced its authority. Yet they did not fight to change feudal society, only retreated to its margins. They did not hasten to bring about the kingdom of heaven on earth, nor did they go in for apocalyptic vision and millenarian tension. They concentrated not on the last things concerning mankind and the world, but on the salvation of the individual in the afterworld. Nor did their concern for the poor go beyond traditional almsgiving. Yet in retreating to the margins and living as a clandestine sect they did on occasion have to transgress against the dos and

---

44 H.Ch. Lea, op. cit., Vol. II, Appendix X, pp. 580–583; P. Biller, ' "Curate infirmos": The Medieval Waldensian Practice of Medicine', in The Church and Healing, ed. W.J. Sheils, Studies in Church History 9 (1982), pp. 55–77.

especially the don'ts of their faith in order to survive. They not only attended church and received sacraments that were not given by the Brothers, but sometimes even made incomplete confessions to the Catholic priests. Some of The Poor of Lyons testified before the courts of the Inquisition that they used to make their confession once a year (as required of Catholics) before a Catholic priest, and receive holy communion at his hands. What they did not confess was their membership of the sect. A Waldensian from the French Alpine valleys added that he had done so upon the advice of the elders (*barbes*).[45] The Poor of Lyons regarded the tithes as extortion and a sign of the Church's greed, but they paid it nevertheless. They kept the Church fast days and festivals, though they did not believe in them, and made pilgrimages to the shrines of saints in whose ability to help the living they did not believe – or, at any rate, were not supposed to as Waldensians. All these made it harder for the Inquisition to track them down. Although The Poor of Lyons unconditionally objected to killing, it happened that they set fire to the houses of Inquisitors and informers or killed them, even in some cases with the knowledge or at the prompting of the Brothers.[46] It seems that the natural vengeful impulse of the weak and persecuted was not eradicated from their hearts, despite the preaching by the Brothers to avoid violence in all circumstances and never repay evil with evil, but only pray to God to turn their enemies' hearts in their favour.[47] The Anonymous of Passau describes a Waldensian, a glover from Tevin (today's Devin, near Pressburg), who cried out as he was

---

45 *Quellen zur Ketzergeschichte Brandenburgs un Pommerns*, pp. 80, 89, 113, 119, 195, 258; J.J. Ign von Döllinger, *op. cit.*, Vol. II, pp. 365–366; P. Paravy, *op. cit.*, Vol. II, p. 1082.

46 T.W. Röhrich, ed., *op. cit.*, Vol. I, p. 43: P.P. Bernard, 'Heresy in Fourteenth Century Austria', *Medievalia et Humanistica* 10 (1956), pp. 60–61; R. Kieckhefer, *Repression of Heresy in Medieval Germany*, Philadelphia, 1979, pp. 58–60, 64; P. Biller, 'Medieval Waldensian Abhorrence of Killing pre c. 1400', in *The Church and War*, ed. W.J. Sheils, *Studies in Church History* 20 (1983), pp. 129–146; P. Paravy, *op. cit.*, Vol. II, p. 1081.

47 *De vita et actibus*, in J.J. Ign von Döllinger, *op. cit.*, Vol. II, p. 94.

being led to the stake, 'If we were not so few, we would use the force you are now employing upon us against your Church, your monks and your laity.'[48] In the years 1488–1489, when the Catholics conducted a crusade in the Dauphiné Alps, they fought as hard as they could to gain military and even political aims.[49] Yet even then they did not seek to change the social system, only to protect themselves and ensure the survival of their sect.

However, such acts of violence were exceptional. The Poor of Lyons were the ones who were persecuted. The Brothers repeatedly quoted the words of Peter and the Apostles that, according to tradition, had been held up by Waldes: 'We ought to obey God rather than men' (Acts 5:29). This was the justification of their duty to wander and preach as Jesus and the Apostles had done: 'Go ye into all the world and preach the gospel to every creature' (Mark 16:15), their break with the sinful Catholic Church and their devotion to their own true church, the successor of the Apostles. The Believers regarded their loyalty to the Brothers and the moral precepts they taught as a condition of transcendental salvation. Their very membership in this community, the successor of the Apostles, was a sign that they were chosen as the poor in spirit and the meek, as against the rich and mighty who ruled this world. The more they were hounded, the more the Brothers stressed that they were elected to undergo suffering and persecution, like the prophets of old, like Jesus and the Apostles, and that this was their fate till the Second Coming.[50] Indeed, many of The Poor of Lyons were put to death for their faith. And while some recanted before the court of the Inquisition and promised to

---

48 The Anonymous of Passau, op. cit., p. 72.
49 See: S.K. Treesh, 'The Waldensian Recourse to Violence', Church History 55 (1986), pp. 294–306; P. Paravy, op. cit., Vol. II, pp. 977–988.
50 Writings of The Poor of Lyons about this: a letter sent in 1368 by Brothers in Italy to their comrades in Austria who had reverted to Catholicism, in J.J. Ign von Döllinger, op. cit., Vol. II, p. 357; and throughout the Waldensian poem, La noble leçon des Vaudois du Piémont, ed. A. de Stefano, Paris, 1909; in the writings of the Inquisitors: Etienne de Bourbon, op. cit., p. 308; David of Augsburg, op. cit., p. 26 (206); Anonymous of Passau, op. cit., p. 76.

return to the Catholic Church and did so, others who were freed lapsed, were again caught and were put to death as lapsed heretics. Still others, men and women alike, withstood their interrogators to the end and were burnt at the stake. The death at the stake of a member of the family did not always deter the rest. They persevered in their faith and their membership of the sect, and brought in other relatives and the next generation.

With the advent of the Reformation and the ending of the Catholic Church's monopoly on religious life, The Poor of Lyons merged with the Calvinist church. This union meant renouncing some of their beliefs which were closer to Catholicism than to the Reformers, as well as their organization, customs and traditional way of life. They no longer had to live clandestinely, pretending to be other than they were, but they also lost their distinction. What the Inquisition had failed to achieve, the Reformation accomplished. It is ironic that they united with the Calvinists, the Protestant movement known for its belief in predestination, a belief that they had rejected at least in the first decades of their movement, as appears from the single Waldensian document of that time – Durand Osca's composition.[51] When The Poor of Lyons, or rather their descendants, were persecuted in France and Italy in the latter half of the sixteenth century, it was as Protestants. Something of their ancient beliefs and a strong sense of their origins in The Poor of Lyons persisted only among the Protestants of the Alpine valleys of Piedmont. They call themselves the 'Waldensian Church' (*Chiesa Valdese*), the only Protestant church in Italy. In the nineteenth century, as freedom of religion became established throughout Italy, they expanded into other cities, such as Turin, Genoa and other cities in northern, central and southern Italy. And following the economic migration from Piedmont in the nineteenth century, Waldensian churches sprang up in France, Switzerland, South America, the United States and South Africa. In 1989 the Waldensian church had about 45,000 members.[52]

[51] See note 5.
[52] For the union with the Calvinists, the persecution during the wars of religion, and the 'Waldensian Church', see: G. Audisio, *Les 'Vaudois'*.

To return to the early days of The Poor of Lyons. The reaction of Waldes' wife to his conversion – at any rate, according to the chronicler of his life – did not presage well for the willingness of women to renounce earthly belongings and follow in his way. He allowed his wife to choose between his movable goods or real estate, and she, who was 'downcast, chose the latter, which included lands, waters, woods, meadows, houses, rents, vineyards, mills and ovens'. She could not accept Waldes' decision to become a dependant, and indeed the archbishop to whom she appealed ordered him to eat only at her house whenever he was in Lyons. In view of the fact that he had destined his young daughters to a traditional career of well-off Catholic girls, it would seem that he did not address his call for total poverty and a life of preaching to women. He set aside a substantial portion of his capital as a dowry to a convent (as was customary) and sent his two young daughters to a convent of the order of Fontevrault.[53] But already in the 1180s there were women among his followers, and hereafter The Poor of Lyons included women. The next

Naissance, vie et mort d'une dissidence (XIIe–XVIe siècles), Turin, 1989, chs 8–9; P. Paravy, *op. cit.*, Vol. II, pp. 1163–1177; a slight migration of Waldensians to North America must have occurred from the seventeenth century. They migrated from the Alpine valleys of Piedmont to other European countries, and thence with other Protestants to North America. A more substantial migration in that direction took place in the nineteenth century. See: G.B. Watts, *The Waldenses in the New World*, Durham, N.C., 1941.

[53] *Chronicon universale anonymi Laudunensis*, in M.G.H. Scriptores, Vol. 26, ed. G. Waitz, Hanover and Berlin, 1931, p. 447.

[54] The sources: With the exception of the work by Durand Osca (note 5), and the letter of 'The Poor of Lombardy' to The Poor of Lyons, following the Council of Bergamo in 1218 (note 13), all the sources about the Waldensians up to the middle of the fourteenth century are Catholic ones. There is a letter written in 1368 by Italian Waldensians to their comrades in Austria who had reverted to Catholicism (note 50). There is also 'Waldes' *Profession of Faith*', dating from 1180 or 1181, but it was not written by him and cannot be regarded as a Waldensian text. It is an early text to which were added portions rejecting Cathar beliefs. A. Dondaine O.P., 'Aux origines du Valdéisme: une profession de foi de Valdes', *Archivum Fratrum Pradicatorum*

chapter is devoted to women in the early days of The Poor of Lyons, before the division into Brothers and Believers and their female counterparts.[54]

[Note 54 starts on the previous page]

16 (1946), Appendix, pp. 231–232. In addition, Durand Osca signed a profession of faith when he returned to Catholicism in 1208 and founded the order of 'The Poor Catholics', and Bernard Prim, when he returned to Catholicism in 1210, and founded the order of 'The Reconciled Poor'. These two statements resemble the one of Waldes, portions were tacked on to them rejecting the deviations which were ascribed to Waldensians at that time: in *Enchiridion fontium Valdensium*, ed. G. Gonnet, Torre Pellice, 1958, pp. 129–140. For Waldensian texts from the latter half of the fourteenth century onward, see: G. Gonnet and A. Molnar, *op. cit.*, ch. 7; P. Paravy, *op. cit.*, Vol. II, pp. 1084–1149; P. Biller, 'Heresy and Literacy: Early History of the Theme', in *Heresy and Literacy 1000–1350*, eds P. Biller and A. Hudson, Cambridge, 1994, pp. 1–18; parts of the Catholic sources about the Waldensians to approximately the end of the thirteenth century (excluding the court records of the Inquisition) in translation: *Heresies of the High Middle Ages*, ed. and trans. W.L. Wakefield and A.P. Evans, New York, 1969. Lutz Kaelber describes the kind of asceticism that characterized not only the Waldensian Brothers but also the Believers in thirteenth-century Austria. He defines this as a rational inner worldly asceticism and precursor of that of some Protestant sects. See: L. Kaelber, *Schools of Asceticism. Ideology and Organization in Medieval Religious Communities*, University Park, Pa., 1998, pp. 129–173.

2

Women in the Early Days of
The Poor of Lyons

Everything that is known about the presence of a female element in the deity of any religion, or the introduction at some stage in its history of a female element into its divine system, or the playing of a positive role by such an element in the history of salvation or in its future, tells us that these have not necessarily been accompanied by gender equality in the religious life. In most polytheistic religions whose pantheons included both male and female deities, though women played some part in the religious rituals, the religious establishment was still headed by men and the rights of women in it were not equal to theirs. The position of the Virgin Mary as the mother of God and the mediator between the faithful and her Son, which was determined as early as the Church councils in the fifth century (in Ephesus in 431 and Chalcedon in 451), and was further developed and given various expressions and rituals from the twelfth century on, did not expand the rights of women in the Catholic Church. In most of the Kabbalistic systems developed from the twelfth century onwards the tree of *Sefirot*, wherein the divine powers are manifested, included a female *Sefirah* (called a daughter, a matron, *Shekhinah*, or a bride). This *Sefirah* was thought of as representing the expansion of the divine power through the world, directing and representing the Godhead, while in the divine world itself it was God's consort.[1]

---

[1] G. Scholem, *Elements of the Kabbalah and its Symbols*, Jerusalem, 1976 (written in Hebrew), pp. 259–307.

Yet this introduction of a female element produced no change in the status of women in the Kabbalists' religious life. Indeed, some Kabbalist circles even laid stress on the demonic powers and uncleanness of woman. According to Rabbi David Ibn Zimra (1479–1575), a Kabbalist of Safed, the reincarnation of a man in a woman's body was a grave punishment, while for a woman to be found worthy of being reincarnated in a man's body was an elevation.[2] Though the presence or introduction of a feminine element at some stage in the history of a religion no doubt helped shape its theological structures (and in the Kabbalah, also gave additional significance to certain ritual obligations), they did not produce a change in the actual position and rights of women in the religious life.

As for sects, we know that they did not necessarily give women any greater rights than did the hegemonic church. It may also be impossible to pinpoint common denominators among the sects which did practise gender equality (except the tendency of persecuted sects, because of their circumstances, to practise greater equality among *all* their members, including women, than did hegemonic churches). But it is possible to point to Christian sects who believed in combined male and female elements in the Godhead, and in the embodiment of the female aspect of the Godhead, and who also maintained a state of equality between men and women in the community. Other sects interpreted the spiritual equality between the sexes since the coming of Christ as calling for equality in the earthly community, and strengthened the rights of women in their communities. It may be worthwhile to divert from our subject, the women of The Poor of Lyons, and briefly examine the histories of some of these sects in order to illuminate, by way of comparison, the case of The Poor of Lyons.

The Guillelmites, a small sect that rose in Milan in the latter

---

2 'And the man thus reincarnated is punished, hence the blessing on not being created a women' (*Menahot* 43:72). But 'woman reincarnated as man is rewarded, for she is raised in sanctity' (*Berakhot* 129–28, 71), quoted by R. Lamdan, *A Separate People. Jewish Women in Palestine, Syria and Egypt in the 16th century*, Tel Aviv, 1996 (in Hebrew), p. 25.

half of the thirteenth century and survived for only a few decades, believed that God combined both male and female aspects. The sect's name derived from that of its spiritual leader who embodied the Holy Spirit – Guillelma. In her lifetime and for some twenty years after her death Guillelma was believed to be not only a righteous woman, but an orthodox saint. She was about fifty when she arrived in Milan from Bohemia in the 1260s. A woman of means, it was said that she was a Bohemian princess. Recent research has shown that she was indeed the daughter of king Premysl Ottokar I of Bohemia. She became renowned as a counsellor, comforter, alms-giver, a denouncer of sins (especially the sins of deceit and of money-lending at interest), and as a worker of miracles. The stigmata appeared on her body in her lifetime, though she took care to hide them. She was connected with the Cistercian monks of Chiarvale, resided in a house that belonged to them, bequeathed her property to them, and in 1281 was buried in their monastery, as she had requested. Her tomb with the chapel that was built over it and contained her portrait became a focus of pilgrimate, with the particular encouragement of one of the monks. (Later he was accused of doing so in order to obtain greater donations to the monastery.) Rumours that Guillelma had been an earthly embodiment of the Holy Spirit began to spread in her lifetime, but it is not clear whether or not she had a share in them, the evidence being contradictory. It is certain that her chosen disciple, Andreas Saramita, reported that Guillelma had informed him of her divine nature, described how she had come down from heaven and would in time rise from the dead to inspire her disciples with tongues of flame and bring about a new age in which the entire world would be saved, including the Jews and the Saracens. Andreas Saramita and Manfreda, his fellow leader of the group, stated that Guillelma had said that since 1262 not only the body of Christ was consecrated in the sacrament, but also the body of the Holy Spirit, namely, her own body, and that she refused to take the Eucharist because she viewed it as her own body. But whether or not she had actually said this, it is clear that only after her death did her disciples organize their doctrine and ritual and act to disseminate them.

The leaders of the group, then, were a man and a woman.

Andreas Saramita was associated with the Cistercians and was familiar with the theory of the Ages of Joachim of Fiore.[3] It was he who wrote what he had heard – as he claimed – from Guillelma, as well as his own ideas and those of his co-leader, Manfreda de Pirovano, in the form of new gospels and epistles. Manfreda was born into the high nobility of Milan, and joined the Humiliati, a lay religious order whose members were active in the cities of northern Italy. They were supported and encouraged by the Church authorities, but were always on the brink of heresy.

The introduction of a female element into the deity, and a belief in an imminent new divine revelation, formed the core of the Guillelmites' faith. It was an extreme feminization of Christianity. They regarded Guillelma as the embodiment of the Holy Spirit, the third person of the Trinity. And this incorporation in a female body indicated to them the coming of the third age, which is promised in the New Testament, just as the fulfilled promise is found in the Old Testament. This was an ontological belief about the nature of God: the deity is a combination of male and female. The significance of the statements attributed to Guillelma concerning the sacrifice of her body in the sacrament together with the body of Christ was that the two were linked in consubstantiation. Just as the Son and the Holy Spirit are a single substance in two divine personae, so Guillelma, the embodiment of the Holy Spirit, and Jesus, the Son of God, were a single flesh in two separate historical persons.

Such a belief in the equality of the male and the female in the deity led the Guillelmites to endow women with equal status to the men, without excluding the latter. In her second coming Guillelma was expected to replace the corrupt Church of Rome with a pure evangelical church. In that new church a woman would become the pope and the cardinals would also be women. But while Guillelma tarried, reverence was made to Manfreda, who saw herself as Guillelma's vicar, and as the pope-designate in the new church. She conducted services in the chapel which was built on top of Guillelma's tomb, and at the Church of Mary Magdalen

[3]   M. Reeves, *The Influence of Prophecy in the Later Middle Ages*, Oxford, 1969, pp. 248–250.

in Milan, ordained women as cardinals and allowed the believers to kiss her hands and feet. She and Andreas commissioned portraits of Guillelma and composed hymns and litanies to her. An especially solemn ceremony was held at Pentecost, the feast at which Christ reappeared to the Apostles after the resurrection, which also happened to be Guillelma's birthday. Men, as noted before, were not denied a place in the rites. When Manfreda conducted the sacrament of Holy Communion, men read the words of consecration. Manfreda headed the ritual, Andreas Saramita was the theologian.

They had but a few dozen followers, and they did not seek to achieve their aim by rebellion. The revolution was expected to take place without a struggle when Guillelma returned. But the Church authorities regarded their beliefs and rituals as a threat. Already in 1284 they were detained, interrogated, ordered to recant, and set free. After the ceremony that was held at Pentecost, which witnesses said was attended by more than a hundred men and women, some from the highest society of Milan, they were once again arrested under pressure from the Dominicans.[4] This time their fate was sealed. Manfreda, Andreas and another woman were burnt at the stake. Some thirty others were ordered to repent, and were freed. Guillelma's bones were disinterred and burnt, and the short history of the sect came to an end.[5]

Another sect which believed in the combined male–female nature of the deity and also gave women complete equal rights

---

4 For the disagreement between the Dominicans and the Cistercians, and the possibility that the former demanded the reopening of the trial in order to harm the latter and seize the property left them by Guillelma, see: G.G. Merlo, *Eretici e eresi medievali*, Bologna, 1989, pp. 113–118.
5 For the fullest and most thorough study of the Guillelmites, see: B. Newman, *From Virile Woman to Woman Christ. Studies in Medieval Religion and Literature*, Philadelphia, 1995, pp. 182–195; my summary is based largely on her analysis. According to Alain Boureau, the Guillelmites developed their faith partly under the influence of the legend about Pope Joan, and their short-lived movement in turn promoted new versions of the legend: A. Boureau, *La papesse Jeanne*, Paris, 1988, pp. 188–192.

was that of the Shakers. They had their origins in a Protestant sect from the Sevennes mountains in the South of France, known as The French Prophets. It was a millenarian sect which awaited the imminent coming of the Saviour in the form of a woman. The French Prophets fled from persecution to England in the 1710s, and a small group that settled in Manchester remained faithful to their beliefs. They were joined by men and women from the Methodist church and especially by Quakers. At first they were called The Shaking Quakers, and later the name Shakers stuck to them, because they expressed their religious ecstasy by shaking, dancing and shouting. In 1758 a woman called Ann Lee joined them, the illiterate daughter of a poor blacksmith from Manchester. She worked in a cotton mill, as a felt-cutter for hatters, in a brewery, and finally in a clinic. She did not wish to marry but was compelled to do so by her family, and married the blacksmith Abraham Stanley, by whom she had four children, who all died in infancy. She regarded their deaths as divine punishment for marrying and having carnal relations. In Manchester she underwent ecstatic experiences, saw visions and prophesied. Her prophecies and sermons called for a life of asceticism and a withdrawal from the vanities of the world, and denounced sinfulness. In 1772, she was arrested on account of her preaching, because she had broken the Sabbath. After her release, Ann announced that she had been ordered in a vision to sail with her followers to America. Though she was recognized as the leader, she had only a handful of followers left, most of them having abandoned the sect because of its increasingly extreme beliefs, its attitude towards other churches, and because of persecution.

In 1774 Ann Lee and eight of her followers (including her husband Abraham, from whom she later separated), migrated to America. The Revival movement over there brought them more followers and the sect grew. In 1787 they built their first communal settlement, Mount Lebanon, which served as the model for later settlements. Unlike the Guillelmites, the Shakers lasted a long time. The authorities did not always regard them favourably – during the American Revolution because they were English, and during the Civil War because of their pacifism. At times they were subject to various pressures, but they were not persecuted. They reached their largest membership and expansion in the middle of the nineteenth century. The decline set in in the 1860s, from a combination of socio-economic and spiritual factors. By the 1980s their total number, in the handful of still extant settlements, did not exceed a few dozen.

Although the French Prophets already expected a female Saviour, and women played a prominent part among them, and though the group in Manchester was led by a man and a woman (the Wardley couple) even before Ann Lee joined them, it was she who fixed the female principle in the Shakers' theology and the lasting gender equality in the sect. She led the community till her death in 1789, and after her a man and a woman led and organized it: Joseph Mecham and Lucy Wright.

The Shakers disbelieved the Trinity in its orthodox connotation. In its place they had a bi-sexual divinity, a heavenly father and heavenly mother who rule over the earth. As Fredrick Evans, one of the leading Shakers in the latter half of the nineteenth century wrote: How could God have created both man and woman in his image (Genesis 1:27), 'if God himself was not in the order of male and female?'[6] Christ personified the male aspect of the Godhead on earth, and Ann Lee the female aspect. Both were annointed and both were divinely inspired. With Jesus began a new age, and likewise with Ann Lee. (In their interpretation of the Revelation of St John, they described the age which began with Ann Lee as the final one, which would last till the End of Days, and in which it was possible to discern the first signs of redemption.[7]) To the Shakers, then, as to the Guillelmites, God was a composite of the male and the female whose attributes complement one another, and earthly man and woman reflect the two aspects of god. In Evans' words: 'Man is to Woman her God in physical and intellectual power as representing and revealing the Father in Deity – Wisdom. And Woman is to Man his God and Saviour in affectional power and in Divine spiritual intuition, as

6 F.W. Evans, *The American Utopian Adventure. Autobiography of a Shaker*, Glasgow, 1888, reprinted Philadelphia, 1972, p. 199.
7 *Ibid.*, pp. 70, 98.

representing the Mother in Deity – Love.' And, turning Aristotelian biology on its head, he adds: 'Woman rising out of man is his superior in the complexity and variety of her physical functions and powers, as also in the superior refinement of her organization generally.'[8] This reasoning meant that men and women were to be equal on earth.

The Shakers were celibate. Before Original Sin, they said, echoing Augustine of Hippo, people might use their genitals for their natural purpose of procreation. But since Original Sin, sexual relations are tainted with lust. With the appearance of Jesus, which marked the end of the age of the 'Law' and the first promise, the commandment to 'be fruitful and multiply' ceased to be valid. The Shakers regarded their celibacy as one of the most important distinctions that set them apart from the world. In the nineteenth century they reinforced the Christian-theological argument against procreation with a theological-Malthusian one: it is better for the world if fewer unfortunate children were born in it, who were fated to die prematurely of disease and poverty. Social injustice is associated with biological ills. Only a new relationship between men and women, without sexual life and childbirth, could change the social-economic system and create a new society.[9]

The Shakers' abolition of the biological family was therefore an outcome of their ideal of celibacy and opposition to procreation, and facilitated the abolition of private property and the realization of communal life, in the spirit of the New Testament depiction of the life of the Apostles. In its place they instituted the Shaker family, numbering eighty to a hundred persons, which formed the basic social unit in every settlement. Married couples who joined the community undertook to live apart, the men with the men and the women with the women. The children were raised and educated apart from their parents, together with the orphans and poor children adopted by the settlement. Every func-

8 *Ibid.*, pp. 101–102.
9 *Ibid.*, p. 201; H. Desroche, *The American Shakers. From Neo-Christianity to Presocialism*, trans. J.K. Savacool, Amherst, Mass., 1971, pp. 16ff., 155.

tion in the cooperative community was filled by a man and a woman. There were Elders and Elderesses, a male minister and a female one, a deacon and deaconess. Women took part in all the social and religious activities of the community, but a strict physical distance was maintained between men and women. Even handshakes were forbidden. In their extreme avoidance of all physical contact between the sexes the Shakers resembled the Cathars, among whom the Perfects did not even eat at the same table with women.[10] And when giving a woman the *consolamentum* (the ceremony in which a person became a Perfect), the male Perfect did not touch her head or her shoulder, but laid a book on her. But the Cathars, whose faith rejected both the male and female bodies as the work of Satan, like the rest of the material creation, in their myths and to some extent in everyday life regarded the female body as especially unclean, whereas the Shakers considered both the male and female bodies as divinely created, and some even wrote in praise of the female body.[11]

Let us now turn to the sect which broadened the rights of women on the basis of the spiritual equality between the sexes after the coming of Christ, as spelled out in the Epistle to the Galatians 3:28: 'There is neither Jew nor Greek, there is neither bond nor free, there is neither male nor female: for ye are all one in Christ Jesus' – namely, the Quakers. In their community in seventeenth century England there were women preachers, missionaries, writers of pamphlets, prophets and organizers. This is how George Fox (1624–1690) justified their status and rights: 'Man and Woman were help meets in the image of God, and in Righteousness and Holiness in the Dominion before they fell, but after the Fall in the Transgression, the Man was to rule over his wife, but in the Restauration by Christ into the image of God and his righteousness and Holiness again, in that they are help meets, Man and Woman, as they were before the Fall.' And further on:

---

10 J. Duvernoy, *Le Catharisme. La religion des Cathares*, Toulouse, 1976, p. 183.
11 Additional bibliography about the Shakers: M.F. Melcher, *The Shaker Adventure*, New York, 1940, reprinted 1975; E.D. Andrews, *The People Called Shakers. A Search for the Perfect Society*, New York, 1963.

'For the Power and Spirit of God gives Liberty to all; for women are Heirs of Life as well as Men, and so stewards of the manifold Grace of God.'[12]

The Poor of Lyons were different. They did not believe in the existence of a female element in the Godhead, nor did they interpret the idea of the spiritual equality of the sexes after the coming of Christ as requiring equality in the religious life in this world. Although there were women preachers among them, they did not regard gender equality as a matter of principle. Contrary to the idea that was widespread among researchers who have studied them (and which has not been entirely abandoned), women did not enjoy equal rights among them, not even in their early days. Until the publication of the revisionist paper by the historian of the Waldensians, Grado Merlo, in 1991,[13] it was the accepted view of historians who considered the standing of women in the sect, that in its early decades women enjoyed equal rights with the men, and only after the sect's 'churchification', the discarding of the egalitarian ideal also among the men, and the division into Brothers and Believers, did the women lose their rights.[14] Unfortunately, these conclusions were based on the accusations leveled by the Catholic authors and the Inquisitors, and ignored the sources which indicated, even if indirectly but still plainly, that this was not the case.

---

12 George Fox, *A Collection of Many Select and Christian Epistles*, London, 1698, pp. 272, 323. Concerning women Quakers, see: R. Ruether Radford, 'Prophets and Humanists: Types of Religious Feminism in Stuart England', *Journal of Religion* 70 (1990), pp. 8–12, 17–18; M. Thickstun Olofson, 'This was a Woman that Taught: Feminist Scriptural Exegesis in the 17th Century', *Studies in Eighteenth Century Culture* 21, eds P.B. Craddock and C.H. Hay, pp. 149–158.

13 G. Merlo, 'Sulle "misere donnicciuole" che predicavano', *Identita Valdesi nella storia e nella storiografia. Valdesi e Valdismi medievali II*, Turin, 1991, pp. 93–112.

14 See inter alia: G. Audisio, *Les 'Vaudois'. Naissance, vie et mort d'une dissidence (XIIe–XVIe siècles)*, Turin, 1989, pp. 120, 127; G. Gonnet, 'La femme dans les mouvements paupéro-evangeliques du bas moyen âge (notamment chez les Vaudois)', *Heresis* 22 (1994), pp. 25–41; P. Paravy, *De la chrétienté romaine à la Réforme en Dauphiné*, Rome, 1993, Vol. II, p. 1037.

The Poor of Lyons did not develop any new theology, let alone about the nature of the Trinity, nor did they believe in the presence of a feminine element in the Godhead. Indeed, all the evidence, from whatever source, shows that they limited the standing and reduced the role of the Virgin Mary. They did not deny her role as the mother of the Redeemer, but did not believe in her power to mediate between the faithful and her son, or to help those who prayed to her. In the poem of The Poor of Lyons (dating probably from the latter half of the fourteenth century), Mary is called 'The Saviour's Mother'.[15] Another poem, entitled 'The Noble Lesson', laments Mary's suffering at her son's death, and calls her 'saint', 'glorious' and 'Our Lady' (*sancta, gloriosa, nostra dona*).[16] Also, according to the Inquisitors, they celebrated the feast of Mary, although they took little interest in the feasts of the other saints,[17] but they did not appeal for her help. According to the Dominican known as the Anonymous of Passau, they never prayed to the saints for help, nor to the Virgin Mary.[18] Some of those questioned in Stettin in the years 1392–1394, and in Fribourg, Switzerland, in the late fourteenth century, explained their reasoning: there is no point in appealing to St Mary and other saints, since they are so joyous, enjoying the bounties of heaven, that they do not think of us and would not intercede for us before God. One of the 'elders' (*Barbes*) from the Alpine valleys of Italy actually testified in the fifteenth century that they did not believe in the efficacy of appealing to the Mother of God. Another who was questioned added that the Virgin Mary and the other saints were human, and therefore men must strive to emulate

---

[15] *Le novel sermon*, in *Six Vaudois Poems from the Waldensian Manuscripts in the University Libraries of Cambridge, Dublin and Geneva*, ed. and trans. H.J. Chaytor, Cambridge, 1930, v. 381, p. 31.

[16] *La noble leçon des Vaudois du Piédmont*, ed. A. de Stefano, Paris 1909. V. 29–30, 214, 218, 220, 326–329, 381.

[17] J.J. Ign von Döllinger, ed., *Beiträge zur Sektengeschichte des Mittelalters*, Munich, 1890, Vol. II, p. 9; Bernard Gui, *Manuel de l'inquisiteur*, ed. and trans. G. Mollat, Paris, 1964, Vol. I, p. 48.

[18] Anonymous of Passau, *Auszuge aus dem Sammelwerk des Passauer Anonymus*, in *Quellen zur Geschichte der Waldenser*, eds A. Patschovsky and K.V. Selge, Göttingen, 1973, p. 97.

them, but to put their trust in God alone.[19] As a rule, The Poor of Lyons did not say the prayer Hail Mary. Though Raymond de la Côte testified that he and other members of his sect did say this prayer,[20] his statement was contradicted not only by the Inquisitors, but also by most of the persons who were interrogated in Stettin, Austria, Fribourg and the Italian Alps. They testified that they did not say this prayer, and that when the Brothers laid penances upon them after confession, these included fasting and repeating the *Pater Noster*, but not the *Ave Maria*. Indeed, some of these witnesses did not know it at all, and many of those who did know the prayer testified that they said it out of habit, or to disguise their sectarian affiliation. Others testified they could not give up this prayer or shake off the belief in the power of the Virgin, and admitted that they prayed to her from time to time, despite the instructions of the Brothers, because they believed that unlike the other saints she would intercede for them.[21] Those who testified in Toulouse in the 1310s, when asked about this, also stated that when praying with the Brothers they said only the *Pater Noster*.[22] Given that The Poor of Lyons rejected the pictures and statues – the visual symbols of the Catholic religion – and reduced their religious rites to a minimalist simplicity, inevitably the Holy Virgin could not be for them the same feminine model and a focus of their beliefs and religious lives as she was to the Catholics, even though they reverenced her as the mother of God and even if some of the Believers retained their faith in her ability

19 *Quellen zur Ketzergeschichte Brandenburgs und Pommerns*, ed. D. Kurze, Berlin, 1975, pp. 79–80, 82, 225; J.J. Ign von Döllinger, ed., *op. cit.*, Vol. II, pp. 306, 363; G. Barnes Fiertz, 'An Unusual Trial under the Inquisition at Fribourg, Switzerland, in 1399', *Speculum* 18 (1943), p. 344; E. Comba, *History of the Waldenses of Italy*, trans. T. Comba, London, 1889, pp. 284–285.
20 *Le registre*, Vol. I, pp. 58, 70–71, 104, 115.
21 *Quellen zur Ketzergeschichte Brandenburgs und Pommerns*, pp. 26, 85, 97, 113, 119, 120, 124, 130, 134, 141, 159, 165, 169, 173, 178, 186, 238, 241, 246, 253, 259; J.J. Ign von Döllinger, *op. cit.*, Vol. II, pp. 306–307, 333, 345, 363, 365; G. Barnes Fiertz, *op. cit.*, p. 344.
22 *Liber sententiarum inquisitionis Tholosanae*, in *Historia Inquisitionis*, ed. Ph. van Limborch, Amsterdam, 1692, pp. 356 (181), 358 (182).

to help them. From all that is known of their writings and their testimonies before the courts of the Inquisition, it appears that they saw no feminine element in the vision of redemption at the Second Coming. It is therefore clear that The Poor of Lyons did not advance the place and function of the female element. Nor, as we shall see, did they interpret the idea of the spiritual equality between the sexes as calling for gender equality on earth. But let us first examine the accusations levelled against them by the Catholic writers in the early days, that is to say, before the division between Brothers or Sisters and Believers (male and female), which seems to have taken place in the second decade of the thirteenth century.

The first Catholic writer who castigated The Poor of Lyons for allowing their female sect members to preach must have been the Cistercian abbot Geoffroy of Auxerre, writing in 1181–1182. These illiterate boors, he wrote, who beg for alms and preach, not only '. . . creep into houses and lead captive silly women laden with sins, led away with divers lusts' (II Timothy 3:6), but those shameless, sinful females actually presume to preach. He expands (quoting the Song of Solomon 3:2 and Proverbs 9:17) about the boldness, laziness and lewdness of two such women who stood up against the bishop of Clermont who had tried to dissuade them from preaching, and who harassed and insulted him for five years.[23] Other writers followed, often quoting the same verses from the Scriptures, among them Joachim of Fiore,[24] Alain of Lille (who also charged them with debauchery),[25] Bernard of Font-caude (to whom we shall return) and Richard of Poitiers.[26] Others charged that not only did their women preach, they also heard

[23] Geoffroy d'Auxerre, *Super Apocalypsim*, in 'Le témoignage de Geoffroy d'Auxerre sur la vie cistercienne', ed. J. Leclerq, *Studia Anselmiana* 31 (1953), p. 196.

[24] Joachim of Fiore, *De articulis fidei*, in *Enchiridion fontium Valdensium*, ed. G. Gonnet, Torre Pellice, 1958, pp. 99–100.

[25] Alain of Lille, *De fide catholica*, PL 210, L. II (Contra Valdenses), C. 1, cols 379–380.

[26] Richard wrote this work between 1181 and 1216. Bernard Gui incorporated it in his biography of Pope Alexander III: *Vita Alexandri Papae*, in *Enchiridion*, p. 165.

confessions and consecrated the body of Christ in the sacrament. This accusation first appears in a letter of Ardizzo, bishop of Plaisance, written before 1199,[27] as well as in a letter attributed to Ermengaud of Beziers.[28] On the other hand, Pope Innocent III referred only to the preaching of women. In a letter he sent in 1198 or 1199 to the faithful of the diocese of Metz, he warned them against the translation of the Scriptures by The Poor of Lyons, and also denounced their clandestine gatherings, at which lay men and women alike preach.[29] Since there is also evidence of women preaching in the testimony of men and women interrogated by the courts of the Inquisition (in which they spoke in the 1240s about events that had taken place some forty years earlier), it is plain that women did indeed preach. This was an obvious violation of the accepted gender roles – the women were fulfilling a function from which they were banned by the Catholic Church. But even in the early phase of The Poor of Lyons, women did not enjoy equality with the men.

As noted above, it was the historian Grado Merlo who undermined the widespread belief that in the early days of The Poor of Lyons women enjoyed equality with the men, and his argument can be supported further. His main argument goes as follows: the early chroniclers, writing soon after the events of 1173–1179, who described Waldes' early career and his appearance with some of his followers before Pope Alexander III at the Third Lateran Council (1179) to ask him to allow them to live in absolute poverty and preach, made no mention of women. Women were not mentioned in the chronicle by the so-called Anonymous of Lyons which described Waldes' conversion and the Third Lateran

27 *Litterae episcopi Placentini de Pauperibus de Lugduno*, in A. Dondaine O.P., 'Durand de Huesca et la polémique anti-Cathare', *Archivum Fratrum Paedicatorum* 29 (1959), Appendix III, p. 274.
28 *Manifestatio hereses Albigensium et Lugdunensium*, in *ibid.*, Appendix I, p. 271; G. Gonnet, 'Waldensia', *Revue d'histoire et de philosophie religieuses* 33 (1953), Appendix, p. 252.
29 This letter was incorporated in canon law and constituted the basis for the ban on distributing translations of the Scriptures among the laity: *Innocenti III romani pontificis regestrorum sive epistolarum*, PL 214, CXLI, col. 695.

Council, nor in the book of Walter Map, who was present at the Council.[30] Nor did Waldes himself refer to women in the profession of faith he declared in 1180–1181. In it he formally undertook, in his own name and on only behalf of his brothers to obey the priests, bishops and other clerics.[31] Durand Osca's work, *Liber antiheresis*, the only extant Waldensian document from the early period, written between 1190 and 1194, defended the right of laymen to preach and the principle of absolute poverty, but said nothing about women.[32] To these observations of Grado Merlo may be added the following facts: according to the Anonymous of Lyons, Waldes made no attempt to bring up his daughters in his own way – we have noted that he sent them to a convent of the Fontevrault order. His call to renounce private property and for laymen to preach penitence were not addressed to women.[33] In 1208 Durand Osca reverted to Catholicism and was also ordered to make a profession of faith. This statement, made some twenty-eight years after Waldes, added several clauses that had not appeared in the latter, with the aim of denouncing the deviations which were then attributed to The Poor of Lyons. These consisted of a rejection of Donatism, a statement that only a properly ordained priest may administer the Eucharist, that the Church may collect tithes, that secular authorities may judge wrongdoers and put them to death, and a clause concerning preaching. This said that preaching is a good thing, and that it is right to dispute with heretics and turn them to the true path, but only properly authorized persons should do so, or one who was empowered by the Pope, or one of the higher clerics in the Church. There is no reference to women preaching.[34] The profession of faith made by Bernard Prim, who reverted to Catholicism two years later, in

30 *Chronicon universale anonymi Laudunensis*, in *M.G.H. Scriptores*, Vol. 26, ed. G. Waitz, Hanover and Berlin, 1931, pp. 447, 449; Walter Map, *De nugis curialium*, ed. and trans. M.R. James, revised by C.N.L. Brooke and R.A.B. Mynors, Oxford, 1983, pp. 125–127.
31 See note 53, chapter 1, first item.
32 See note 5, chapter 1; Merlo's article, note 13, above.
33 See note 30, above.
34 *Innocenti III romani pontificis regestrorum sive epistolarum*, PL 215, CXCVI, cols 510–513.

1210, does contain a clause that denies women the right to preach or to teach,[35] but the fact that it does not appear in Durand Osca's statement seems to suggest that preaching by women did not strike the Church authorities (unlike the various authors who sought to denounce The Poor of Lyons) as a central issue, and that women preaching was a less widespread phenomenon than the polemical writings implied. Finally, before 1190 a public debate was held between Waldensians and Catholics, following which Abbot Bernard of the Cistercian monastery of Fontcaude (north of Narbonne), composed his well-known polemic, entitled 'Against the Waldensians'. The Prologue describes the debate, and it is plain than just as no women took part in the debate on the Catholic side, nor did any on the Waldensian.[36]

This work of Bernard Fontcaude shows that the Poor of Lyons did not interpret the idea of spiritual equality after Christ as meaning that equality must rule on earth. The eighth chapter of this polemic[37] contains the most exhaustive discussion by a Catholic author on women preaching among The Poor of Lyons, and is the most thorough source on the subject as a whole, seeing that there are no Waldensian documents on this issue. The chapter opens in a relatively mild tone. It states that 'they [Waldensians] say that women may preach',[38] and proceeds to quote all the usual verses from the Epistles of St Paul with which the Church denied women the right to be clerics or to preach;[39] also on the First Epistle of Peter 3:1, and on the resolution of the Church Council of Carthage (318). He refers to St Mary's silence, who kept 'in her heart' all that she had heard, and did not speak of it with anyone (Luke 2:51). He further notes that Mary Magdalene and the other faithful women who followed Christ neither taught nor preached. He quotes from the Book of Genesis to expand on woman's secondary place in creation and her part in

---

35 *PL* 216, cols 292–293.
36 Bernard Fontcaude, *Adversus Waldensium sectam*, PL 204, cols 793–840; The Prologue: cols 793–795.
37 *Ibid.*, cols 825–828.
38 '. . . quod mulieres praedicare posse dicunt', *ibid.*, col. 825.
39 I Corinthians 13:34–35; I Timothy 2:11–15; Ephesians 5:22–24.

the Original Sin, recalls the (failed) attempt of Job's wife to get him to curse God (Job 2:9), to show that the 'cunning tempter' may again use woman to bring down man, and reiterates that it is unthinkable that the woman, who is commanded to cover her head – in memory of her sin and as sign of her servitude – who may not teach even her own husband verbally, but may at best serve him as an example in deed, might be allowed to teach other men.

The second half of the chapter is more aggressive. Bernard no longer says that according to The Poor of Lyons women may preach, but that 'the enemies of truth say that women must teach[40] and quotes what he claims were the authorities on which The Poor of Lyons based their permitting of women to preach, then proceeds to invalidate them. But while he produces a large number of authorities to justify the banning of women from preaching, he brings in only two sources which he claims were used by The Poor of Lyons. The first is taken from the Epistle of Paul to Titus (2:3–5): 'The aged women likewise, that they be in behaviour as becometh holiness, not false accusers, not given to much wine, teachers of good things. That they may teach the young women to be sober, to love their husbands, to love their children. To be discreet, chaste, keepers at home, good, obedient to their own husbands . . .' The other authority which he claims was cited by The Poor of Lyons was the story of Anna at the Temple, as related in Luke 2:36–39. He has no difficulty disproving the application of these quotes. As for the statement in the Epistle to Titus, he explains that it referred only to teaching young women at home, not teaching men, let alone in public. About the case of Anna, he states that she was a virtuous woman endowed with the gift of prophecy, and therefore spoke in public – she prophesied about Jesus and praised him, but neither taught nor preached. Quoting St Paul in I Corinthians 12:5–12, he notes the distinction between the various gifts of the Holy Spirit, to show that the gift of prophecy is not the same as teaching the faith. His arguments imply the common acceptance of the spiri-

[40] 'Dicunt inimici veritatis muliere debere docere.' Bernard Fontcaude, *op. cit.*, col. 826.

tual equality between the sexes, since he takes pains to stress that women must be silent in the 'earthy church' in which there can be no equality between the sexes. Therefore in the earthly church women may pray and praise God, but may not teach.[41]

According to Bernard Fontcaude, these two excerpts – from the Second Epistle to Titus 2:3–5, and the story of Anna in Luke 2:36–39 – were the only Scriptural authorities The Poor of Lyons used to justify preaching by women. He did not ascribe to them a reliance on the Scriptural text that declares the spiritual equality between men and women (Galatians 3:28) as meaning that such equality must prevail in the earthly Church (as the Quakers would do in the seventeenth century), and hence justify preaching by women. Yet such an interpretation had actually been made before. Some four centuries before the Quaker George Fox, Pierre Abelard propounded this unusual and subversive interpretation, but unlike Fox he stopped short of drawing practical conclusions from this interpretation, and did not call for greater rights for women in the Church. Referring to this verse in an Easter sermon, he wrote:

> Who is so singular in dignity as Christ, in whom the Apostle says there is neither male nor female? (Galatians 3:28). In the body of Christ, which is the Church, difference of sex therefore confers no dignity; for Christ looks not to the condition of sex, but to the quality of merits.[42]

---

[41] '. . . Apostolus jubet, ut mulieris taceant in ecclesiis materialibut, vel in congregationibus fidelium, non quidem ab oratione vel laude dei, sed a doctrina,' Bernard Fontcaude, *op. cit.*, col. 825. For an analysis of the rhetorical structure of the writing of Geoffroy d'Auxerre and Bernard Fontcaude, their use of authorities and their arguments in the context of the history of opposition to women preaching, see: B.M. Kienzle, 'The Prostitute-Preacher. Patterns of Polemic against Medieval Waldensian Women Preachers', in *Women Preachers and Prophets Through Two Millennia of Christianity*, eds B.M. Kienzle and P.J. Walker, Berkeley, 1998, pp. 99–113.

[42] 'Quis enim unicus et dignitate singularis ita ut Christus in quo quoque nec masculum, nec feminam Apostolus esse dicit (Gal. 3:28)? Quia in Christi corpore, quod est Ecclesia, nullam dignitatem diversi-

The Church – the body of Christ – is the earthly church. This is not Abelard's only statement in favour of women. He often sang their praises, and was sometimes carried away beyond the rhetoric on spiritual equality that was common in texts in praise of women. (The Catholic discourse about women was not unequivocal.) Writing about Anna in the Temple according to Luke 2:36–39, he went so far as the state that the Apostle was meticulously describing 'her preaching in public about Him, the promise and the birth of the Saviour'.[43] But, again, he stops short of drawing conclusions from this interpretation. In his instructions to Héloïse concerning the best kind of convent, he opposes not only a 'double monastery' headed by an abbess, but even an autonomous women's convent headed by an abbess who is not subject to a man. Quoting St Paul, '. . . the head of every man is Christ, and the head of the woman is the man' (I Corinthians 11:3), he states: 'I want women's convents to be always subject to men's monasteries.'[44]

It is generally assumed that Bernard Fontcaude's work was based on arguments made in the public dispute. While we cannot be certain that The Poor of Lyons did not bring up other arguments and authorities that Bernard did not care to contend with in his book, it is nevertheless reasonable to assume that they had not referred to the verse about spiritual equality with its subversive interpretation – otherwise it it unlikely that Bernard would have shied away from rebutting it with the standard interpretation. As noted before, there are scarcely any Waldensian sources

tas sexum operatur, nec sexum qualitatem, sed meritus Christus attendit . . .' Petrus Abaelardus, *Sermo XIII, PL* 178, col. 488; translated in M.M. McLaughlin, 'Peter Abelard and the Dignity of Women: Twelfth Century Feminism in Theory and Practice', in *Pierre Abelard – Pierre le Venerable*, eds R. Louis and J. Jolivet, Colloques Internationaux du CNRS, No. 546, Paris, 1975, p. 305.

43 '. . . et publicam eius praedicationem de promisso et nato salvatore diligenter expressit', J.T. Muckle C.S.B. ed., 'The Letter of Heloise on Religious Life and Abelard's First Reply', *Medieval Studies* 17 (1955), p. 263.

44 T.P. McLaughlin C.S.B. ed., 'Abelard's Rule for Religious Women', *Medieval Studies* 18 (1956), pp. 258–259.

from the first decades of the movement, and the sole extant one, Durand Osca's book, makes no mention of women. In later years, when they sought to represent their self-image vis-à-vis that of the Catholic clergy, they mentioned their poverty, their devotion to their evangelical role, and their willingness to suffer persecution and hardships, but not gender equality in their community.

In summary, it may be said that while women did preach in the early days of The Poor of Lyons, they did not enjoy equal rights with the men. In their first enthusiasm for the spreading of the word of God in the spirit of the Apostles, the Waldensians licensed preaching by women, but this was not one of their aims and raising the status of women in the religious life was not one of their tenets. It is probable, too, that the Catholic writers exaggerated the extent of preaching by women. Thus, if there was a reduction in the rights of women following the establishment of the sect and the formation of a hierarchy among the Brothers, it was less significant than most historians believed. The division between Brothers and Believers was paralleled by a similar division between female Believers and Sisters. The next chapter discusses the continuity of the status of Sisters, their standing and rights.

3

The Sisters

The previous chapter dealt with the accusations that Catholic polemicists levelled against The Poor of Lyons. Some writers accused them only of allowing women to preach, while others charged that some of their women also heard confessions and consecrated the eucharist. Until the end of the second decade of the thirteenth century the reference was simply to 'women' (*mulieres*), but later, with the rise of the distinction between Brothers and Sisters from Believers, even when the Catholic writers used the term 'women' rather than 'Sisters' (*sorores*), or 'Waldensian women' (*mulieres Valdenses*) by which they also denoted the Sisters, the reference was to Sisters. The accusations appeared regularly until about the fourteenth century, and thereafter, while they did not altogether cease, they became less and less frequent. And just as in the earlier period, some writers such as Moneta of Cremona (who completed his work a little before 1241), accused them only of allowing women to preach,[1] while others also charged that the women heard confessions and consecrated the eucharist. But not all the writers, either early or late, were equally firm in making these accusations.

The chronicler Pierre of Vaux-de-Cernay, who probably completed his work in 1213, and was informed on the subject of the Cathars as well as The Poor of Lyons, noted inter alia that the latter believe that any one of them, so long as he is 'shod in

---

1 Moneta of Cremona, *Adversus Catharos et Valdenses, libri quinque*, ed. T.A. Ricchini, Rome, 1743, L.V., pp. 403, 441–442.

sandals' may consecrate the body of Christ in the sacrament.[2] This suggests that early in the second decade of the thirteenth century, even if the hierarchy that would later be described by Raymond de la Côte and after him the Inquisitor Bernard Gui was not yet established, there was already a division between the 'sandalled ones', who alone were authorized to administer the sacrament, and the rest of the sect. Were there any 'sandalled' women in the second decade of the century? The Inquisitor Anselm of Alessandria wrote in the late 1260s that the women (by which he certainly meant the Sisters) were living in poverty like the men, surviving on alms and preaching, but were not ordained to serve as priests, could not impose penance following confession, were not authorized to consecrate the body of Christ in the sacrament and did not wear sandals.[3] The sandals were a visible identifying mark in a society in which clothing or a particular part of it served to indicate social and religious status. We cannot conclude with certainty from Anselm's statement that already in the time of Pierre of Vaux-de-Cernay women were barred from wearing sandals, which meant that they were not included among those authorized to administer the sacrament. Nevertheless, the fact that he makes no mention of women suggests that he probably did not think they were so empowered. The Cathar Rainier Sacconi, who reverted to Catholicism and became a Dominican Inquisitor, wrote in the mid-thirteenth century: 'They say that an ordinary layman may consecrate the Lord's body. I believe they say this also of the women, since they did not deny this in speaking to me.'[4] The impression created is that he was less certain about the women than about the men. Nor was the Anonymous of Passau, writing in the late 1260s, unequivocal on

---

2 Pierre de Vaux-de-Cernay, *Hystoria Albigensis*, eds P. Guebin and E. Lyon, Paris, 1926, pp. 18–19.
3 Anselme of Alessandria, *Tractatus de hereticis* in A. Dondaine O.P., ed., 'La hiérarchie cathare en Italie II: Le "Tractatus de hereticis" d'Anselme d'Alexandrie O.P.', *Archivun Fratrum Praedicatorum* 20 (1950), pp. 318–319.
4 *Summa fratris Raynerii de ordine Fratrum Praedicatorum de Catharis et Pauperibus de Lugduno*, in A. Dondaine O.P. ed., *Un traité néo-manichéen du XIIIe siècle*, Rome, 1939, p. 78.

the subject. First he wrote that they believed that a sinful priest might not administer the eucharist, whereas a virtuous layman or even a woman who knows the words might do so, but further on, in reference to confession and the imposition of penance, he made no mention of women.[5] However, Stephen of Bourbon, writing in the 1250s, stated that he had been told by one of the leaders of The Poor of Lyons (*magnus magister et legatus*) that they were divided over the question of women's rights. Some of them held that only men might be ordained, while others maintain that if a woman was truly virtuous she too may serve as a priest. Further on he reported seeing a woman, who would later be burnt at the stake, about to conduct the sacrament of the eucharist on a chest made to look like an altar.[6] This statement of Stephen of Bourbon is unique – to the best of my knowledge, none of the other ecclesiastical writers and Inquisitors described actually seeing a woman about to conduct a sacrament. Bernard Gui, whose book was completed in 1323 or 1324,[7] the Inquisitor of Aragon Nicolas Eymeric in the middle of the fourteenth century,[8] and the Inquisitor Ricardino who composed the list of the 'errors' of The Poor of Lyons in Pesana in the early sixteenth century,[9] all attributed to women the right to administer the sacrament unreservedly.

However it would seem that while this accusation did not cease until the early sixteenth century, it had certainly become rarer. A

---

5 Anonymous of Passau, *Auszuge aus dem Sarnmelwerk des Passauer Anonymus*, in *Quellen zur Geschichte der Waldenser*, eds A. Patschovsky and K.V. Selge, Göttingen, 1973, pp. 82, 86.
6 Etienne de Bourbon, *Tractatus de diversis materiis praedicabilis*, in *Anecdotes historiques, légendes et apologues tirés du recueil inédit d'Etienne de Bourbon*, ed. A. Lecoy de la Marche, Paris, 1877, p. 296; according to Anselm, the majoral used a box instead of an altar once a year: Anselme d'Alexandrie, *op. cit.*, pp. 320–321.
7 Bernard Gui, *Manuel de l'inquisiteur*, ed. and trans. G. Mollat, Paris, 1964, Vol. I, pp. 36, 42.
8 G. Gonnet, *Le confessioni di fede dei Valdesi prima della Riforma*, Turin, 1967, pp. 116–117.
9 G. Gonnet, 'Waldensia', *Revue d'histoire et de philosophie religieuses* 33 (1953), pp. 236–237.

text composed in 1399 and attributed to the Inquisitor of Silesia Giovanni di Gliwice, attacks the deviations and errors of The Poor of Lyons and disputes with them, but makes no mention of women preaching or serving as priests.[10] The same holds true for the polemical work of the Inquisitor Peter Zwicker, 'While Men Sleep' (Cum dormirent homines), written in 1395.[11] Even more significant than the lack of reference to women in the polemical writings is the fact that the Inquisitors ceased to ask about them. In the list of questions to be put to The Poor of Lyons, prepared by Peter Zwicker in the 1390s, there is not one question concerning the status and rights of the Sisters, and not once in the 195 interrogations which he himself conducted as Inquisitor of Stettin in the years 1392–1394 did he ask a question on this matter.[12] The same holds true for Gallus of Neuhaus' interrogations in the 1350s.[13] Bernard Gui's manual for Inquisitors, following Stephen of Bourbon, still stated that women preached (though the men disseminated more errors than they did), and administered the eucharist.[14] But the 1320s records of his court in Toulouse mention only one Sister by name, and none of the many men and women who were interrogated mentioned Sisters preaching, hearing confessions or administering the eucharist, and apparently none was questioned about this.[15] Jacques Four-

---

[10] Tractatus bonus (pars prima contra hereticos qui Valdensis dicuntur, quorum magistri heresiarche, Fratres nuncupantur), in R. Cegna, ed., 'La condizione del Valdismo secondo l'inedito Tractatus bonus contra haereticos del 1399 attribubile all'inquisitore della Slesia Giovanni di Gliwice', in I Valdesi e l'Europa. Collana della società di studi Valdesi 9, Torre Pellice, 1982, pp. 39–65.

[11] Peter Biller, 'Les Vaudois dans les territoires de la langue allemande vers la fin du XIVe siècle: le regard d'un Inquisiteur', Heresis 13–14 (1989), pp. 203–228.

[12] Quellen zur Ketzergeschichte Brandenburgs und Pommerns, ed. D. Kurze, Berlin, 1975, pp. 73–75, 77–261.

[13] Verhorsprotokolle der inquisition des Gallus von Neuhaus (1335 bis ca. 1353/55), in Quellen zur Böhmischen Inquisition im 14. Jahrhundert, ed. A. Patschovsky, Weimar, 1979, pp. 173–255.

[14] See note 7, above.

[15] In this collection, the verdicts are preceded by short, standardized descriptions of the charges admitted by the accused, and the answers

nier, who interrogated our four Poor of Lyons about the same time and in the same region, did put questions about the position of women in the sect both to Raymond de la Côte and to Huguette. Raymond was asked if they admitted women into their rank (*status*) – meaning, did they admit Sisters in the same way as Brothers – and he replied categorically that they did not admit virgins into their rank. When asked why not, he replied: 'Because women may not preach the word of God, nor can they serve as presbyter, deacon or majoral'.[16] When Huguette was asked if she had seen the majoral Jean of Lorraine holding the sacrament of the eucharist, she replied that she had not, and added that she herself had not conducted the sacrament nor heard anyone's confession.[17] Though we cannot be certain, it is reasonable to assume that she had been asked about it but the question was not recorded. Possibly, if less probably, she believed that the Inquisitor thought that women sometimes heard confessions and administered the sacrament, and therefore saw fit to reply as she did. At her next interrogation 'she was asked if [according to their faith] she or any other woman might hear confessions, and she said no'.[18] (This does not preclude the possibility that she had been asked about it in the previous interrogation; Jacques Fournier habitually repeated his questions.) In view of the paucity of references to Sisters in the Catholic writings from the late fourteenth century and their virtual disappearance from the records of the Inquisitorial courts, and in the light of the unequivocal testimony of the deacon Raymond de la Côte, some historians concluded that the rank of Sisters had altogether disappeared. But it did not.

Peter Biller, who more than any historian of the Waldensians

which are mostly stereotypical. Yet it is possible to deduce from these what the accused were questioned about, and it appears that they were not questioned about the Sisters. *Liber sententiarum inquisitionis Tholosanae*, in *Historia inquisitionis*, ed. Ph. van Limborch, Amsterdam, 1692, pp. 200–201, 207–217, 221–224, 228–229, 231, 263–265 and more.

16 *Le registre*, Vol. I, p. 74.
17 *Ibid.*, p. 525.
18 *Ibid.*, p. 527.

researched the role of the Sisters in the sect, has pointed to the continuous, if sporadic, references to the Sisters in the various sources, and tried to account for their disappearance from the records of the Inquisitorial courts. The letter sent by The Poor of Lombardy to The Poor of Lyons following the conference held in Bergamo in 1218, with the purpose of healing the rift between them, addresses 'our dear Brothers and Sisters in Christ, our [male and female] friends across the Alps'.[19] During the 1240s witnesses in the courts of the Inquisition in Languedoc testified about the Sisters.[20] The famous work known as *De vita et actibus*, composed in Languedoc at the end of the thirteenth or beginning of the fourteenth century, states that The Poor of Lyons admitted both men and women and called them Brothers and Sisters, and describes their customs.[21] The records of the Inquisition of Strasbourg for the year 1400 include the interrogation of men and women who described the ordination of men and women as male and female teachers (the latter: *meisterin*).[22] To these references noted by Biller we may add the opening of the prayer that was

---

19 'Fratribus ac sororibus, amicis et amicabus . . .' *Rescriptum heresiarcharum Lombardiae ad Pauperes de Lugduno*, in *Enchiridion fontium Valdensium*, ed. G. Gonnet, Torre Pellice, 1958, p. 171.

20 P. Biller, ' "Thesaurus Absconditus": The Hidden Treasure of the Waldensians', in *The Church and Wealth*, eds W.J. Sheils and D. Wood, *Studies in Church History* 24 (1987), p. 142; P. Biller, 'The Preaching of the Waldensian Sisters', notes 12–13, 38–39, 40–41 and Appendix; Dr Biller has kindly enabled me to read the manuscript of this paper before publication, hence the reference to notes rather than pages. The paper is due to appear in *La prédication sur un mode dissident: laics femmes, hérétiques (XIe–XIVe siècles)*, Actes de la 9e session d'histoire mediévale organisée par le C.N.E.C./ R. Nelli, 26–30 août 1996, ed. M.B. Kienzle, Carcassonne, forthcoming; see also Y. Dossat, 'Les Vaudois méridionaux d'après les documents de l'inquisition', in *Vaudois languedociens et Pauvres Catholiques. Cahiers de Fanjeaux* 2 (1967), p. 224.

21 *De vita et actibus*, in J.J. Ign von Döllinger, ed., *Beiträge zur Sektengeschichte des Mittelalters*, Munich, 1890, Vol. II, pp. 93–95.

22 T.W. Röhrich, ed., *Factum hereticorum*, in *Mitteilungen aus der Geschichte der evangelischen Kirche des Elsasses*, Paris–Strasbourg, 1855, pp. 42, 51–52.

attached to a Provençal translation of a Waldensian text from the late thirteenth or early fourteenth century, known as *The Waldensian Rule Book*. It opens with a prayer for the Brothers and Sisters.[23] Likewise, in the testimony of the nobleman Jean Draedorf, who was either a Hussite or a Waldensian and was burnt at the stake in Heidelberg in 1425 – he reported that in the 1420s, while travelling in Germany, he stayed in the hospices of The Poor of Lyons, in one of which lived a widow and two virgins. He added that those women (most likely Sisters) knew that the Catholic priests were greedy and lascivious, and stated that he slept in their house but not in the same room with them.[24] The sisters were mentioned again, and for the last time, on the eve of the union with the Calvinists. In 1530, an exchange of letters between the Swiss Reformists and the Waldensians Georges Morel and Pierre Mason, in which the latter described their beliefs, organization and customs, they also referred to the status of the Sisters. This was ended, under pressure from the Reformists, in the resolutions of the conference at Chanforan in 1532.[25]

There is no doubt that mention of the sisters had grown very rare, but Biller suggests that the scanty mention and the virtual disappearance from the records of the Inquisitorial courts does not mean that the Sisters had ceased to exist. He maintains that they disappeared from the records because the Inquisitors lost interest in them and so did not ask questions about them and were therefore not informed about them. This is proved by the fact that people from the Alpine valleys of Piedmont in the fifteenth century made no mention of the Sisters when under interrogation by the Inquisition, although the letters of Georges Morel and Pierre Mason clearly show that there were Sisters

---

23 *Regula secte Waldensium*, ed. A. Molnar, in 'Les Vaudois et l'unité des Frères tchéques', *Bolletino della società di studi Valdesi* 118 (1965), p. 3.
24 In G. Gonnet and A. Molnar, *Les Vaudois au moyen âge*, Turin, 1974, p. 227, note 82.
25 V. Vinay, ed., *Le confessioni di fede dei Valdesi Riformati con documenti del dialogo fra 'prima' e 'seconda' Riforma*, Collana della facoltà Valdes di Teologia 12, Turin, 1975, pp. 36–38, 46, 58–60, 68, 76–78, 89; G. Gonnet and A. Molnar, *op. cit.*, Ch. 6.

there. Biller also noted other factors which might explain their disappearance from the records of the Inquisitorial courts: more men than women testified before these courts, and the men knew less about the Sisters than did the women; the Sisters did not move from one Believer's house to another, as did the Brothers, but resided in the hospices, so that fewer Believers knew them. Moreover, those interrogated often used terms that could apply to both men and women (e.g. 'He said he saw the Waldensians'). As for the testimony of Raymond de la Côte,[26] from which researchers concluded that by the second decade of the fourteenth century there were no more Sisters in Languedoc: Biller argues that Raymond was trying to defend the Sisters in the few remaining hospices in the region, as there is no doubt that there were some. This is borne out by the text De vita et actibus, which was composed during the time when the four Waldensians were in prison, or a little earlier, and which contains the most detailed extant description of the life of the Sisters.[27] It seems to me that Biller's supposition that the rank of Sisters persisted throughout the period – i.e. until the union with the Protestants – is well-based. However, the question remains why the Inquisitors lost interest in them and consequently stopped asking questions about them. The Inquisitors in their interrogations did not engage in polemics or propaganda. Their purpose was to determine the degree of the accused individual's deviation and adherence to heresy; if found guilty to induce him or her to recant, to punish (even if the method was described as an act of atonement rather than punishment), and to obtain further information about the sect's beliefs and customs and about other heretics. By the fourteenth century they already had reliable information about The Poor of Lyons, so it would seem that they stopped asking questions about the Sisters because they realized that they were few and their activity was limited.

What can be gleaned from the sources about the Sisters' way of life, their prerogatives and functions? Let us start with what they most probably were not authorized to do, namely, administer the

[26] See note 16, above.
[27] P. Biller, 'The Preaching of the Waldensian Sisters', notes 74, 75, 77.

sacrament of the eucharist. As we have seen, some Catholic writers and Inquisitors accused The Poor of Lyons – categorically or with some reservation – of permitting women to administer the eucharist. Yet it is extremely unlikely that this was the case, for several reasons. Although both Durand Osca and Bernard Prim, in their declarations of faith, denounced the administering of the sacrament by laymen, it is not certain how widespread this was, from what time and in which communities. The testimonies of the fourteenth century, as mentioned in the First Chapter, show that only the head of the hierarchy of Brothers, the majoral, was authorized to conduct the sacrament, and that he too did this very rarely. By and large, the Brothers encouraged the Believers to receive the sacrament in the Catholic church. While evidence given in the courts of the Inquisition (in the mid-thirteenth century) testified to the Sisters, teaching and preaching, there is not one testimony about their administering the sacrament. As we have seen, one of the principal issues on which The Poor of Lyons and The Poor of Lombardy failed to agree at the Bergamo conference in 1218 was the validity of a sacrament administered by a sinful priest. The letter sent by The Poor of Lombardy to The Poor of Lyons, following the conference, which detailed all the positions taken by both sides, made it clear that neither side believed that women could administer the sacrament. It stated that The Poor of Lyons did not question the validity of a sacrament administered by a Catholic priest, even a sinful one, and maintained that no layman or woman, but only a priest ordained in the Catholic church was empowered to do so; whereas The Poor of Lombardy held that the sacrament was valid only if administered by a priest who was free of sin, or else by a virtuous laymen. It stated explicitly that The Poor of Lyons did not acknowledge a sacrament administered by a woman, while as for The Poor of Lombardy, there is no unequivocal statement that they did acknowledge such a sacrament, and there is no reference to women.[28]

While it is impossible to state categorically that nowhere and at no time did a woman administer the eucharist (as we have seen,

[28] *Rescriptum heresiarcharum Lombardiae ad Pauperes de Lugduno*, p. 177.

Stephen of Bourbon claimed to have seen a woman preparing to do so), it was obviously not an accepted custom. It is exceedingly unlikely that The Poor of Lyons, who from the start excluded women from their delegations to the pope and the bishops and from public debates, and later – as we shall see – also from their conventions, and Durand Osca in his writing did not even defend their right to preach, actually allowed women to administer the eucharist, which was the central symbol of Christianity at that time. Unlike other sacraments – baptism, marriage and extreme unction, which in dire emergencies might be administered by laymen – and in which God was present only in spirit, the eucharist offered the body of Christ to the faithful.[29] We should keep in mind that the Catholic polemicists and Inquisitors accused The Poor of Lyons of other offences, some of which were standard elements in the stereotype of the heretic. The heretic was regarded not only as deviant because of his presumptuous and erroneous interpretation of the Scriptures, but also as one who overturned all the accepted norms. Thus The Poor of Lyons were also accused of ignorance, of disregard for the laws of incest, of sexual profligacy, lying, hypocrisy – revealed, inter alia, by the Brothers' ostensible devotion to poverty whereas in reality they were misers who amassed fortunes – and in the fifteenth century also of witchcraft. None of these accusations is accepted uncritically by any modern historian. Even if some Catholic writers believed that Waldensian women administered the sacrament – which intensified their anxieties and their feeling that the established social and religious order was threatened by the undermining of the hierarchical distinctions between men and women – they did not pull these accusations out of the air. The Catholic writers had a standard pattern of bad, corrupting women, much like the pattern of heretics going back to the time of the Church Fathers. Thus in the rhetoric of denunciation used against The Poor of Lyons they recycled familiar textual patterns and gave them a new content: women administering the sacrament. Later writers and Inquisitors repeated their predecessors' words.

---

[29] See M. Rubin, *Corpus Christi. The Eucharist in Late Medieval Culture*, Cambridge, 1991, p. 36.

As noted before, the most detailed description of the life of the Sisters and the roles they played is found in the work known as *De vita et actibus*. The author stated that in some hospices two or three old women lived alone, but were frequently visited by the Brothers, whose food they prepared. In other hospices lived two or three men and two or three women, who pretended to be married couples or brothers and sisters. Men and women who wished to learn the Scriptures met in the hospices, where they were taught by the *doctores*, received their blessings and listened to their sermons. The teachers would read the texts aloud over and over, until their hearers knew them by heart. The ceremonies of ordination of the Brothers and Sisters were also held in these hospices, after which the men gave the kiss of peace to the new Brother and the women to the new Sister, and this was also done when Brothers or Sisters arrived at a hospice from elsewhere. The hospice was headed by a man, called a *gubernator*, who led the prayers, the sermon and the rituals. The author proceeds to describe the general conventions which The Poor of Lyons held annually,[30] and specifies who was not entitled to participate in them: Believers, young Perfects (he uses the terms Brothers and Sisters interchangeably with Perfects, male and female), Perfects who were not obedient or did not serve the sect wholeheartedly, even if they were old, or women, even if they were Perfects and old.[31] Sisters did not take part in the conference of Bergamo, either. The absence of Sisters from the gatherings meant that they had no part in the decisions concerning the allocation of funds to the different hospices. These descriptions supplement the information gathered from the testimonies at the Inquisitorial courts during the 1240s, which referred to events of some forty years before – i.e. the end of the first decade of the thirteenth century – which have been studied and published by Peter Biller. It is clear from these testimonies that the Sisters did not work outside the hospices, where they resided for relatively long stretches. One woman testified that in Castres, Sisters lived in the house of a

---

[30] See chapter 1, notes 33, 34.
[31] *De vita et actibus*, in J.J. Ign von Döllinger, ed., *op. cit.*, Vol. II, pp. 93–96; he calls the leading Brothers *sandaliati*.

woman Believer, and Believers from nearby villages provided them with grain and meat. Others testified about a house in Beaucaire which they had leased for Sisters for a year, and still others about a house in Montcuq that was leased for two years. A woman stated that she had lived with Sisters in a house in Castelnaudary for three years.[32] At that time the Brothers were still openly active in the region. After the sect moved underground, only the Brothers continued to wander between the houses of the Believers, and the road and the open country became theirs alone. Already in the first decade of the thirteenth century the Sisters were confined to the hospices, the space thought appropriate for women. They became cloistered at about the same time as the Poor Clares were cloistered by the Franciscans. When Raymond de la Côte described the ceremony of Maundy Thursday, in which the Believers did not participate (nor, according to him, were they even supposed to know about it), he spoke about the participation of the Brothers (socii) only.[33] But it is possible that this was not the case, and that Raymond left out the women's presence as part of his overall denial of their status.

The above already makes it clear that the Sisters were restricted. They did teach, and some of them also preached, at least in some regions some of the time. A few of the women interrogated in Languedoc in the 1240s testified about being taught by the Sisters. One Believer described to the court of the Inquisitors Peter Durant and Ferrier in 1244 how the Sisters read to a sick Believer at her house from the Athanasian Creed and the Gospel of St John.[34] Another woman who testified before the court of Peter Seila, also in the 1240s (about events that had occurred several decades earlier), how she had heard a woman preach about the Passion of Christ,[35] and a builder from Montauban testi-

---

32 See note 20, above.
33 Le registre, Vol. I, p. 68.
34 Quellen zur Geschichte der Waldenser, p. 63; testimonies about the Sisters: ibid., pp. 58, 59, 61, 69.
35 Mentioned in G. Merlo, 'Sulle "misere donnicciuole" che predicavano', Identità Valdesi nella storia e nella storiografia. Valdesi e Valdismi medievali II, Turin, 1991, p. 106.

fied that he had heard Waldensian women preaching in public.[36] The Sisters did not as a rule preach on formal or solemn occasions, and did not usually expound on the Scriptures. They generally taught in the hospices those of the Believers who attended, almost exclusively women.[37] The Anonymous of Passau described all The Poor of Lyons, men, women and children, as studying diligently, and noted that the women studied and taught.[38] The persons interrogated by the court of the Inquisition in Strasbourg in 1400 described the ordination of men and women as teachers (*meister, meisterin*) as being identical, and likewise their vows to a life of celibacy poverty and devotion to the faith. The men chosen for ordination had to be such as had never known a woman carnally, and the women, virgins. There are no testimonies describing the work of the female teachers, but the female witnesses stressed their existence and one testified explicitly that she had been taught her faith by a woman teacher.[39] The number of Sisters who taught varied no doubt from region to region and over time. As we shall see in the next chapter, Huguette described in detail her contacts with the Brothers and what she had learned from them, but made no mention of contact with a Sister. When asked if she had taught her errors or discussed them with anyone, she replied that she had discussed them with her husband Jean and with a woman named Jeanne of Montpellier, but it is clear

---

[36] In A. Brenon, 'The Voice of the Good Women. An Essay on the Pastoral and Sacerdotal Role of Women in the Cathar Church', in *Women Preachers and Prophets Through Two Millennia of Christianity*, eds B.M. Kienzle and P.J. Walker, Berkeley, 1998, p. 122 and note 28.

[37] P. Biller, 'The Preaching of the Waldensian Sisters', notes 60–64 and Appendix.

[38] Anonymous of Passau, *op. cit.*, pp. 70–76; Pseudo-Reinerius, *Tractatus*, in M. Nickson, ed., 'The "Pseudo-Reineius" Treatise: The Final Stage of a Thirteenth Century Work on Heresy from the Diocese of Passau', *Archives d'histoire doctrinale et littéraire du moyen âge* 42 (1967), p. 292; see also David of Augsburg, *Tractatus de Inquisicione hereticorum*, ed. W. Preger, Munich, 1878, pp. 29, 209.

[39] *Factum hereticorum*, in T.W. Röhrich, ed., *op. cit.*, pp. 42, 51, 52; see also the article analyzing this text: P. Biller, 'What did Happen to the Waldensian Sisters? The Strasbourg Testimony'. This article is due to be published in *Mélange Giovanni Gonnet*, ed. F. Giacone.

from the context that she was referring to a Believer in the sect, not a Sister who taught her.

The final reference to the Sisters occurs in the report of Georges Morel and Pierre Mason to the Swiss Reformists. They wrote about *nostrae mulierculae*, who were called Sisters and who lived as virgins in the Alpine valleys of Piedmont. For, they said, young women who wished to remain virgins took vows to live in celibacy and entered a religious order (in *religionem introducte*). The Sisters lived apart and subsisted on donations allocated by the Brothers, but the young men who were training to become Brothers lived for a year or two in their vicinity. It is not clear if the purpose was for them to do the heavier chores (as the lay brothers did in the Catholic monasteries), or that they received their spiritual training in such an isolated place before being sent out to work among the Believers. A late Waldensian work, a commentary on the Song of Solomon written in the Piedmontese dialect, enjoined the Brothers to maintain a holy and honourable relationship with the Sisters (*serors*), and the Sisters were told to submit to the Brothers modestly and humbly. In describing their way of life, the author reiterates those statements: 'The Brothers treat the Sisters with respect and love, and the Sisters submit to them and obey them nimbly.'[40] This injuction to obey the Brothers, which accorded with the traditional subordination of women in the Church and in society, was exceptional in the writings of The Poor of Lyons. As a rule, there was no discourse on the subject of women in their writings. What the sources reveal – usually by implication – was how they were restricted in practice. The Protestant Reformists reacted with severity to the report of Morel and Mason, and brought up a series of objections to the status of Sisters: such virgins were usually inclined to commit sin, and the proximity of the Brothers, however modest, exposed them to temptation; the cost of maintaining them was substantial and of little usefulness; if they were true Sisters, they ought not to live at the expense of the church; it would be best for them to

[40] *Cantica*, ed. and trans. J. Herzog, *Zeitschrift für die historische Theologie* 31 (1861), pp. 493–559.

marry, despite their foolish vows, which were not binding and had not been ordained by God. And indeed at the conference in Chanforan in 1532 it was decided to abolish the rank of Sisters.[41] Sisters did not take part in the negotiations with the Reformists, nor in the conferences which revolved upon the union with them and on the abolition of their rank.

Gabriel Audisio regarded the presence of Sisters in the Piedmontese valleys in the early sixteenth century as a mere vestige of the old equality which had existed in the early days between the Waldensian men and women.[42] But, as we have seen, there had never been any such equality. However, the report undoubtedly reveals a further decline in the position of women compared with the thirteenth century in Languedoc, or even the early fifteenth century in Germany. By this time, their sole distinction was virginity, and there was no mention of teaching. The text written in that region calls on the sisters to submit humbly to the Brothers – the emphasis shifting from virginity to obedience. There was also an irony in the use of the term *mulierculae*, a humiliating diminutive of marked paternalistic connotation, a word used by the early Catholic writers (in a quote from the Vulgate translation of the Second Epistle to Timothy 3:6, translated in the King James Version as 'silly women') when they denounced the Waldensian women preachers.[43] Since it has been suggested that it was the formal establishment and hierarchization that reduced the rights of women among The Poor of Lyons, it should be pointed out that in the fifteenth century the establishment was in fact simplified by the abolition of the positions of deacon, presbyter and majoral, and all the Brothers became Elders (*barbes* in the Romance languages and *meister* in the German-speaking lands). Yet the

---

41 See note 25, above.
42 G. Audisio, *Les 'Vaudois'. Naissance, vie et mort d'une dissidence (XIIe–XVIe siècles)*, Turin, 1989, p. 127.
43 '. . . they which creep into houses and lead captive silly women laden with sins, led away with divers lusts'; the verse is quoted by Geoffroy d'Auxerre – see note 23, chapter 2, and also in Alain of Lille, *De fide catholica PL* 210, LII, c. 1, col. 380.

process did not enhance the position of the Sisters – if anything, rather the reverse.

Peter Biller sees a resemblance between the Sisters, especially in the ultimate phase, and the nuns in the female orders which rose parallel with the Mendicant orders: the Poor Clares and the female order corresponding to the Dominicans.[44] Indeed, the nuns in those orders were expected to lead an introspective religious life, in contrast to the men in the parallel male orders or to the Waldensian Brothers who operated as preachers, teachers and missionaries. Saint Clare herself, the founder of the Poor Clares, had hoped to be sent to Africa as a missionary and be martyred there, but this did not come about, and she and her companions complained that Francis had imprisoned them for all time.[45] Before long, the way of life in these female orders became indistinguishable from that of the Benedictine monasteries. But whereas the Church authorities would not allow the Poor Clares to realize the ideal of utter poverty as they wished, excepting a handful of convents – chiefly because the Franciscans refused to undertake the burden of begging on their behalf – the Waldensian Sisters were allowed to realize it as much as the Brothers. (The fact that the Brothers had to allocate to the Sisters some of the funds donated to their sect displeased the Reformists, who mentioned this among their arguments for the abolition of their status.[46]) On the other hand, both in the Benedictine convents and in those of the new orders, the nuns enjoyed a measure of autonomy unknown to the Sisters. There were the abbesses, who enjoyed extensive prerogatives in their community, even though they were forbidden to preach and conduct religious services. I believe that the condition of the Sisters resembled more closely that of the nuns in the 'double orders' headed by a man, such as that of the Premonstratensians when it was still a 'double order'

[44] P. Biller, ' "Multum ieiunantes et se castigantes": Medieval Waldensian Asceticism', in Monks, Hermits and the Ascetic Tradition, ed. W.J. Sheils, Studies in Church History 22 (1985), p. 220.

[45] In J. Moorman, The Franciscan Order from its Origins to the Year 1517, Oxford, 1968, p. 35.

[46] V. Vinay, ed., op. cit., p. 66.

(i.e. until 1141). These monasteries were headed by an abbot to whom the prioress was subordinate. The joint prayers, contemplation and reading took up less of the nuns' time than they did in the autonomous convents, because they also had to look after the monks' clothes and devote time and labour to sewing, weaving and laundry, much as the Sisters in the hospices were expected to take care of the Brothers' meals. They had a separate section of the convent chapel, and according to the Rule they had to pray silently and listen to the monks chanting hymns on the other side of the partition. Their only books were a psalter and a breviary containing some of the prayers. The Rule explicitly forbade them to learn anything else. These two specifics distinguished the Waldensians from the Premonstratensians. So far as we know, the Sisters prayed with the Brothers, and there was no strict physical separation between the sexes. Moreover, The Poor of Lyons, who devoted themselves to teaching the Believers, must surely have seen to the Sisters' education. There is no telling if they were taught as much as the men training to become Brothers, but the Waldensians certainly could not have discriminated against women as much as did the Premonstratensians. Yet there is a marked similarity between the two (in addition to the fact that the Waldensian hospice was headed by a man, like a Premonstratensian house) in that the Sisters, like the nuns of that order, were excluded from the conferences and councils which discussed and resolved the future direction of their movements, including decisions affecting their own fate.[47] It is worth noting that Ardizzo, bishop of Plaisance, writing towards the end of the twelfth century, claimed that The Poor of Lyons did not hesitate to entice

---

47 *Les premiers statuts de l'ordre de Prémontré*, ed. R. van Waefelghem, *Analectes de l'ordre Prémontré* V8 (1913), pp. 63–67; A.E. Praem, 'Les soeurs dans l'ordre de Prémontré', *Analecta Praemonstratensia* 5 (1929), pp. 5–6, 10, 16–18; the 'double order' came to an end in 1141; in 1198 the order decided not to create more women's convents; in 1270 it resolved not to admit more women into the existing convents. A ruling of the Second Lateran Council (1139) prohibited nuns from singing psalms alongside canons or monks in the same choir: J.D. Mansi, ed., *Sacrorum conciliorum nova et amplisssima collectio*, Florence–Venice, 1798, reprint Graz, 1961, canon 27, col. 533.

nuns out of their convents to join them.[48] We do not know if nuns did in fact leave their convents to join the sect in Ardizzo's time, but a case is known of a nun who supported The Poor of Lyons at a later time. In 1246 a nun of the convent at Lespinasse, of the order of Fontevrault in the diocese of Toulouse, was tried by the court of the Inquisition in Toulouse. She was accused of listening frequently to the Brothers' sermons, of giving them alms and offering them hospitality, and believing that they were good people. Her prioress determined her penance – confinement in an isolated cell in the convent, without contact with the rest of the community.[49]

But while the sources tell us something about the position of the Sisters, they reveal nothing about their spiritual life. Was there ever a written work, among the few Waldensian texts, that was produced by a Sister? During the High and Late Middle Ages women mystics – most of them nuns – created a language of spirituality, religious symbolism and devotion that greatly enriched Christian mysticism. Some of their writings were subversive, others were found free from deviations from orthodoxy. But there is no extant text known to have been written by a Waldensian Sister. Were there any Sisters who maintained special contacts with Brothers, as did some nuns and mystics, such as Hildegard of Bingen, who maintained a close connection with the monk Volmar? Were there any relations between Sisters and Brothers like those of some female mystics with their spiritual instructors to whom they generally dictated their visions and mystical experiences?[50] These questions remain unanswered. The sources tell us nothing about the circumstances and the reasons that made any of the women choose to become a Sister, nothing to enable us to reconstruct a biography, even a partial one, of such a Sister (as we

[48] *Litterae episcopi Placentini de Pauperibus de Lugduno*, in A. Dondaine O.P., 'Durand Huesca et la polémique anti-cathare', *Archivum Fratrum Praedicatorum* 29 (1959), Appendix III, p. 274.

[49] Mgr. Douais, ed., *Documents pour servir à l'histoire de l'inquisition dans le Languedoc*, Paris, 1900, reprint: 1977, Vol. II, XI, p. 31.

[50] *Gendered Voices. Medieval Saints and their Interpreters*, ed. C.M. Mooney. Philadelphia, 1999.

can for Agnes and Huguette – see chapter 4), or to know if they were satisfied with their way of life and found spiritual fulfilment in it. Nevertheless, the substantial difference between the ways that a young woman became a Waldensian Sister or a Catholic nun suggests that most of the Sisters found a greater spiritual satisfaction than did many of the Catholic nuns. It is known that many of the latter came from the nobility or the wealthy town dwellers, as part of a strategy by which most of the family resources were devoted to the dowry of one daughter, or some of the daughters, in order to arrange a marriage contract with a suitable family, while other daughters were given smaller dowries and destined for a convent. But a young woman who became a Sister did so from choice; her very membership of the sect, even as a Believer, was voluntary. There may have been women who chose to become Sisters because of economic hardship, or because their parents could not provide them with a dowry, but they cannot have been many, because the cost – membership of a persecuted community – was high.[51] We may therefore assume that few if any Sisters would have fitted the description which the Dominican Humbert de Romans applied to certain Catholic nuns: some are sunk in depression, which troubles the peace of their companions in the convent, while others are cantankerous like dogs which have been chained too long.[52] A consciousness of choice and the voluntary participation in a persecuted community, requiring a major commitment from its members, and the tension of clandestine life, probably shielded them from monotony and inner dissatisfaction.

The Sisters were a minority; most of the women of the sect were Believers. The next chapter will cover the arrest and interrogation, and a partial biography of two of the latter. Though Sisters did teach and sometimes preach – at least some of the time and in some regions – essentially the same hierarchy and gender roles

---

[51] It seems to me that Koch overstated the economic factor inducing women to join heretical movements, including The Poor of Lyons: G. Koch, *Frauenfrage und Ketzertum im Mittelalter*, Berlin, 1962, C.X.

[52] Humbert de Romans, *Sermones*, Venice, 1605, XLV, p. 47.

prevailed between the Brothers and Sisters as between the nuns and the monks or canons in the Catholic Church. This was not the case among the male and female Believers. Here a certain neutralization of the standard gender roles occurred, or, in other words, a certain blurring of the women's 'otherness'. The story of Agnes and Huguette is an individual story seen in particular context, namely, the Inquisitorial interrogation, with all its limitations and difficulties as an historical source. Neither their biographies nor the way they withstood the interrogation can be regarded as representing those of all female Believers. While most of The Poor of Lyons belonged like them to the working class, being peasants, artisans and journeymen, there were men and women from other social strata too. Women joined the sect at various stages and in various circumstances in their lives (as may be seen in the biographies of Agnes and Huguette); they varied as to individual personality, degree of devotion to the sect's faith and moral code, and no doubt their commitment to the sect varied too. Nevertheless, the relatively detailed record of their interrogation is revealing not only about them personally, but also about the attitude of the Brothers towards women of their sect, and even how the latter internalized the moral precepts. The next chapter will focus on them. Chapter Five, which deals with the female Believers as a whole, will return to certain particulars of their testimonies which may be regarded as typical and which complement other testimonies found in the Inquisitorial and other records.

4

Agnes and Huguette: Two Believers

There were three ways of bringing a person in for questioning by the Inquisition. The first of these was the least frightening. The Inquisitor regularly sermonized the parish about the true faith and against heresy, on which occasions he would also threaten with excommunication anyone who attempted to disrupt the work of the Inquisition by means of bribery, by contradicting honest testimony or withdrawing one's own honest testimony, or even by refusing to aid the Inquisition with the 'help and advice'. At the same time, he would announce a period of grace of a 'general summons' (*citatio universalis*), during which anyone who had become involved with any kind of heresy could come and confess as well as inform on others, with the promise of no greater penalty than a minor act of penance.[1] (Informers were asked what motivated them to testify – was it hatred, fear, love, or hope of financial reward, and they were supposed to reply that all they wished to do was tell the truth.[2]) The second way was to send the suspect a personal summons, generally as a result of a denunciation, to come to the court for questioning. The Inquisitorial summons (*citatio*) was given to the parish priest and signed with his seal, and sometimes notarized. The priest would take the summons to the house of the man or woman in question and

---

1 An example of such a sermon by Jacques Fournier: *Liber sententiarum inquisitionis Tholosanae*, in *Historia inquisitionis*, ed. Ph. van Limborch. Amsterdam, 1692, p. 148(b).
2 *Le registre*, Vol. I, pp. 171–172.

deliver it in the presence of witnesses, after which he had to announce the summons publicly in church every Sunday for three weeks. If the person summoned appeared in court as required, he or she was often allowed to go home between interrogations, and was free to move about the diocese. Whoever failed to appear, and did not send a representative, was labelled disobedient and temporarily excommunicated. At the end of a year from the set date, if the person had still failed to appear, he or she was fully excommunicated and anyone who knew their whereabouts had to report it, on pain of excommunication. Once the whereabouts were known, soldiers of the secular authority were sent to seize him or her. The third way was immediate imprisonment. A representative of the secular authority (in Pamiers it was the bailiff of the count of Foix[3]) was ordered to dispatch soldiers directly to fetch the suspect to the prison of the Inquisition.

It was in this last way that Raymond de la Côte and Agnes, Jean of Vienne and Huguette were seized and taken to the Allemans prison. It seems that Jacques Fournier, who had only recently begun to act as Inquisitor, wanted to make sure they did not escape. The four were probably arrested as a result of information brought against them. Regarding Agnes, it was said only that she was greatly suspected of being a heretic; Huguette and Jean were greatly suspected following information brought against them; as for Raymond, he was suspected because of things he had said and the books found in his possession.[4] After their preliminary interrogation, Jacques Fournier sent the four to Avignon, either at the request of the Inquisitor Bernard Gui, who also wished to question them, or because he was not certain that he was empowered to try them, having only recently arrived in Pamiers. But Pope

---

3   For the Count of Foix and the county nobility of that time, see J. Duvernoy, 'La noblesse du comté de Foix au début du XIVe siècle', in *Pays de l'Ariège, archéologie-histoire-géographie*, Actes du XVIe congrès de la fédération des societés académiques et savantes Languedoc–Pyrenées–Gascogne. Auch, 1961, pp. 123–140.

4   About Jean: *Le registre*, Vol. I, p. 508; about Raymond: *Ibid.*, Vol. I, p. 40. The Alemans prison was built by Jacques Fournier. It is today's Tour de Crieu.

John XXII, who resided in Avignon, ordered them sent back to Pamiers, to be tried by Jacques Fournier.[5]

We can only surmise in what kind of conditions the four detainees were held. Prisoners were supposed to pay for their own upkeep, as well as the guards' wages. Direct payment was made by the secular authorities, who reimbursed themselves from the prisoners' confiscated property. Since Agnes, Huguette and Jean, at any rate, were quite poor, and had only recently come to Pamiers, they obviously did not have property worth confiscating, nor enough money with which to pay the prison guards. Raymond, as we shall see, did have some financial means and perhaps was able to provide for himself and his companions. If he did not, then they probably were very poorly fed, and the guards would scarcely bother to maintain them in decent conditions. In 1376, responding to an appeal from the Inquisitor of the Dauphiné, Pope Gregory XI called on the Catholic faithful to contribute to the upkeep of poor heretics who were held in prison, despite the abomination of their heresy, because otherwise they would perish.[6] He was referring to men and women who had been tried and sentenced to prison terms by way of penitence, but it is possible to infer from it what condition the poor detainees were held in while being interrogated. Some Inquisitors even proposed, among various means of inducing suspects to confess and inform on other members of the sect, to isolate and barely feed them.[7] It is known that it was sometimes permitted to visit the detainees and bring them food. David of Augsburg, listing the signs by which supporters of the heretics might be identified, named as the first sign the fact that they visit the detainees, speak with them in whispers and bring them food.[8] Also, the records of the court of Toulouse for the 1310s reveals that some

5 *Bullaire de l'inquisition française au XIVe siècle*, ed. J.M. Vidal, Paris, 1913, p. 55; *Le registre*, Vol. I, p. 18 and note 31.
6 *Bullaire de l'inquisition*, pp. 407, 435.
7 A. Dondaine O.P., 'Le manuel de l'inquisteur (1230–1330)', *Archivum fratrum Praedicatorum* 17 (1947), p. 105.
8 David of Augsburg, *Tractatus de inquisicione hereticorum*, ed. W. Preger, Munich 1878, p. 41 (221); see also: *Tractatus de haeresi Pauperam de Lugduno auctore anonymo. De libro Stephani de Bella-villa accipiuntur ista*,

people succeeded in providing for the detainees by means of messengers with both money and clothes.[9] But even if it was permitted to visit our four detainees, it is doubtful that there was anyone to do so, or to bring them food. Those of their small group who were not caught had fled from Pamiers. They had only recently arrived in the town, and probably had little truck with people who did not belong to their sect, certainly not such as would risk visiting them and providing for them. We do not know if the four were held together in one cell (women and men were generally kept apart), with or without other prisoners.

The sociologist Talcott Parsons, discussing methods of influence and persuasion, stated that the likeliest way of persuading the other to accept one's viewpoint is by opening the discussion not with a head-on confrontation, but with a presentation of those views and positions that both sides agree on, thus creating confidence.[10] But the interrogation of the four Poor of Lyons, which was supposed to lead them eventually to recant, opened with an unavoidable clash. For even if Jacques Fournier had shared the sociologist's opinion, he had to follow the accepted procedure in Inquisitorial interrogations and require the suspects to swear on the Gospels that they would tell the truth about their beliefs, customs and history, as well as about their co-believers in the sect. And indeed Jacques Fournier, like other Inquisitors, began the first interrogations by demanding that the four swear on the Gospels. They all refused and lied about their reasons for refusing. Raymond de la Côte, Jean of Vienne and Agnes gave the same false reason for refusing, while Huguette cited a different one.

Raymond de la Côte said that he did not dare to swear, because once when he had sworn to the truth he fell seriously ill, and that a Catholic cleric (whose rank and function he said he could not recall), by name of Pierre, who had died ten years previously, had

in *Thesaurus novus anecdotorum*, eds E. Martène and M. Durand, Paris, 1717, Vol. V, col. 1786.

9   *Liber sententiarum*, p. 232 (100–100b).

10 T. Parsons, 'On Concepts of Influence', *Public Opinion Quarterly* 27 (1963), pp. 32–62.

told him that it was a sin to swear, and it was that which had caused him to fall ill.[11] Jean of Vienne, too, said that he had once fallen ill after swearing and suffered great pains in his head and arm. He stated that he had heard several times from the Franciscans and Dominicans that it was a sin to swear.[12] Agnes said that the previous year she had been gravely ill at Vermelle, and a chaplain who came to hear her confession and give her the extreme unction told her that under no circumstances must she swear. Asked if she believed that it was a sin to swear to the truth, she said she did, because she had been told as much by the chaplain. Still lying, she added that she would not tell lies from fear of death, but would answer all questions truthfully.[13] The close resemblance between the reasons given by the three suggests that they had agreed in advance that in the event they were captured, they would give such a reason for refusing to swear. Certain records of the Inquisitorial courts show that some people became Believers under the influence of a Waldensian friend or relative when they were seriously ill and thought they were dying, or when their lives were otherwise in danger, and sought to ensure their salvation in this way.[14] But it is evident from the rest of the testimonies given by the three that they had learned of the Waldensian prohibition of swearing in quite different circumstances. Needless to say, they had not been warned not to swear by Catholic clerics. There were other cases when it is evident that a group of The Poor of Lyons agreed what they would say to the Inquisitor in the hope of saving themselves. A serving-woman in Steier in Upper Austria testified before the Inquisitor Gallus of Neuhaus that upon the arrival of the Inquisitors the Believers consulted their *magister* as to what they should say, and he told them: 'If you are asked if people have visited your house in order

---

11 *Le registre*, Vol. I, pp. 40–42.
12 *Ibid.*, pp. 508–509.
13 See Appendix, p. 132.
14 *Verhorsprotokolle der Inquisition des Gallus von Neuhaus (1335 bis ca. 1353/55)*, in *Quellen zur Böhmischen Inquisition im 14. Jahrhundert*, ed. A. Patschovsky, Weimar, 1979, pp. 86, 106; *Quellen zur Ketzergeschichte Brandenburgs und Pommerns*, ed. D. Kurze, Berlin, 1975, p. 86.

to hear confessions and to preach, you must say that people did indeed visit your house, but only in order to sell objects required by the women for the housework.' However, unlike our Poor of Lyons, they agreed to swear and were acquitted. According to the servant, none of them was even sent to prison.[15]

Huguette, however, gave a different reason. She said that once when she was pregnant she did swear and then miscarried, and she feared that if she swore she would again miscarry. She also said that it had been a Catholic cleric, a priest from Arles, who had forbidden her to swear any more. Clearly it was no priest from Arles who had forbidden her to swear. But whether she really was pregnant at the time of the interrogation we do not know. It was the custom in the secular courts that pregnant women were not put to the torture; when a woman who was sentenced to death claimed that she was pregnant, she was examined by 'matrons', and if they confirmed that she was pregnant the execution was postponed till after she gave birth, so as to spare the unborn child.[16] The courts of the Inquisition also honoured this custom, and avoided turning pregnant women over to 'the secular arm' – i.e. having them burnt at the stake. One woman who belonged to The Poor of Lyons but later reverted to Catholicism, testified in the court of the Inquisitor Peter Zwicker that both she and her husband had previously been tried and sentenced to be burnt at the stake; her husband was indeed burnt, but she was spared (and apparently released) because she was pregnant. She was only deprived of her husband's confiscated property. And the Anonymous of Passau even castigated the priests who imposed fasts on pregnant women by way of penance, thus causing them to miscarry.[17] A testimony given in Toulouse in the 1310s reveals that consideration was also shown to a nursing mother. One of

---

[15] *Quellen zur Böhmischen Inquisition*, p. 199.

[16] About the matrons: see M. Green, 'Documenting Medieval Women's Medical Practice', in *Practical Medicine from Salerno to the Black Death*, eds L. Garcia-Ballester et al., Cambridge, 1994, pp. 339–340.

[17] *Quellen zur Ketzergeschichte Brandenburgs und Pommerns*, p. 220; *Auszuge aus dem Sammelwert des Passauer Anonymus*, in *Quellen zur Geschichte der Waldenser*, eds A. Patschovsky and K.V. Selge, Göttingen, 1973, p. 89.

the women suspects was told she could return home, even though she had not yet fully confessed and recanted her errors, nor was a penance imposed upon her, because she had a baby at the breast.[18] Huguette was burnt at the stake, but whereas Raymond and Agnes were sent to the stake after nine months of imprisonment and interrogations, Huguette and her husband, who were summoned for questioning far fewer times than Raymond, were burnt at the stake only after two years. At her second interrogation Huguette retracted the false admissions she had made before, but not what she had said about her pregnancy. Was her execution delayed because she was pregnant? And if she was, did she miscarry, give birth to a child that died, or a child that survived and was put in some foundling home, but the court clerk not bothering to refer to the matter? Or was the delay due to some hesitation on the part of Jacques Fournier – who had already sent two Waldensians to the stake soon after he had begun to serve as Inquisitor – and perhaps a hope that these people would repent of their errors? The court records provide no answer to these questions.

The difficulty of getting suspects to admit to membership in The Poor of Lyons troubled the Inquisitors, who discussed it at length. They described them as disingenuous and devious persons, who avoided direct answers to questions, pretended not to understand a question or answered it with another, gave ambiguous answers and even feigned madness.[19] Yet in reality, even Raymond's answers were hardly cunning, much less the answers given by the other three. They gradually retracted some of the statements they had made at the first interrogation, and told the truth about their reasons for joining the sect and about their beliefs. Jean and Agnes said they did not know the answers

---

18 *Liber sententiarum*, p. 345 (174b).
19 David of Augsburg, *op. cit.*, p. 49 (229); Etienne de Bourbon, *Tractatus de diversis materiis praedicabilis*, in *Anecdotes historiques, légendes et apologues tirés du recueil inédit d'Etienne de Bourbon*, ed. A. Lecoy de la Marche, Paris, 1877, pp. 311–313; Bernard Gui, *Manuel de l'inquisiteur*, ed. and trans. G. Mollat, Paris, 1964, Vol. I, pp. 64–70, 72–76; Bernard Gui relied for some of his material on David of Augsburg.

to some of the questions, and all four avoided giving details about other members of the sect. Clearly, the clerk of the court did not record all their answers precisely, nor even all the questions. Some of the questions can only be inferred from the answers. For example, the record states that Agnes 'had been asked who had taught her that to swear, even to swear to tell the truth, was opposed to the Lord's commandment, since, as she herself had said, she could not read'.[20] Yet neither the question nor the answer appear in the preceding record. However, had their answers really been cunning and sophisticated, it should have been possible to discern these qualities even in the clerk's selective record. The most naive of the four, who also knew least about the sect's beliefs, was Agnes. When she first refused to swear, she declared at once that she would not do so even to save her life, adding that the chaplain had not only prohibited it, he had also warned her against walking barefoot. In the sect's early days, the Catholic writers described them as going about naked and barefoot, following the naked Christ.[21] Perhaps they did at first go barefoot to express their renunciation of all property and their following of Christ and the Apostles. Later the Brothers renounced shoes, following the commandment of Jesus to his disciples (St Mark 6:9 and St Luke 10:4), and wore sandals (for which they were sometimes known as *Sandaliati*). Ultimately, they wore shoes whose uppers were cut in the style of sandals, or else wore a distinguishing mark in the form of a shield. But by the early fourteenth century, when they had become a clandestine movement and sought to disguise their identity, they probably avoided displaying any distinguishing marks. Indeed, Raymond testified to that effect.[22] Agnes had probably heard about this and ascribed the prohibition to the chaplain.

The Inquisitors often noted that a willingness to swear was not in itself proof that the suspect was innocent or sincerely willing to recant. They reiterated that the leaders of the sect permitted the

[20] See Appendix p. 136 and note 7 in Appendix.
[21] Walter Map, *De nugis curialium*, ed. and trans. M.R. James, revised by C.N.L. Brooke and R.A.B. Mynors, Oxford, 1983, Dist. I, c. 31, p. 126.
[22] *Le registre*, Vol. I, p. 105.

Believers to swear in order to save their lives, or the lives of their fellow sectarians, provided they later confessed this sin and did penance for it. Bernard Gui's manual (which was based in part on the work of his predecessors) stated that if the person being interrogated suddenly agreed to swear, he or she should be addressed as follows:

> You are swearing in order to be freed, but rest assured that I shall not be satisfied with a single oath. I may ask of you any number of oaths: two, ten or even a hundred. I know that you are allowed to swear so as to save yourself. Moreover, you may swear many oaths, yet if witnesses swear to statements that contradict you, you shall not escape.

He then describes cases of suspects who swore only to save themselves.[23] But if willingness to swear did not ensure an acquittal, on more than one occasion it led to a relatively mild penance and saved the subject from the stake. Huguette herself testified that she had once sworn in order to save herself. She had already been aware that it was a sin, but hoped to confess it and do penance, and did not think that she would be consigned to hell for it.[24] Agnes was asked if she would swear provided Jacques Fournier promised to release her if she did, but she still refused.[25] It is not clear what Jacques Fournier was getting at. Was he trying to trick her, to induce her to swear by deluding her that she might thereby save herself, then hold it against her (in accordance with the Inquisitors' warnings), when in fact he had no intention of letting her go? It was not considered a moral duty to keep a promise

---

23 Bernard Gui, op. cit., Vol. I, pp. 70–72; some of his predecessors and successors on this subject: David of Augsburg, op. cit., pp. 28 (208), 51 (231–232); Etienne de Bourbon, op. cit., p. 294; J.J. Ign von Döllinger, ed., op. cit., Vol. II, p. 7; Tractatus bonus (pars prima contra hereticos qui Valdensis dicuntur, quorum magistri heresiarche Fratres nuncupantur), in R. Cegna, ed., 'La condizione del Valdismo secondo l'inedito Tractatus bonus contra hereticos del 1399, attribubile all'inquisitore della Slesia Giovanni di Gliwice', in I Valdesi e l'Europa, Collana della società di studi Valdesi 9, Torre Pellice, 1982, p. 60.
24 See Appendix p. 142.
25 See Appendix p. 134.

given to a heretic. Yet it must be remembered that Agnes' sole 'error' was her refusal to swear, which amounted to disobedience to the representatives of the Church, when such obedience was the touchstone of orthodoxy. But unlike the other three, she did not deny the existence of Purgatory, did not declare that her primary obedience was due to the Waldensian majoral rather than to the Pope, and even stated that no layman was empowered to absolve people of sins or to administer the sacrament of the eucharist. On the whole, judging from the record of the court, Jacques Fournier did not put tricky or complex questions to her. Perhaps he really was willing to impose an easy penance on the old woman and to set her free. But Agnes would not swear. All four chose not to swear at their first interrogation, and remained unshaken in this refusal in the subsequent interrogations, in which they retracted most of their previous statements. But if will-ingness to swear did not necessarily acquit a person of suspicion and punishment, refusing to swear was in canon law,[26] and in the eyes of the Inquisitors, an overwhelming proof that the person was a heretic. This was a foregone conclusion. Even if Raymond, Huguette and Jean had not admitted to other Waldensian beliefs, Jacques Fournier would have had to condemn them as heretics, just as he condemned Agnes who had only refused to swear.

Agnes

In the fourteenth century membership of the sect passed mostly vertically through families, from parents to offspring. Most of the persons interrogated in the court of Peter Zwicker in Stettin, in the late fourteenth century, testified that their parents had been members of The Poor of Lyons. The phrases 'Born in the sect' or 'Brought into the sect' by the parents, appear frequently in the records.[27] 'Brought into the sect' meant that the person had been taken at an early age to a Waldensian Brother to make confession,

[26] *Decretales Gregorii IX*, L.V. tit. VII, c. XIII, *Corpus iuris canonici*, ed. A. Friedberg, Leipzig, 1879, Vol. II, col. 789.
[27] *Quellen zur Ketzergeschichte Brandenburgs und Pommerns*, pp. 79, 80, 107, 118, 119, 122, 140, 154, 164, 165.

sometimes also to hear him preach. Similarly, in Bernard Gui's court in Toulouse many of the persons interrogated stated that they had first encountered the Brothers in their home and their parents' home alike. Others were influenced to join the sect by their contemporaries in the family – siblings or cousins. However, Waldensian missionarizing had not entirely ceased even in the fourteenth century, and there were still men and women who had been introduced into the sect by Waldensians who were not related to them. Sometimes they were taken to meet one of the Brothers, and sometimes they joined the sect after a direct encounter with a Brother. Such an introduction into the sect did not prevent a young man from being trained to become a Brother, provided his personality was deemed suitable.[28] Agnes, who had been Raymond's wet-nurse, came to the sect under his influence.

Asked at her first interrogation how long she had known Raymond, she replied, for about a year-and-a-half. But at the second interrogation she admitted that she had known him almost since he was born. She stated that Raymond's mother had died in childbirth, or shortly thereafter, and his father brought her to his village of Côte Saint-André[29] to wet-nurse him. Asked why she had gone to the town of Beaumont de Lomage[30] before settling in Pamiers, she replied that, being a poor woman, she had gone there to look for work. But we may doubt that she went there for this purpose. She stayed there less than a month and then joined Raymond in Toulouse. She was already an old woman, and it is doubtful that anyone would have hired her. Raymond, who had joined the sect some twenty-seven years before his arrest, while still a schoolboy living in his father's house, was now in his early forties, and Agnes, his old nurse, was about sixty. It is probable that she stayed in Beaumont de Lomage hoping to join Raymond. But she was telling the truth when she

---

28 J.J. Ign von Döllinger, op. cit., Vol. II, p. 368; Liber sententiarum, p. 227 (107).
29 Côte Saint-André in the Bas Dauphiné: a region which at that time was ruled by the Counts of Savoy.
30 Beaumont de Lomage – in today's department of Tarn et Garonne. It was originally called a Bastida, a new fortified town.

said that she was a poor woman. At the time of her arrest she was a widow. The heading of the record of her interrogation describes her as 'widow of Etienne Francou', since women were identified by their connection with a man, the father or the husband. But there is no mention of her husband's occupation or when he died. Nor do we know if, when she came to Raymond's father's house she had left her own baby to a cheaper wet-nurse, or weaned it ahead of time, or whether her own child was dead. But the fact that she consented to be a wet-nurse indicates that she was a poor woman. Only women who needed additional income sold their milk. By contrast, Raymond's father must have been a man of some means, since he brought the wet-nurse to his house, which was more costly than leaving the baby in the wet-nurse's house.[31] Raymond attended school for several years. At his first school he acquired the basics of Latin philology as part of the *trivium*, and later studied at one of the Franciscan schools. He was not sent out to work at an early age. During his stay in Pamiers he arranged the marriage of his sister Jeanne, and saw to it that she was assured a widow's dower. He could hardly have arranged a dower unless he had also given her a dowry, and in southern France in those days the dowry had to be large in relation to the dower.[32] Having answered the question of where he had lived before coming to Pamiers, he added that while living in Pamiers he went several times to Vienne to collect monies owing to him; he also admitted that he had bought with his own money one of the three books that were found in his possession at the time of his arrest.[33] Moreover, Huguette testified that living with their group in the house in Pamiers there had also been a manservant of Raymond's by name of Etienne. As a Waldensian Brother, Raymond was supposed to renounce his private property, but perhaps he had not done so. Otherwise, it is possible that he had not paid his

---

[31] S. Shahar, *Childhood in the Middle Ages*, London, 1990, Ch. 4.

[32] In southern France at that time the dower (*dos*) customarily corresponded to ¼ to ½ of the value of the bride's dowry. See J. Mundy, *Men and Women at Toulouse in the Age of the Cathars*, Toronto, 1990, Ch. 5.

[33] *Le registre*, Vol. I, pp. 102, 105–106.

sister's dowry but had only made the marriage arrangements concerning the size of the dowry and the dower, while the property in question was actually his sister's. He might also have paid for the book with money from the donations he received, and used the money from the debts he collected to pay for the needs of his fellow sectarians. It appears that there was nothing extraordinary about a Brother having a servant of his own. Huguette also mentioned the servant of the majoral, Jean of Lorraine, whom the latter used to send on errands and to deliver money. The picture is not clear, and it is not certain that Raymond had indeed renounced all his personal property, which, as a Waldensian deacon, he ought to have done. But whether he did or not, he had the means to support Agnes, either with his own money (if he did not give it all up) or from the donations fund, which was quite proper, since some of it was destined for the support of poor Believers.

There is no direct evidence that Raymond supported Agnes, but he clearly kept in touch with her after he had grown up. At first she spoke only of her meetings with him in the months preceding their arrest, how they met at Castel-Sarrasin,[34] spent some time in Toulouse together, then came to Pamiers, where they resided in the same house. But at her fifth interrogation Agnes admitted that it was Raymond who had told her that it was forbidden to swear, and that for the past twenty years she had believed that it was a sin. That would have been about the time that Raymond became a deacon (some seven years after joining the sect), and it was then that he brought her into the sect. At that time she had been about forty years old. It appears that they did not always live in proximity. During his studies and his training as deacon Raymond moved from place to place, but they kept in touch, and he may have supported her financially. It was not unusual for prosperous, or moderately prosperous people to look after their old wet-nurses and governesses. These often stayed on in their employers' houses, especially if they were childless widows, as governesses and members of the household. In the

---

34 Castel-Sarrasin, in today's Tarn et Garonne.

Lives of the Saints the *nutrix* (which meant both wet-nurse and nanny) is frequently mentioned as present in the homes of long-weaned children and even in their households as adults.[35] A man of Toulouse mentions in his will a woman whom he describes as his 'wet-nurse and mother'.[36] Raymond, being a Waldensian deacon, had no family of his own, no wife or children, for whose material and spiritual welfare he would have beeen responsible. It would appear that his nurse–mother and the majoral Jean were the two persons to whom he was most attached. It was only natural that he cared not only for Agnes' material comfort, but also for her soul's salvation, which was why he brought her into the sect. This was also a vertical introduction into the sect, but in reverse: the son bringing the faith to the woman who had been a mother to him.

While in Pamiers, Raymond, Agnes, Huguette and Jean lived in one house together with others of their sect, both men and women. One of the women was Raymond's sister and another a relative of his, and there was also a sister of Huguette's husband, and those two were also related to Raymond. When Raymond was asked if a Waldensian deacon, a presbyter or a majoral, were allowed to take a wife, he replied that not only was it utterly forbidden, they were also supposed to keep as far apart as possible from women: 'They may not kiss their hands and may not sleep in the same room with a woman, unless it is impossible to avoid doing so.' Later he added that they were not allowed to share quarters with a woman, even if she was the mother, sister or other female relative.[37] (This conflicts with what is known of the

---

[35] *Acta Sanctorum*, ed. The Bollandist Fathers, Paris, 1863, July I, p. 514; September V, p. 699, September VII, p. 540; see also: *The Fifty Earliest Wills in the Court Probate of London*, ed. F.J. Furnivall, London, 1882, p. 20; M.Th. Lorcen, *Vivre et mourir en Lyonnais à la fin du Moyen Age*, Paris, 1981, p. 111; I. Origo, *The Merchant of Prato. Francesco di Marco Datini*, Harmondsworth, 1963, pp. 195, 345; S. Epstein, *Wills and Wealth in Medieval Genova 1150–1250*, Cambridge, MA, 1984, p. 130.

[36] J. Mundy, *op. cit.*, p. 73 and note 32.

[37] *Le registre*, Vol. I, pp. 74, 76–77. He also said that they did not admit widowers as Brothers, for fear that they would be unable to withstand celibacy, having been accustomed to the 'act of the flesh' in their

hospices of The Poor of Lyons, where both Brothers and Sisters usually lived together.) We do not know if Raymond had a separate room in the house where so many people resided, or whether he regarded his stay in Pamiers and having to sleep in the same room with women as a case when it was 'impossible to avoid doing so'. Certainly during the month or two prior to their arrest, Raymond and Agnes were sharing quarters.

We have noted that Agnes was simple and naive. Not only was she illiterate (like many of the Believers), it is also clear that she had not learned much about the beliefs of The Poor of Lyons from listening to the Brothers. When she responded to various questions by saying that she did not know the answers, it appears that she really did not know. But she had learned and internalized the prohibition against swearing, something that for her represented her faith in God, obedience to the Redeemer's commandments, and loyalty to the sect and to Raymond, who had been like a son to her and had brought her into the sect. Her answers reveal the weariness felt by this simple, elderly woman as she repeatedly faced the learned interrogators and their questions. At one of the interrogations, when ordered to swear, she turned her face away from the book of the Gospels. At another interrogation she begged the Inquisitor not to continue talking to her about the oath. But she held out and never broke down. The case of Agnes perfectly fits the mocking phrase that Salvo Burci, a Catholic aristocrat from Piacenza, put in the mouth of The Poor of Lyons regarding the Church leaders: 'Look at them putting people to death for the crime of the refusing to swear!'[38]

married life. Testimonies from Strasbourg also show that the Brothers had to be virgins. However, this requirement was not applied in all communities through the entire period: K.V. Selge, *Die Ersten Waldenser*, Berlin, 1967, Vol. I, p. 138.

38 Salvo Burci, *Liber supra stella*, in J.J. Ign von Döllinger, *op. cit.*, Vol. II, p. 72.

Huguette

At the time of her arrest, Huguette was a young woman of about thirty. She was not a child of Waldensian parents either, but said she had been brought into the sect by Brother Gerard of Arles (known as the Provençal) at the age of twelve. In the High and Late Middle Ages there was no consistent concept of legal adulthood. The minimum age for marriage, or the age at which a man was deemed capable of controlling his own property without a guardian, of suing or of testifying in court, of being held responsible by law, capable of being appointed or elected to an ecclesiastical or secular office – all these varied and were also gender-dependent. Moreover, the right to dispose of property also varied from region to region and according to types of property. Nevertheless, the age of twelve was widely considered to be the end of the second phase of childhood (*pueritia*) in girls, and fourteen in boys.[39] The Inquisitors regarded girls of twelve and boys of fourteen to be responsible for their faith. When an entire community was arrested, like the villagers of Montaillou, who were suspected of Catharism, all the males over fourteen and all the females over twelve were detained. In 1254, the Church council of Albi resolved, inter alia, that a profession of faith and a rejection of heresy would be required of everyone at those ages.[40] David of Augsburg, for his part, expatiated on the Waldensian custom of teaching to very young girls (*puellas parvulas*) the Gospels and the Epistles, with their own interpretation, in order to inculcate their erroneous beliefs from an early age.[41] The Inquisitors were correct in their arguments and demands that boys and girls at that age should profess their faith, because it was not unusual to admit or introduce children to the sect at the age that Huguette was brought to it. (Even if she was not precise in her testimony, she had clearly been a very young girl.) Raymond, too, testified that he had been brought into the sect at the age of thirteen, and the

[39] S. Shahar, *op. cit.*, Ch. 2.
[40] E. Le Roy Ladurie, *Montaillou. Village occitan de 1294 à 1324*, Paris, 1975, p. 320.
[41] David of Augsburg, *op. cit.*, p. 33.

testimonies at Stettin reveal that many of the Believers had been brought into the sect – i.e. had first made a confession to a Brother – at the age of twelve or even earlier.[42] As far as we know, The Poor of Lyons did not consider the first confession to be a rite of passage, that is to say, a ritual constituting a public, religious and social recognition of a significant change of status. Only ordination as deacon, according to Raymond, or as *meister* or *meisterin*, according to the testimonies of Strasbourg from 1400, were regarded as a rite of passage. Children made their first confession at their parents' house (or barn, as one witness reported), or at the house of neighbours or friends who belonged to the sect, and listened to a reading from the Scriptures and a sermon. But unlike others of her age who were introduced into the sect by their parents, Huguette had first been drawn to it and then joined it of her own volition, following a meeting with a Brother.

Like Agnes, she too was born to poor people. The heading of the record of her interrogation identified her by her husband: '. . . wife of Jean of Vienne . . .', but in the course of her questioning she also talked about her parents. Her father had been the village baker, that is, an artisan, and perhaps while he lived the family belonged to the village middle stratum. But he died when she was very young, and she and her mother moved from their village at Côte Saint-André to Arles. Well-off peasants or artisans did not usually migrate, nor did propertied widows. It was the poorest villagers who moved to the towns in the hope of earning a living wage there. After staying for several years in Tarrascon, she returned to Arles and there, some six years before her arrest, she married Jean of Vienne, when she was about twenty-four. In her testimony she mentioned a family house and an inn where she had lived. She may well have worked in those places as a maidservant, and perhaps even saved up enough for a little dowry. Jean and Huguette belonged to the same social class. Jean was an artisan, like her father, a carpenter who was also a skilled cooper, who had at some time – as Huguette testified – gone to sea,

---

42 *Quellen zur Ketzergeschichte Brandenburgs und Pommerns*, pp. 79, 82, 83, 84, 95, 107, 117, 121, 123, 132, 143; there were also some older ones, aged between 14 and 19: pp. 88, 122–123.

probably as a ship's carpenter. They had come to Pamiers in order to join the little group which had already gathered there, Jean hoping to find work in his trade, since the town was known as 'a good market for foodstuffs'. Raymond, too, when asked why he had brought his companions to Pamiers, replied that the town had a good market, and he had hoped that they would be able to make a living at weaving and other trades, and moreover he wanted to have their company.[43]

Nothing is known about the circumstances of Huguette and Jean's marriage, if it was a marriage of love (which was not unheard of even in the Middle Ages, especially among the working classes), or had been arranged by relatives in the nearby villages of their native Dauphiné. But it is known that they were both Waldensians at the time of their marriage, some six years before their arrest. Huguette had approached the sect some eighteen years before the arrest, and Jean had joined some twelve years before. Religious endogamy characterized most marriages among The Poor of Lyons,[44] as it characterized their contemporaries, the Cathars, and the Lollards in fifteenth-century England.

As mentioned above, the first Brother to introduce Huguette to the sect was Gerard of Arles, the Provençal, though she had probably heard of the sect before. (Jean testified that he had heard of the sect before he ever met the Brothers.[45]) As we shall see in the next chapter, many of the Believers welcomed the Brothers to their homes. However, the Brothers did not visit Huguette at her place in Arles – evidently the conditions and the proximity of Catholic neighbours made it impossible. According to her testi-

---

[43] *Le registre*, Vol. I, pp. 44–45.

[44] *Quellen zur Ketzergeschichte Brandenburgs und Pommerns*, pp. 80, 100, 120–122, 127; Audisio's research has shown that 89% of all the Waldensians in Louveron in the latter half of the fifteenth century married among themselves: G. Audisio, *Les 'Vaudois'. Naissance, vie et mort d'une dissidence (XIIe–XVIe siècles)*, Turin, 1989, p. 113; in the Haut Dauphiné in the final decades of the fifteenth century whole families, rather than individuals, were put on trial: parents, offspring and their servants: P. Paravy, *De la chrétienté romaine à la Réforme en Dauphiné*, Rome, 1993, Vol. II, pp. 1015–1018, 1030.

[45] *Le registre*, Vol. I, p. 513.

mony, Gerard only called on her once, and she gave him food and drink. After their first meeting, she went on meeting him and other Brothers. Her testimony sheds light on the place the sect occupied in the young woman's life, and on various details of the daily existence of a female Believer and the Brothers.

Two years after their first meeting, Gerard told her that the majoral Jean of Lorraine had come to Montpellier, and she went there to see him. He agreed to speak to her and together they went to a house of one of the Believers in the town and talked there. While in Vauvert,[46] she decided to see Jean once more and returned to Montpellier for that purpose. Jean of Lorraine wandered about the region, and at some point reached St-Gilles-du-Gard and the inn where Huguette was staying at the time (most probably as a maidservant). He met her there and told her to return to Arles. But they met most frequently during her five-year stay in Arles, and on those occasions she would make her confession to him. Jean of Vienne had been brought into the sect by Jean of Lorraine some time before his marriage to Huguette. At Montpellier she also met Gerard the Provençal once again, as well as another Brother by name of Jean Cerno. She stated that she had spent the whole night in their company at the house of a family of Believers, and listened to their talk, and they gave her food and drink. She kept in touch with them and met them on many more occasions. But they never did visit her at home, nor did she give them anything, though they gave her small gifts. She only testified that she had given Jean of Lorraine half a pound of dates when she met him in the garden of the house where she lived in Arles, and that when she was in Montpellier she wanted to give him two silver coins of Tours, but he did not accept them, saying that he did not carry any money. But in all probability he did not want to take her money because he knew she was very poor. (There are other known cases of Brothers refusing to accept money from Believers.[47]) The following day he sent her three silver coins with his servant, so he obviously could have accepted her money by the same means. She stated that he sent her the money so that she

---

[46] It was a place of pilgrimage (in today's department of Gard).
[47] *Liber sententiarum*, p. 241 (116).

could buy stockings – perhaps he noticed that she was not
wearing any – but instead she bought herself two linen shawls.
On another occasion he gave her a scarf as well as a belt of white
linen thread. Jean Cerno gave her a scarf of coarse cloth, and
Gerard the Provençal, a single silver coin.

Like the other Waldensians, Huguette also attended church,
since the sect's separation from the Catholic Church was more a
matter of principle and feeling than of practice. We have seen that
they received most of the sacraments in church. Huguette testified
that when she went to meet Jean of Lorraine in Montpellier, she
took the opportunity to spend a night's vigil at the church of St
Mary of the Tablets, which was a place of pilgrimage.[48] Perhaps
she also went to Vauvert on pilgrimate. Her interrogators did not
ask if she considered pilgrimage to be an act of religious piety, or
believed in the grace that accrued from it, so we cannot tell if she
did these things to disguise her affiliation with the sect, or because
she was unable to discard a belief she had grown up with. The
difficulty of discarding familiar beliefs and customs was sometimes shown by Believers in other matters. We have seen that
though the Brothers rejected the prayer to the Virgin, nevertheless
some Believers did not give it up. Yet despite Huguette's attendance in church and her pilgrimage to sacred shrines, the sect
clearly occupied the central place in her religious and social life.

Huguette first asked to meet the majoral Jean of Lorraine when
she was a girl of about fourteen, and neither as a young girl nor as
a young woman did she hesitate to go to meet him and other
Brothers. There was nothing irregular about her going alone to
such meetings. In contrast to the aristocracy or prosperous bourgeoisie, unmarried women of the working classes were free to
come and go unchaperoned. More significant is the fact that the

---

[48] *Ecclesia beate Marie de Tabulis.* The Inquisitors in the south of France
sometimes ordered recanted heretics to make a pilgrimage to that
church as part of their penance. Some Catholic writers claimed that
the refusal of The Poor of Lyons to make pilgrimage to the shrines of
the saints was not categorical, despite their open disavowal. The
Anonymous of Passau, among others, wrote about it: Anonymous of
Passau, *Auszuge aus dem Sammelwerk des Passauer Anonymus*, p. 101.

Brothers were willing to meet her, to talk to her and instruct her, and to take her to the houses of the Believers and let her listen to their discussions through the night. At the same time, Jean of Lorraine was concerned about her virtue. When he met her at the inn in St-Gilles-du-Gard, he ordered her to return to Arles, for fear that she might otherwise 'do something improper' – which in this case meant a sexual sin. As a child of poor parents, Huguette had received no education before she joined the sect, and apparently she did not attend any of the sect's 'schools' or hospices, of which there were very few left by then. What she knew, she learned from her talks with the Brothers and her meetings with them at the houses of various Believers. Though unable to read, and without any continuous teaching, she nevertheless learned and took to heart the beliefs and moral precepts of The Poor of Lyons. Having lied at her first interrogation, she withdrew the lie at the start of the second session and offered another, absurd one (namely, that at the time of her arrest it was the pope's emissaries who had told her to say what she had said), but from a certain point in that interrogation and throughout the subsequent ones she told no more lies and expressed her adherence to all the beliefs and moral precepts of The Poor of Lyons: that it is a sin to lie; that there is no Purgatory in the afterlife, and therefore all the prayers, masses, alms, or anything else that is done for the dead, are entirely pointless; that it is forbidden to execute, mutilate or even judge anyone; that excommunication by the Church is meaningless, and the papal indulgences are worthless; and that the Brothers are empowered to hear confessions and impose penances. She understood the difference between the Catholic concept of the role of the confessor and that of The Poor of Lyons, saying that God alone can absolve sins, while the confessor may only advise a person how to atone for his or her sin. She also stated that she owed her primary obedience to the majoral of their sect, rather than to the pope. Unlike Raymond, she was unable to describe the hierarchy of the Brothers, but she did know that Jean of Lorraine was the majoral, and that he alone was authorized to consecrate the body of Christ in the sacrament. The Believers admired the wisdom and spiritual power of the Brothers so much, that in some regions a belief spread that once in seven years the Brothers ascended to heaven to hear the word of God and renew their wisdom, before returning to earth.[49] Huguette did not adopt this belief. She said only that she knew the majoral Jean was the wisest of them all, that he had died, and she believed that his soul was in paradise. She refused to say where he had died and was buried. It seems that Jean of Lorraine was a person who aroused not only respect and trust, but also love. Raymond described spending two years with him while he trained to become a deacon, and even journeyed with him to Italy, and said that he still loved him after his death. While Jean was alive, Huguette worried about his safety. Seeing him sitting in the garden of the house where she lived in Arles, she told him to leave because there were many people in the house at the time. The heading of the record of her interrogation says: 'The confession of Huguette, wife of Jean of Vienne, a *perfecta* of the heretics of the Waldensian sect or The Poor of Lyons'.[50] The use of the term *perfecta* is curious, since she certainly was not a Sister (or *perfecta* in the Inquisitors' vocabulary), if only because she was a married woman. If this was not merely a copier's error, it is possible that she was described in this way because of her knowledge of the beliefs and moral precepts of The Poor of Lyons – which was not only more extensive than that of Agnes, but also of her husband Jean – and her adherence to them.

Nevertheless, the loyalty of Huguette and Jean, no less than that of Agnes, to their sect and its beliefs was also human loyalty to one another. The journeyman Jean, who may or may not have had a child by Huguette, testified that before he married her she had told him about her affiliation with the sect, which 'made him love her more'.[51] When Huguette was asked with whom she had talked about the errors of The Poor of Lyons, she replied that it was mostly with her husband. Asked if she had convinced him to believe in them, 'she replied that she had done to the best of her

---

[49] *Quellen zur Ketzergeschichte Brandenburgs und Pommerns*, pp. 229, 231, 248.

[50] 'Confessio Huguete uxoris Iohannis de Vienna heretice perfecte secte Valdencium seu Pauperum de Lugduno'.

[51] '. . . et ex hoc ipse eam plus diligebat', *Le registre*, Vol. I, p. 513.

abilities, and that she had been very pleased and was still pleased that Jean believed and still now believed in the said errors'. And at her final interrogation, when she stated that nothing would dissuade her from her errors, she also stated that 'she wished to live and die in the faith in which her husband Jean Fustier believed, for she knew that they were of one faith'.

*

Raymond, Agnes, Jean and Huguette were not interrogated an equal number of times, and not all the questions were put to each of them. Yet Jacques Fournier's interrogation reveals no gender perspective. The differences in the number of interrogations and questions arose not from gender, but from Jacques Fournier's correct estimation of what each of the four suspects knew, and what information could be obtained from them individually. Raymond de la Côte was summoned for interrogation twenty-four times, because he was a deacon and a learned one. Agnes was interrogated only five times, because Jacques Fournier soon realized how little she knew. Huguette was interrogated nine times and her husband Jean ten. In reality, however, he was interrogated only six times, as on the last four occasions he was only warned to recant. More questions and in greater detail were put to Huguette than to Jean. (The record of her interrogations covers fourteen pages of the printed *Registre*, and Jean's only ten.) Also, the subject-matter of the questions did not vary according to gender, not even that relating to the position of women in the sect. Jacques Fournier put questions about it to Raymond and Huguette, but not to Jean and Agnes.

Peter Dronke has noted the individual and 'feminine voice' in the testimonies of some women (Cathars and Catholics) who were interrogated by Jacques Fournier.[52] Yet in the case of Huguette and Agnes it is very difficult to discern a 'feminine voice', or to pinpoint a distinctive feminine identity, or even a 'feminine' manner of speech. It cannot be determined if Jean and

---

52 P. Dronke, *Women Writers of the Middle Ages. A Critical Study of Texts from Perpetua (d. 1230) to Marguerite Porete (d. 1310)*, Cambridge, 1985, pp. 202–215, 265–274.

Huguette responded in the same 'heretical language', since their replies were translated into Latin, including the clerk of the court's formulations, but with regard to contents and basic positions, they were virtually identical. Indeed, the pace of admissions was similar in all four suspects. All four contradicted themselves, both logically and in the details they gave about themselves and their fellow sectarians. In all four there was a gradual transition from admitting to something that affected them alone -- e.g. having promised never to swear, for it was a sin to do so – to admitting to an absolute truth that is enjoined upon everyone – i.e. the Lord has commanded us not to swear. All four talked in a similar way about their companions, striving to mention only those who were already in prison, or who they knew had already fled from Pamiers, or had died.[53] Regarding those who had fled, they tried to avoid naming their surnames or the exact place they had fled to, and as for the dead, they refused to say where they had died or been buried. (A person who was known in his or her lifetime to have been a heretic, or who was posthumously discovered to have been a heretic, was exhumed and the remains were burnt at the stake.) All four strove to be fairly polite and restrained in speaking about the Catholic Church, though Huguette was somewhat less reserved and more direct than were Raymond and Jean. Agnes, as noted above, was asked fewer questions, and admitted only that swearing was prohibited. Those of the questions that were put equally to Raymond, Huguette and Jean were answered in much the same way.

The only issue on which Huguette's replies differed from Raymond's was that of the right of the authorities to use violent means, while Jean's replies were vague and expressed no clear-cut position. When Raymond was asked if the secular authorities were entitled to execute or mutilate a person for committing theft, murder or any crime which is a mortal sin, he replied that they

---

[53] The Inquisitors were aware of this evasion. David of Augsburg wrote that when they could not avoid giving names, they would name those who had already died or moved elsewhere a long time before, or had already been tried and convicted. David of Augsburg, *op. cit.*, p. 40 (220).

were so entitled, for otherwise there would be no more peace and security among men. Asked if an individual might prosecute a person for such crimes, knowing that the penalty would be mutilation or death, he replied that he believed that it would be a sin for him to do so, and that although he did not know if it was a mortal or a venial sin, he would certainly never do so. Asked if the Church might put to death a Christian who erred in his beliefs, even if not in deeds, he replied that it would not be just to put him and his fellow sectarians to death, even though they refused to return to the fold of the Roman Church. But as for other heretics, such as the Manichaeans, he believed it was just to put them to death. Asked whether, assuming he had the authority to put to death a heretic who refused to return to the true faith, he would have that person killed, or delivered to others for execution, he replied that under no circumstances would he do so, for he would have been committing a sin. He would have arrested the person and kept him in prison, and provided all his needs so as not to shorten his life. He was asked, what if a robber tried to rob and kill him, and he physically prevented him from doing so, would that have been a sin? Raymond replied that he would have tried to stop the robber with his hands, with a stick or a sword (if he had one), but would not seek to kill him. He said that those who sentenced heretics and bad people to death were right to do so, but anyone who sentenced him or another person of his sect to death would go to hell, unless he atoned for this sin. In response to a question, he stated that there were 'just wars' (*bellum justum*): e.g. Christians may go to war against idolaters, infidels and heretics, provided those people had been given fair warning but refused to be converted. Furthermore, a Christian prince, or the Church, might make war against other Christians if they were guilty of acts of injustice or violence, broken trust and disobedience. But it would be wrong for the Church to make war against his sect, even though they disobeyed it.[54] In sum, Raymond did not deny the prohibition of violence, but confined it to a prohibition that affected only him, and by implication the

---

[54] *Le registre*, Vol. I, pp. 75–76.

rest of his fellow sectarians. As for warfare, he enumerated all the cases which were usually cited as justifying violent response and war, and even went further than the Church's official position by saying that when infidels refused to be converted to Christianity it was right to make war upon them. The only exception he allowed was the right to attack his own sect. Jean did not deny that violence was prohibited, but avoided giving a straightforward answer. At his first interrogation he refused to swear, but denied all the beliefs of The Poor of Lyons about which he was asked, and said that the secular authorities might justly and without sin judge and execute murderers, robbers and other criminals. At the second interrogation, when he was beginning to admit to his beliefs, he replied to the same question by saying that he did not know, but was certain that he had heard that God said: Thou shalt not kill. Asked about it once more at his fourth interrogation, he said that he did not know if the authorities had the right and might judge criminals and execute the guilty ones without sin, nor did he know what to believe about it.[55] But Huguette's answers were unequivocal, rejecting not only the use of violence, but even putting people on trial. In reply to Jacques Fournier's questions, she said that 'no man has the right to kill or injure criminals', that 'if she were to sentence a man to death or life imprisonment she would be a sinner, and if she did not confess and atone for the sin she would be condemned to hell', that 'she did not want to judge anyone, because by doing so she would be transgressing the Lord's commandment', and that 'anyone who kills a Christian in any war whatsoever has committed a sin'. Had Huguette taken to heart the prohibition of violence more than did the deacon Raymond and her husband Jean?

On the basis of testimonies from Quercy before 1241, and from Stettin between 1392 and 1394, Peter Biller has speculated that the women, who did not fight and did not sentence people to death (and we may add: accounted for a tiny percentage of the murderers and other violent criminals),[56] put greater emphasis on this prohibition, which was taught them mainly by the Sisters,

---

[55] *Ibid.*, pp. 509, 511, 513.
[56] J.B. Given, *Society and Homicide in Thirteenth Century England*, Stan-

than did the male sectarians.[57] A different degree of internalization may account for the difference between Huguette's statement, on the one hand, and those of Raymond and Jean, on the other. But it may also have been due to their individual capacity to withstand the interrogations. It goes without saying that all three, as well as Agnes who was not asked about this matter, were extremely brave people who did not break down and who went knowingly to their death, though they could have escaped it be recanting. But of all of them, Huguette was the most decisive and consistent in her answers. Some of the answers Jean gave were also direct and unequivocal, but unlike Huguette, even after he began to tell the truth, he lied at least once, and evaded several questions by saying that he did not know the answer. He denied he had ever confessed his sins to Jean of Lorraine, which was certainly a lie. Asked if the papal indulgences had any value, he said he did not know. Asked if he believed that the majoral, Jean of Lorraine, could absolve him of his sins, he said he did not know, and gave the same answer when asked for the last time about the right of the authorities to execute criminals.[58] As for Raymond, it is possible that he had not taken the prohibition of killing so much to heart as he took other moral precepts of The Poor of Lyons, which he described as binding upon all Christians. But it is also possible that, despite his courage and consistency, he was sometimes seized with weakness and anxiety, which caused him to meet the Inquisitor halfway. The records of the Inquisitorial courts show other cases when persons under interrogation wavered between blunt, unequivocal answers and diffident,

---

dord, 1977, pp. 48, 117, 134–149; N. Gontier, *Délinquance, justice et société dans le Lyonnais mediéval*, Paris, 1993, pp. 113–135.

[57] P. Biller, 'Medieval Waldensian Abhorrence of Killing pre-c. 1400', in *The Church and War*, ed. W.J. Sheils, Studies in Church History 20 (1983), pp. 139–140; idem, 'The Preaching of the Waldensian Sisters', in *La prédication sur un mode dissident: laics, femmes hérétiques (XIe–XIVe siècles)*, Actes de la 9e session d'histoire mediévale organisée par le C.N.E.C./ R. Nelli, 26–30 août 1996, ed. M.B. Kienzle, Carcassonne, forthcoming, notes 67–69.

[58] *Le registre*, Vol. I, pp. 512–513.

evasive ones.[59] In any case, even if Huguette did internalize the prohibition of killing more than did Raymond and Jean, it was not because she had been taught by a Sister – she testified about the Brothers who had taught her, and never once mentioned a Sister.

All we know about Huguette and Agnes comes from what they told the Inquisitor, and they only spoke in response to questions. Perhaps if they had openly expressed their thought and anxieties about such basic human matters as sex, childbirth,, and motherhood, which were also shaped by their religious beliefs, there would have been a discernible 'feminine voice' in their statements. But all we have is their answers to the questions put to them by the Inquisitor, and in these the dominant voice is the Waldensian one – the gender aspect is less significant than the sect affiliation.

The next chapter is devoted to the female Believers: what characterized their position in the sect (which would define the general as opposed to the individual in the cases of Huguette and Agnes); what they were denied by comparison with women in the Catholic Church; the blurring of their 'otherness' as women in the sect, and the crossing of the usual gender boundaries in the attitude of the Inquisitors towards them.

[59] Raymond and Jean's vacillations did not prevent the judges from including their objection to killing in the list of their errors. (The final record of confessions was more stereotypical than the record made in the course of the interrogations.) Among Jean's errors was stated that he believed that when authorities condemned criminals they were committing a sin. Among Raymond's, that he believed that if he had condemned a person as a result of which he was put to death or mutilated, he would have sinned; moreover, that he quoted the words of Christ in St Matthew 5:21, forbidding all killing. *Le registre*, Vol. I, pp. 112, 515.

5

The Female Believers: A Deviation from the Gender Culture of the Age

Let me open this chapter with what the women members of The Poor of Lyons were deprived of – they were deprived of the worship of the Holy Virgin and of the other saints, male and female, as well as of the opportunities for social-religious activity in the community. We have seen that The Poor of Lyons regarded St Mary as the mother of God, but did not believe in her power to mediate between the faithful and her Son; they reduced her worship, and rejected her artistic depiction in paintings and statues, and even the prayer 'Hail Mary'. This meant that the female Poor of Lyons were deprived of a central focus in the religious life of Catholic women – a female element and symbol, and an object of identification which fulfilled a profound emotional need, an expression of a transcendent feminine ideal and a return to the mother, as well as a refuge from a male deity and male priesthood. The spokesmen for the Church knew how to utilize St Mary as the model for the feminine role, whose humility and resignation supported the social and symbolic order. Yet at the same time, the Virgin was occasionally depicted as a powerful matriarchal and subversive image which challenged masculine theology. This was what the Waldensian women lost. The spiritual life of the Sisters and female Believers had no use for the imaginary matriarchate whose artistic expression, in painting and sculpture, was a female dynasty consisting of St Anne, St Mary and the infant Jesus (known in German as *Anna Selbdritt*); and in the figures known as the 'Open Virgin': a sculpture of St Mary nursing the infant Jesus which opened to reveal the entire Holy Trinity nestling in her body as in a shrine. According to Erich Wolf, St Mary, who expressed people's emotional needs, stood for the private and familial area which, though governed by the male, had the female at its focus. Jesus, on the other hand, symbolized the public arena, namely, the world of men. Mary's worship expressed the inward, private world, which was especially meaningful for women, an antithesis to the instrumental relationships which dominated the political, financial and labour arenas.[1] Along with the worship of the Virgin, St Anne and Mary Magdalen, the Waldensian women were also deprived of the flexible and accessible worship of the male and female saints, which gave the Catholic women another outlet for their religious feelings and a source of hope and strength in their daily lives. Being deprived of the cult of female saints was especially significant, since women tended to worship the non-military, non-political saints, which most of the female saints were.[2] The number of such female saints had been growing steadily since the twelfth century, and by the early fourteenth an even greater proportion of them had been lay women.[3] But among The Poor of Lyons no such object for identification existed, nor a feminine cult to replace the worship of the Virgin and other female saints.

The male Waldensians were also deprived by the diminution of the status of St Mary and the abolition of her worship and of other female saints. The Virgin Mary, being the female element,

---

[1] E.R. Wolf, 'Society and Symbols in Latin Europe and in the Islamic Near East: Some Comparisons', *Anthropological Quarterly* 42 (1969), pp. 287–301.

[2] R. Finucane, *Miracles and Pilgrims. Popular Beliefs in Medieval England*, London, 1977, pp. 121–151.

[3] D. Weinstein and R. Bell, *Saints and Society. The Two Worlds of Christendom 1000–1700*, Chicago, 1982, pp. 200–201; A. Vauchez, *La sainteté en occident au derniers siècles du Moyen Age d'après les procès de canonisation et les documents hagiographiques*, Rome, 1988, pp. 243–299, 316–318, 402–410; B. Bolton, ' "Vitae Patrum": A Further Aspect of the Frauenfrage', in *Medieval Women. Dedicated and Presented to Rosalind M.T. Hill*, ed. D. Baker, *Studies in Church History*, Subsidia 1, Oxford, 1978, p. 250.

an archetype of the subconscious, or *anima* in K.G. Jung's terms, answered the needs of men too. It enabled them to relate to the link between mother and child in a religion of a male divinity. Hence men also turned to her for help and consolation, and male mystics also saw her in their visions. Men no less than women frequented the shrines of saints, both male and female. But the Waldensian women's loss was greater. They (and their male co-sectarians) could only experience the feminine element and the connection between mother and child through Jesus, the male divinity, instead of through Mary, regarding him as the mother, fulfilling her maternal role – as indeed did Catholic men and women whose writings have been analyzed by Carolyn Walker Bynum.[4] But we have no way of knowing if Waldensian women experienced the feminine and maternal through Jesus. Nor do we know if the Waldensian Brothers in their sermons tended, like Martin Luther, not only to depreciate the role of the Virgin, but also to downplay Jesus' feminine and maternal qualities and stress his masculine image.[5] And if so, whether or not the women accepted this image, since, as noted before, not a single written work by a Waldensian woman, either Believer or Sister, has come down to us.

Following the eleventh-century reform, the extended and struc-tured Church apparatus, having intensified the demand for conformity and established new boundaries, also strove from the late twelfth century to formalize the inferiority of women. In the thirteenth century, Aristotelian anatomy and physiology under-lined the theory about woman's natural inferiority. Fears of female impurity were also widely expressed during the twelfth

---

4 C. Walker Bynum, *Jesus as Mother. Studies in the Spirituality of the High Middle Ages*, Berkeley, 1982; *idem*, 'The Body of Christ in the Later Middle Ages: A reply to Leo Steinberg', in *Fragmentation and Redemp-tion. Essays on Gender and the Human Body in Medieval Religion*, New York, 1991, pp. 79–117.
5 About Luther in this connection: M. Wiesner, 'Luther and Women: The Death of Two Marys', in *Disciplines of Faith. Studies in Religion, Poli-tics and Patriarchy*, eds J. Obelkevich, L. Roper and R. Samuel, London, 1987, pp. 295–308.

century,[6] and the control of women grew tighter, from a closer supervision of the authority of abbesses in the convents to confining and regulating prostitution (in partnership with the signiorial or royal authority).[7] Nevertheless, the discourse on the subject of women was not unequivocal, and women did have outlets for religious activity in the parish entailing female companionship. Women stood godmothers at baptisms, took part in the network of charitable activity within the parish, listened to the sermons of the friars in the town square, watched the religious plays that were staged periodically in the towns, marched in the religious processions through the fields, led by a priest carrying the eucharist in order to banish pests and bring about bumper crops, or to end a plague. They also participated in processions in honour of the Virgin Mary and the patron saints of the city or the guild. (For example, the statutes of the city of Lille ruled that men and women taking part in the processions in honour of the Virgin Mary, which lasted nine days, could not be arrested or sued during that time.[8]) Women were also known to be especially devoted to the worship of the eucharist. The concept of the body of Christ being actually present in the sacrament also meant a connection between him and the Virgin, between the eucharistical body reborn in the Mass and the original body formed in the Virgin's womb. Women took part in the processions of the feast of Corpus Christi, which became established in the latter half of the thirteenth century, the brainchild of the mystic nun, Juliana of Liège. They took part in preparations for the event, such as spreading sawdust on the roads to prevent slipping, and making the floral decorations.[9] Women also had a central role in the feast commemorating the purification of St Mary at the temple (St

6 J. Dalarum, 'The Clerical Gaze', in *A History of Women in the West*, ed. Ch. Klapisch Zuber, London, 1992, pp. 15–42.
7 L.L. Otis, *Prostitution in Medieval Society. The History of an Urban Institution in Languedoc*, Chicago, 1985; R.M. Karras, *Prostitution and Sexuality in Medieval England*, New York–Oxford, 1995.
8 *Le livre Roisin. Coutumier lillois de la fin du 13e siècle*, ed. R. Monier, Paris–Lille, 1932, p. 138.
9 M. Rubin, *Corpus Christi. The Eucharist in Late Medieval Culture*, Cambridge, 1991, pp. 142–147, 164ff.

Luke 2:21–40), known variously as *Purificatio, Hypopanti* and *Candalaria*, in which women marched in procession, dressed in white and carrying lighted candles.[10] The ritual was associated with and resembled the ritual of the churching of women forty days after childbirth – the sole liturgical ritual in the Middle Ages that the priesthood held specifically for women, with an element of 'the imitation of Mary' (*imitatio Mariae*). The clerics as a whole regarded the ritual as a thanksgiving for the confinement which had passed safely, and a blessing for the future, but also as a rite of purification following which the childbearing woman could rejoin the mixed male and female society and take up her usual tasks. But to the women – the new mother, the midwife, the mother's friends and neighbours who had helped her during and after the confinement – it was also an expression of their shared feminine identity and temporary power.[11] Though more men than women belonged to religious fraternities, there were also many fraternities which admitted women and assigned them the same tasks as the men in the cult of the patron saint, in maintaining the fraternity chapel, in external charities and in mutual aid among the members. As we have said, the discourse about women was not all of a piece, either. There was an extensive list of 'good women.' The Franciscan Berthold of Regensburg, a disciple of David of Augsburg who preached all over Germany, lauded the women for attending church more willingly, praying and listening to the

10 In English: Candlemas, in German: *Lichtmess*; G. McMurray Gibson, 'Blessing from the Sun and Moon', in *Bodies and Disciplines. Intersections of Literature and History in Fifteenth Century England*, eds B.A. Hanawalt and D. Wallace, Minneapolis–London, 1996, pp. 139–154.
11 For a description of the ritual and its various meanings for the clergy and for the women, and historians' evaluations, see: A. Wilson, 'The Ceremony of Childbirth and its Interpretation', in *Women and Mothers in Pre-Industrial England. Essays in Memory of Dorothy McLaren*, ed. V. Fields, London, 1990, pp. 68–107; S.C. Karant-Nunn, *The Reformation of Ritual*, London–New York, 1997, pp. 72–90; though the ceremony was regarded also as an act of purification, the women who had given birth were not prohibited from entering the church before the ceremony: *Decretales Gregorii IX*, in *Corpus iuris canonici*, ed. E. Friedberg, Leipzig, 1879, Vol. II, Lib. III, tit. LXVII, col. 652.

sermons more attentively than did the men.[12] Women in the
nobility and upper bourgeoisie enjoyed a richer religious life than
did the women of the lower social strata. Many of the castles had
chapels with their own chaplains to serve the noble family. Many
of the noblewomen and women in the wealthy burgher stratum
had aunts, sisters, daughters or other female relatives who were
nuns or abbesses in convents which had been founded and
patronized by an ancestor, and which served as a centre for the
family's religious life and received its donations. They visited
these convents during religious feasts and memorial days, and in
their old age, or when they were widowed, they often retired to
the same convents, where they could, if they wished, take part in
its religious life. Moreover, being literate, some of them were able
to read religious works that were written or translated for women,
or had been translated personally for them. In religious literature
there was a particular genre known as *Sermones ad status*, that is
sermons designed for the different social groups. The sermons
meant for women were generally adapted to a purely spiritual
hierarchy, that is, virgins, married women and widows, rather
than according to a social or occupational status like the men. But
the religious literature, which was written or translated for
women was intended for those who could read, which meant
almost exclusively women in the upper strata of society. Indeed, it
was expected of them to study such works. The religious literature
intended for women, some of which was especially translated and
adapted for them, included selected passages from the Scriptures,
prayer books (especially 'Books of Hours'), moral literature and
the lives of the saints, chiefly 'The Golden Legend' of Jacob of
Voragine. However, women also commissioned translation of
works outside the recommended genres, such as portions of the
writings of St Augustine and Boethius, and some women of these
strata owned libraries that contained religious as well as secular
literature.[13]

---

[12] Berthold of Regensburg, *Vollständige Ausgabe seiner deutschen Predigten*,
eds F. Pfeiffer and J. Strobl, Vienna, 1862–1880, p. 324.

[13] A. Hentsch, *De la littérature didactique du moyen âge s'adressant spécialement aux femmes*, Cahors, 1903, reprint: Geneva, 1979; G. Hasenohr,

Did the Waldensian Believers forgo all this? We have seen that the Believers attended church now and then, confessed to a Catholic priest (though not about their sectarian affiliation), and received the eucharist from his hands, with the Brothers' approval. No doubt some of them stood godfathers and godmothers, since this sacrament took place only in the Catholic Church. Some, like Huguette, did not stop making pilgrimages to the shrines of saints – though they were not supposed to – and others did not give up the Hail Mary. We have no way of knowing if some of The Poor of Lyons took part in other parochial religious activities, either because they were unable to tear themselves away from the surrounding beliefs and rituals (especially if they had been brought up in them and only joined the sect as adults), or in order to disguise their membership of the sect. Be that as it may, when taking part in such events they must have felt a mental reservation, if not complete alienation.

Comparing the position of the female Believers among The Poor of Lyons, and the attitude towards them, with those of lay women in the Catholic Church, one is struck by the neutralization of the customary division of gender roles among The Poor of Lyons, or, in other words, the blurring of the 'otherness' of women. They did not develop a female stereotype; they gave the same tuition to male and female Believers and involved them in similar tasks for the Brothers. There is no discourse about women in the literature of The Poor of Lyons, and neither egalitarian nor discriminatory imagery. The instruction to the Sisters to obey the Brothers humbly and nimbly, which appears in the commentary to the Song of Solomon,[14] was exceptional, and was addressed to the Sisters, who indeed did not enjoy equality with the Brothers, for much the same gender hierarchy obtained among them as in

'Religious Reading among the Laity in France in the Fifteenth Century', in *Heresy and Literacy 1000–1350*, eds P. Biller and A. Hudson, Cambridge, 1994, pp. 205–221; S. Bell Groage, 'Medieval Women Book Owners: Arbiters of Lay Piety and Ambassadors of Culture', in *Women and Power in the Middle Ages*, eds M. Erler and M. Kowaleski, Athens, Ga., 1988, pp. 188–212.

14 See chapter 3, note 40.

the Catholic Church. But as a rule, the teaching of the Brothers did not refer to gender, showing neither a gender concept nor gender boundaries. We know of no writings that were considered as especially appropriate to women, nor of any sermons that were composed for them. The Brothers preached to mixed groups of men and women. Literate female Believers read the Scriptures like their male counterparts, and all were taught mainly by listening to the Brothers and learning by heart, this being the predominant form of study among The Poor of Lyons. The well-known Waldensian poem, The New Sermon (Lo novel sermon), enumerates the virtues which marriage was supposed to cultivate: 'Keeping matrimony faithfully and in goodness, departing from all evil, performing virtuous labour, and teaching their children to fear the Lord'.[15] There were no special instructions for the women – not even the usual commandment for the wife to obey her husband. We saw in the first chapter that the Brothers were es-pecially concerned about teaching the Believers: men, women and children. At various times and places they maintained schools in which men, women and children were taught by both men and women – as Catholic writers and Inquisitors noted enviously.[16] Once there were no longer such schools, they taught in the hospices, in the homes of Believers, or in direct meetings with individuals, as may be gathered from the testimonies of Huguette and her husband Jean. And there was no difference between what those two were taught, only she was firmer in giving evidence than he was. It seems that for the Brothers the female sectarian was first and foremost a human being, who had chosen the true faith and needed to be fortified in it. Raymond de la Côte's state-ment that the Brothers kept physically as far apart from women as possible is not supported by other testimonies in the Inquisitorial courts, or any other source. It would seem that, unlike the Cathar

[15] Lo novel sermon, in Six Vaudois Poems from the Waldensian Manuscripts in the University Libraries of Cambridge, Dublin and Geneva, ed. and trans. H.J. Chaytor, Cambridge, 1930, pp. 29–30.
[16] See chapter 1, note 38.

Perfects,[17] the Waldensian Brothers did not recoil from women for fear of pollution. (According to one Inquisitor, the Waldensians did not even believe that women needed to be purified in church after childbirth.) In the hospices as in the homes of the Believers, men and women dined together at the same table, the shared meal being a customary expression of solidarity, and they also prayed together.[18]

The Catholic discourse on women, which was not single-minded, and sometimes praised women for attending church more regularly and paying more willing attention to sermons than did the men, also sometimes used the image of the woman whose conduct serves as a model for her husband to emulate, as in the verse, 'For the unbelieving husband is sanctified by the wife . . .' (I Corinthians 7:14). Yet by contrast they excoriated the women among The Poor of Lyons who taught that false doctrine and Eve-like, tempted their husbands to follow a heresy. As Bernard Fontcaude wrote: 'Women should win their husbands [to the faith],' and at the same time: 'They [the Waldensians] tempt first the women and through them the men, just as Satan tempted Eve first, and through her Adam.'[19] A hundred years later, the Franciscan David of Augsburg described how they taught little

---

17 J. Duvernoy, *La Catharisme. La religion des Cathares*, Toulouse, 1976, p. 183.

18 About Brothers and Sisters who resided in the same hospice, see Chapter Three, note 31; in the records of the court of the Inquisition in Toulouse, the testimonies of men and women alike conclude with the formula: '. . . comedit cum eis in eadem mensa per eos benedicta et oravit cum eis . . .' *Liber sententiarum inquisitionis Tholosanae*, in Ph. van Limborch, ed., *Historia Inquisitionis*, Amsterdam, 1692, pp. 222–223 (104b), 225 (106), 333 (111); see also *Quellen zur Geschichte der Waldenser*, eds A. Patschovsky and K.V. Selge, Göttingen, 1973, p. 63; about there being no need for purification after childbirth: '. . . dicunt quod femina post partum non egeat benedictione et introductione'. *Pseudo Reinerius*, in M. Nickson, ed., 'The "Pseudo Reinerius" Treatise: The Final Stage of a Thirteenth Century Work on Heresy from the Diocese of Passau', *Archives d'histoire doctrinale et littéraire du moyen âge*, 42 (1967), p. 299.

19 Bernard Fontcaude, *Adversus Waldensium sectam*, PL 204, c. VII, col. 821, C. VIII, col. 826.

girls (*puellas parvulas*) the Gospels and Epistles with their own interpretation, to ensure that they cleaved to these errors from infancy. They puff them up with vanity, promising that if they learned what they were being taught they would know more than all the scholars in the land, would understand the secrets of Heaven and see the angels with their own eyes. And the foolish females, he added, believe what they are told, as Eve believed the serpent. They study enthusiastically and later they teach. And since they can readily approach women, they lead them astray first, then use them to mislead their husbands, as the serpent used Eve to mislead Adam.[20] Needless to say, both the depiction of the Catholic wife who serves as a model and example for her husband and that of the Waldensian woman who turns her husband away from the true faith, as well as other women and through them their husbands, derived from the symbolic dual image of woman in medieval culture. But the testimonies gathered in the courts of the Inquisition show that there were in fact women who brought into the sect not only their children, but also their husbands and even men and women who were not closely related to them. Most but not all the marriages were endogamous.[21] However, just as in the 'mixed' marriages the wife sometimes followed her husband into the sect, it also happened that the husband was influenced by his wife to join.[22] Moreover, the offspring were brought to the sect by both fathers and mothers. Men testified in the court of Bernard Gui in Toulouse that they had first heard that the Brothers were good people from both their mothers and fathers.[23] In the latter half of the fifteenth century, a Waldensian of the Upper Dauphiné testified that he had learned from his mother that there was no Purgatory in the next world. Another testified that as a

---

[20] David of Augsburg, *Tractatus de inquisicione hereticorum*, ed. W. Preger, Munich, 1978, pp. 29 (209), 33 (213).

[21] See, for example: *Verhörsprotokolle der Inquisition des Gallus von Neuhaus (1335 bis ca. 1353/55)*, in *Quellen zur Böhmischen Inquisition im 14. Jahrhundert*, ed. A. Patschovsky, Weimar, 1979, pp. 252–253; *Quellen zur Ketzergeschichte Brandenburgs und Pommerns*, ed. D. Kurze, Berlin, 1975, pp. 132–133, 142, 254.

[22] *Quellen zur Ketzergeschichte Brandenburgs und Pommerns*, pp. 163, 165.

[23] *Liber sententiarum*, pp. 221 (104), 222 (104b).

child he heard his grandmother explain why the priests of the Catholic Church could no longer give absolution from sins. She had said that since the time of a certain pope, whose name she had forgotten, sanctity had departed from the lives of the Catholic clerics, and they could no longer give absolution. She therefore urged her grandson to confess his sins to a Waldensian elder (barbe).[24] The female Believers were equally active in bringing in men and, chiefly, women who were not of their immediate family. In 1335, at one of the courts of the Inquisition thirty-one of the persons interrogated testified that they had been brought into the sect by men, and twenty-four – by women.[25] The women had learned the beliefs of The Poor of Lyons, remembered and internalized them, and passed them on to others. Huguette was not the only woman Believer who was knowledgeable about the principles of the faith and the moral precepts of the sect. They were preoccupied with questions of religion, and discussed and argued about them both in the family and with other women. Huguette also testified that she had discussed matters of religion with her husband and with one of her women friends. Etienne de Bourbon wrote that the women were in the habit of arguing among themselves about their errors, each in keeping with her knowledge of the errors as she had been taught them. He described a mother and daughter who were both very knowledgeable about the sect's errors and argued about them with each other. He added that because of their obduracy and refusal to recant, they were both burnt at the stake.[26] A woman who was questioned in the court of Peter Zwicker about the circumstances of her joining the sect, related that the woman who had led her to it had told her that if she wished to join, she would teach her 'what advances the soul's salvation.'[27] Among the women who

24 P. Paravy, De la chrétienté romaine à la Réforme en Dauphiné, Rome, 1993, Vol. II, pp. 1030–1031.

25 G. Merlo, Eretici e inquisitori nella società piemontese del trecento, Turin, 1977, p. 49, and note 82.

26 Etienne de Bourbon, Tractatus de diversis materiis praedicabilis, in Anecdotes historiques, légendes et apologues tirés du recueil inédit d'Etienne de Bourbon, ed. A. Lecoy de la Marche, Paris, 1877, p. 299.

27 Quellen zur Ketzergeschichte Brandenburgs und Pommerns, p. 126.

testified in the court at Strasbourg in 1400, and described the
ordination of men and women as *meister* and *meisterin*, there was
an older woman, probably a well-off widow who was called 'the
old Hirzte' (*Die alte zum Hirzte*) who stood out. The teachers maintained a 'school' in a cabin she owned which stood behind her
house. She was familiar with the history of The Poor of Lyons,
starting from Waldes and his trip to Rome to seek permission to
live a life of absolute poverty, to wander and preach. She also
distinguished between preaching and teaching.[28] There were
other Waldensian women who knew the sect's history, either the
real or the legendary one.[29] Most of the female Believers could not
read, and, like Huguette, were taught without books. But some of
them could read and owned translations of the Gospels and the
Epistles of St Paul.[30] When Huguette's husband Jean was asked
from whom he had learned about the seven principles of the faith
and the seven sacraments, and that there were only three degrees
in the clerical hierarchy (bishop, presbyter and deacon, as
customary among The Poor of Lyons), he replied that he had
learned these things in Avignon from a woman named Jacoba,
two years before his arrest. He stated that she was a woman of
about forty, who could read and who ran an inn.[31] This woman,
who could only have been a Believer since she ran an inn, was
familiar with the principles of the faith, the theory of sacraments
and the clerical hierarchy of the sect. It was not she who brought
Jean into the sect, as he had joined it twelve years before he was
arrested, but she expanded his knowledge, as Huguette strengthened his faith. The verdict in Huguette's case stated that she had
strengthened her husband's devotion to his false religion.[32] An

28 T.W. Röhrich, ed., *Factum hereticorum*, in *Mitteilungen aus der Geschichte
der evangelischen Kirche des Elsasses*, Paris–Strasbourg, 1855, Vol. I, pp.
49–54, 69.
29 See: P. Biller, 'Medieval Waldesian Construction of the Past', *Proceedings of the Huguenot Society* 25 (1989), pp. 39–40; P. Paravy, *op. cit.*, Vol.
II, p. 1045.
30 See G. Gonnet and A. Molnar, *Les Vaudois au moyen âge*, Turin, 1974,
p. 199 and note 343.
31 '. . . tenebat hostalarium'. *Le registre*, Vol. I, p. 514.
32 *Liber sententiarum*, pp. 289–291 (146b).

Austrian Waldensian who had succumbed and promised to recant, declared that no longer would either man or woman teach him or guide him on a path of life and faith which did not correspond with those of the Catholic Church.[33] It is not known if he made this statement voluntarily because he had in the past learned from one or more women, or if the Inquisitor had put these words in his mouth. If the latter, it would suggest that the Inquisitors (who by then were no longer asking questions about the Sisters) were aware of the role played by the female Believers in spreading the faith and in strengthening other Believers of both sexes in their faith. It would seem that the female Believers, who were free to come and go, played a greater part in spreading the beliefs of The Poor of Lyons than did the Sisters, who were confined to the hospices and apparently only taught the Believers, chiefly the women, who came to them. In his work, *While Men Sleep (Cum dormirent homines)* the Inquisitor Peter Zwicker, who knew a great deal about The Poor of Lyons, described the missionary work done by the women. According to him, they informed and prepared those who were drawn to the sect ahead of their meeting with the Brothers, when these came to their parts. He regarded the women as the agents of the Brothers.[34]

The female Believers were taught the same as the men, and like them spread the faith and assisted the Brothers. The only assistance given by men alone was handling the Brothers' finances and accompanying them when they set out on their journeys. Male Believers collected the donations for the Brothers, sold those which were in the form of crops, changed monies for them and rented the houses that served as hospices. One who was interrogated in Toulouse testified that he often marketed the crops that Believers had donated to the Brothers, and passed on the

---

[33] '. . . nec per quamcumque utriusque sexus personam . . .' J.J. Ign von Döllinger, ed., *Beiträge zur Sektengeschichte des Mittelalters*, Munich, 1890, Vol. II, p. 347.

[34] P. Biller, 'Les Vaudois dans les territoires de la langue allemande vers la fin du XIVe siècle: le regard d'un inquisiteur', *Heresis* 13–14 (1989), p. 219 and notes 63, 95.

proceeds.[35] Jean of Vienne related that he had been sent to change small coins for florins for the Majoral Jean of Lorraine, who was then in Toulouse.[36] Also, as a rule it was the men who accompanied the Brothers who had stayed at their home as they set out again. But in Piedmont the Brothers were sometimes accompanied by women (*mulieres*), and it is not clear if these were Sisters or Believers, though most probably the latter, since by walking along with the Brothers they helped to disguise their identity.[37] Women played a central role in accommodating the Brothers in the Believers' homes. Both married women and widows testified to have put the Brothers up at their homes, provided them with food and donations of money when they left, and also about what they were leaving them in their wills. One woman stated that she regretted being unable to give them better food and drink. Another, a widow (apparently a well-off one), said that the Brothers had stayed at her house for several weeks, rather than days, and that she was willing to have them stay as long as they wished.[38] For their part, the Brothers who stayed in the houses of Believers would give them small sums of money, probably to the poorest ones, as they had done with Huguette, since the donations made to the Brothers were intended also to help maintain poor Believers. It appears that the Brothers also declined to accept donations from these poor women, just as Jean of Lorraine would not take the two silver coins from Huguette. But they mainly gave the women small gifts: pins, needles, shoes and toys for their children,[39] the way the Brothers gave Huguette articles of clothing.

---

35 *Liber sententiarum*, p. 233 (111).
36 *Le registre*, Vol. I, pp. 512–513.
37 G. Merlo, *op. cit.*, p. 50.
38 *Quellen zur Ketzergeschichte Brandenburgs und Pommerns*, pp. 117, 134, 143; *Quellen zur Geschichte der Waldenser*, pp. 63, 68–69; *Liber sententiarum*, p. 222 (104b).
39 The author of *De vita et actibus*, in J.J. Ign von Döllinger, *op. cit.*, Vol. II, p. 97; in testimonies before courts of the Inquisition: *Quellen zur Ketzergeschichte Brandenburgs und Pommerns*, pp. 119, 126, 134, 153, 172, 195; T.W. Röhrich, ed., *op. cit.*, Vol. I, p. 48; *Liber sententiarum*, pp. 233 (111), 240 (115), 241 (116), 242 (115b).

Occasionally these little gifts were given to the poorer women Believers with no end in mind and without any reciprocity. (We noted that Huguette did not even accommodate the Brothers at her home.) They might be given in gratitude for hospitality, a reciprocity which strengthened the friendship. But the gifts might also have been intended to please those women whose commitment to the sect, or willingness to accommodate the Brothers was still uncertain. For there is no doubt that their cooperation was essential for the Brothers to carry out their work, in other words: for the sect's very survival. It was a Cathar Perfect who spoke explicitly about how vital was women's cooperation. Addressing male Believers at San Mateo, Tarragona, he said that they should only marry women of their faith, since when they were not, they prevented the Perfects from entering the house of moribund Believers to give them the *consolamentum*.[40] On another occasion he gave the same personal advice to a Believer, resorting to a parable. He suggested to the man to marry a certain young woman who was a Cathar Believer, adding: 'Do men gather grapes of thorns, or figs of thistles?' (St Matthew 7:16). Women who were not of their faith would, like thistles, prevent access to them for the purpose of the *consolamentum*.[41] Here the Cathar Perfect was concerned with the last rite given to dying men, even though women, too, received it on their deathbed, and sometimes at an earlier stage in their lives, just like the men. While worrying only about the ability of men to receive it, he does acknowledge that women, even in the patriarchal world, could bar the Perfects from entering their own sphere, namely, the home. This was a statement of a Cathar Perfect. Perhaps a Waldensian Brother, speaking of the importance of female cooperation, would also have mentioned how important it was that women hear the sermons and make confession as much as the men, and not only to ensure the spiritual salvation of the latter. What is certain is that the Waldensian Brothers were no less dependent on the women's goodwill than were the Cathar Perfects when they came to family homes to hold common prayers, to teach, preach and hear confes-

[40] *Le registre*, Vol. III, p. 189.
[41] *Le registre*, Vol. III, p. 210.

sions. Their cooperation was equally essential for hiding the whereabouts of the Brothers wherever they happened to abide (e.g. Huguette's warning to Jean of Lorraine to leave the garden where he was sitting, because too many people were in the house at the time), or to disguise their identity if their presence was discovered (e.g. the Brother of Steier telling the men and women Believers, if questioned about the visiting Brothers, to say that these men had come to sell the women household goods.)

It is known that in a persecuted, voluntary group which exists underground and depends on the active consent of its members, the class and gender divisions are partly eliminated. The Poor of Lyons were such a group, in which the 'otherness' of women was diminished and the traditional gender categorization was neutralized, despite the fact that male–female equality was not a principle of faith, and that the women's roles did not involve a formal status or official appointment. Affiliation with the sect had to come with awareness, and it seems that the awareness, combined with the active participation in the life of the sect, affected women's self-identity. They appear to speak for themselves as Believers, rather than as women, gender being less significant than affiliation with the sect. The question arises, whether the polarization between men and women would have been so reduced, and the deviation from the period's gender culture so marked as the sources indicate, had not The Poor of Lyons been such a persecuted fringe group. There is no certain answer, but it is highly doubtful. The Protestant Reformation also denied women their principal objects of identification: the Virgin Mary, Mary Magdalene and the other female saints, as well as the religious ceremonies in which they played a part,[42] and in some of which they enjoyed a relative autonomy. However, unlike the fringe community of The Poor of Lyons, the mainstream Protestant movements did not compensate the women by reducing the hierarchical and patriarchal opposition – rather the reverse.

The Inquisitors, too, for their part, blurred the standard division between men and women, or rather, suspended the

---

[42] See note 5, above: article by M.E. Wiesner.

women's social identity. This is evident not only in Jacques Fournier's interrogation of Agnes and Huguette, which was free from gender perspective, and not only with regard to The Poor of Lyons, but in the Inquisitors' general manner of interrogating all heretics. Women were not supposed to discuss matters of faith, certainly not in public, and were generally expected to keep silent. As Bernard of Fontcaude wrote: 'They must not put questions to the religious teachers, and had best avoid being seen in public.'[43] The courts limited their right to give evidence, except in matters on which only women could testify. Yet the Inquisitor, in front of his advisers and others present at the interrogation, some of them senior churchmen, questioned lay women about matters of doctrine and liturgy, debated with them, sought to obtain the most detailed answers from them, and heard (or strove to hear) their testimonies about other members of the sect. This was an obvious deviation from the norm of the period and of later times. As late as the sixteenth century, John Foxe (1518–1587), writing about what he saw as the violations and iniquities of the English bishops' courts, which had tried the Lollards in their time, was as outraged by the judges' acceptance of women's testimonies as by those of 'usurers, ribalds . . . , yea and common harlots'.[44] The method of interrogation allowed the women to have their say. A suspected female heretic by name of Na Prous Boneta, who would be burnt at the stake in 1325, testified about her visions and the heterodox doctrines she had constructed about God and the imminent coming of the Redeemer. The answers she gave the Inquisitor comprise her spiritual and doctrinal autobiography, and serve as the sole source about her and her small group of

---

[43] Bernard Fontcaude, *op. cit.*, VIII 2, col. 825.
[44] John Foxe, *Acts and Monuments*, London, 1684, Vol. II, p. 534; the Inquisition was not introduced in England. People suspected of heresy were tried before the courts of the bishops, who dealt with heretics and witches in much the same way as the courts of the Inquisition. Foxe was a Protestant martyrologist who wrote mainly about the persecution of the Protestants under Queen Mary, but also about the Lollards.

disciples.[45] Similarly, all that is known about the Guillelmites is contained in the Inquisition's interrogations of the men and women of that group. Some Inquisitors went so far as to base their summaries about heretical sects on the testimonies of women. Anselm of Alessandria, writing in the 1260s about the common and disparate elements in The Poor of Lyons and The Poor of Lombardy, based his summary on the testimonies of two women who had been longtime members of the Waldensian sect but later recanted and atoned for their sin by living in seclusion in Alba.[46] The Inquisitors were more anxious to obtain what they wanted in their interrogations than to abide by the normative manner. They regarded the women they interrogated as primarily the heretical 'other', rather than as the 'inner other', namely, the female. This divergence from the usual gender boundaries, and the view of men and women who belonged to the heretical movements primarily as heretics, suspending the usual gender and class categories, was also applied in the method of executing the condemned heretics. The next chapter will deal with this aspect.

---

[45] *Na Prous Boneta*, in *Medieval Women's Visionary Literature*, ed. and trans. E. Alvida Petroff, Oxford, 1986, pp. 34–35.
[46] Anselme of Alessandria, *Tractatus de hereticis*, in A. Dondaine O.P., ed., 'La hiérarchie cathare en Italie II: le tractatus de hereticis d'Anselme d'Alexandrie O.P.', *Archivum Fratrum Praedicatorum* 20 (1950), p. 318.

6

Martyrdom

During the High and Late Middle Ages, in some parts of western Europe, men and women who were convicted of the same crimes were executed in different ways. In Brabant, Germany and France men were usually hanged, or if they were nobles, decapitated with an axe, but women were either burnt at the stake or buried alive. This custom was established by law and various statutes, and became embodied in the operating legal system.[1] Only in the late fifteenth century were these methods of executing women, gradually and at a varying pace in different places, changed to hanging. The cruelest forms of putting people to death, devised with the explicit intention of intensifying and prolonging the condemned person's agony, were imposed upon those who were convicted of high treason (*crimen laesae maiestatis*). And since the ritual of execution had a special symbolic and educational meaning, their bodies were also specially degraded. One way of doing so was to burn the corpse, or only its internal organs (especially the heart,

---

1   Executions of women by this method appear in the court records of various regions. The following are some examples from France and Flanders: *Le registre criminel de la justice de Saint Martin des Champs à Paris au XIVe siècle*, ed. L. Tanon, Paris, 1877, pp. 43, 220; *Le registre criminel du Châtelet de Paris du 6 septembre 1389 au 18 mai 1392*, ed. Duplès-Agier, Paris, 1861–1864, Vol. I, pp. 48, 268, 327, 363, Vol. II, pp. 60, 64, 337, 393, 436–437; L. Tanon, *Histoire de la justice des anciennes églises et communautés monastiques de Paris*, Paris, 1883, pp. 30–31, 334, 364, 447; G. Espinas, *La vie urbaine de Douai au moyen âge*, Paris, 1913, p. 753.

in which the villain had plotted his treason). But even those convicts were not burnt alive.[2] As a rule, high treason was not a feminine crime, though there were cases of women who were charged with a type of murder that was equated with treason – e.g. when a vassal murdered his seigneur, a servant his employer, or a woman her husband.[3] Women who were convicted of such a murder were burnt at the stake, even in England, where as a rule women were not executed by this method for other crimes. A woman who was convicted of a (failed) attempt to murder her husband was burnt at the stake. A thirteen-year-old maidservant who was found guilty of murdering her mistress was also burnt alive. But in those same days, four menservants who had strangled their master to death were dragged through the streets, hanged and then decapitated.[4] According to one of the Castilian penal codes, a woman who murdered her husband was to be burnt at the stake, whereas a man who murdered his wife was to be hanged (and if it transpired that he had killed her because she had committed adultery, he was to be acquitted.)[5] According to the English jurist who composed the work known as *Fleta* in the late thirteenth century, women convicted of counterfeiting (a crime which was sometimes categorized as high treason) were also to be burnt at the stake.[6] In certain regions the body of a woman suicide was treated differently from that of a male suicide. In 1397 a man and a woman committed suicide in the city of Douai in Flanders. The city authorities ordered the woman's body to be burnt, and the man's to be dragged and hanged.[7] The penal code

---

2 J.G. Bellamy, *The Law of Treason in England in the Later Middle Ages*, Cambridge, 1970, pp. 13, 21–39, 46–47, 51, 136, 172; A. Boureau, *Le simple corps du roi*, Paris, 1988, pp. 52, 57–60.

3 The terms 'misprision' or 'petty treason' came to designate this crime among others: J.G. Bellamy, *op. cit.*, pp. 225–238; W.S. Holdworth, *A History of English Law*, London, 1909, Vol. II, p. 373, note 3.

4 J.G. Bellamy, *op. cit.*, pp. 226–227.

5 *Fueros castellanos de Soria y Alcala de Henares*, ed. G. Sanchez, Madrid, 1919, no. 551, p. 198.

6 *Fleta*, ed. and trans. H.G. Richardson and G.O. Sayles, London, 1955, Vol. I, Bk 1, ch. 22, pp. 58–59.

7 G. Espinas, *op. cit.*, p. 751 and note 5; J. Gessler, ' "Mulier suspenda":

of the city of Lille, from 1344, stipulated that the corpse of a man who committed suicide (which, it stated, was to be regarded as that of a murderer), was to be dragged and hanged, and the body of a woman who committed suicide was to be burnt below the gallows.[8] Thus it may be said that either in respect of any capital crime, or only for specific ones, burning at the stake was a capital punishment generally reserved for women. There were two crimes, however, for which men too were sentenced to the stake: homosexuality and heresy. But while the law (which occurs in most penal codes from the latter half of the thirteenth century)[9] was hardly ever implemented with regard to homosexuals, men who were turned over by the Inquisition to the 'secular arm' were burnt at the stake just like the women.

The compilers of the penal codes and the medieval jurists did not explain the choice of this or that form of punishment, or its stages, for particular crimes. It was assumed that their symbolic meaning was understood by all. Thus they did not explain their choice of specific methods of execution for women. Legal historians who have tried to address this issue attributed the custom to the modesty of medieval people: hanged corpses were left to swing for many days, as an object lesson for the public, and it would have seemed inappropriate to leave a woman's body in this same way. This reason was first brought up in the sixteenth century, and legal historians repeated it until recent times.[10] E. Cohen has proposed a different reason, suggesting that the underlying cause was fear of the evil power of women in general, and of female criminals in particular. This was why the men of the

---

à délit égal peine differente?', *Revue belge de philologie et d'histoire* 18 (1939), pp. 974–988.

8 J. Gessler, *op. cit.*, pp. 986–987.

9 J. Boswell, *Christianity, Social Tolerance and Homosexuality*, Chicago–London, 1980, pp. 281–295. Burning at the stake was also the legal penalty for sexual congress with animals.

10 P. Viollet, *Le droit du XIIIe siècle dans les coutumiers de Touraine-Anjou*, Paris, 1881, p. 164; J. Gessler, *op. cit.*, p. 975; Y.B. Brissaud, 'L'infanticide à la fin du moyen âge:Ses motivations psychologiques et sa repression', *Revue historique de droit français et étranger* 50 (1972), pp. 248 and note 78, 256 and note 88.

period preferred to burn them at the stake or bury them alive, believing that this would ensure that they could not return in spirit form to haunt and harm the living. She rightly notes that keeping the woman's body hidden was not a concern of the age. Women were often subjected to humiliating public punishments in which their bodies were exposed to public gaze. (For example, the statutes of several cities ordered an adulterous couple to run through the streets naked and tied together, being flogged all the way.)[11] Moreover, burning at the stake in public did not ensure modesty. It too crossed the boundary between the intimate-feminine and the publicly revealed. It did not prevent the body and the corpse from being exposed – the clothes burned first, revealing the naked body – combining sex and violence. It is also significant that the modesty explanation was raised only in the sixteenth century, at a time when the method of executing women was already in the process of being changed (and raised mainly by the opponents of change). So far as it is known, there is only one medieval source, a late, indirect equivocal one, suggesting that the reason women were not hanged was to avoid exposing their bodies. The successor of the Burgundian chronicler Enguerrand de Monstrelet, writing in the latter half of the fifteenth century, described the hanging of a woman in Paris, which he said was the first time a woman was executed in this way in France.[12] The woman and the man who was hanged with her had been convicted of a vicious murder of a two-year-old infant who had been entrusted to their care. The chronicler stated that a vast crowd, mainly women, gathered to watch the execution on account of the novelty of hanging a woman. The two gallows were set on a high stage, for everyone to see the punishment for the vile crime. The woman was hanged wearing a long dress, with her legs tied together below her knees. Some of the spectators said,

[11] E. Cohen, 'Symbols of Culpability and the Universal Language of Justice: The Ritual of Public Executions in Late Medieval Europe', *History of European Ideas* 11 (1989), pp. 410–413; *idem, The Crossroads of Justice. Law and Culture in Late Medieval France*, Leiden, 1993, pp. 94–99.
[12] There is a record of an earlier hanging of a woman – in Limoge in 1414: J. Gessler, *op. cit.*, p. 983.

according to the chronicler, that it was she who had asked to be put to death this way, claiming that it was the custom in her country. Others said that she was hanged so that the crime and the punishment would be engraved in women's memory [seeing her hanged body], and because her crime was so heinous that she deserved the worst punishment.[13] Thus, according to this chronicler, some people regarded the unaccustomed hanging of a woman as an especially severe punishment, because her body was exposed. He attributed the long dress and the tying of her legs together to the executioners, who wished to avoid exposing her lower parts. But, again, this indirect testimony is both unique and late.

Unfortunately, the other explanation – namely that women were executed as they were because of fear of their spirits' haunting – has no foundation in the historical sources. But even if the sources suggested that women were burnt at the stake or buried alive because of such anxieties, the question remains, why were homosexuals and heretics also sentenced to be burnt at the stake?

It seems highly unlikely that there was greater fear of homosexuals and heretics returning to haunt the living than any other executed convicts. With regard to the heretics, it is clear that one reason for burning them was the wish to avoid a cult of their remains. While Cathars and The Poor of Lyons alike were not greatly concerned with the dead body and with burial in consecrated ground, we have seen that some of the Believers did not entirely forgo the beliefs and customs rejected by the Brothers. The Franciscan David of Augsburg wrote that people who collected the bones of those who had been burnt at the stake did so because they believed that they were saints, and could therefore be assumed to belong to The Poor of Lyons.[14] Also, a woman

---

13 Although written by Enguerrand's successor, the text is included in *The Chronicle of Enguerrand de Monstrelet*, trans. Th. Johnes, London, 1809, Vol. VIII, ch. CXXXVI, p. 406.

14 David of Augsburg, *Tractatus de inquisicione hereticorum*, ed. W. Preger, Munich, 1878, pp. 42 (222), 48 (228); see also *Tractatus de haeresi Pauperum de Lugduno auctore anonymo. De libro Stephani de Bella-villa accipi-*

who belonged to the Lollard sect, which likewise rejected the veneration of saints, testified that while she did not support such veneration, she did pray to the Lollard martyr Thomas White, because she believed that he would intercede for her before God.[15] There are other cultures which attribute special powers to those who had been killed unjustly. An unjust murder or execution violates the true social order, which is restored by attributing powers to the victim. The concern to avoid a cult of heretical saints could therefore be a partial explanation for burning heretics at the stake, but it cannot apply to the case of homosexuals and women.

It seems to me that executing women by a different method than men was but another form in which the distinction between the sexes was translated into codes of custom. Applying a different custom to women than to men (for reasons that were not always conscious) was like those codes of behaviour that were rooted in the political, social or religious ideology which characterized society as a whole in many areas of life. Thus the manner of executing women was also different. And since women were the 'other' in society, whose legal status was different and whose rights were restricted by comparison with those of the dominant male centre which determined the methods of execution, a different method was devised for putting them to death; one which was longer and more agonizing, and was also considered more undignified, because of the total destruction of the corpse. This also expressed the conscious and unconscious ambivalence towards women. We know that there was particular fear of the spirits of women who died in childbirth and were therefore 'unclean', because they had not been churched, as well as of the spirits of babies, both male and female, who died before joining the community of the living, in the Christian sense – i.e. before they had been baptized. The same anxiety existed with regard to those who were unjustly killed, or even died prematurely (which

untur ista, in *Thesaurus novus anecdotorum*, eds E. Martène and M. Durand, Paris, 1717, Vol. V, cols 1787–1788.

15 *Heresy Trials in the Diocese of Norwich 1428–1431*, ed. and trans. N.P. Tanner, Camden Fourth Series 20, London, 1977, pp. 14, 47.

might be explained psychologically as reflecting the guilty feelings of the living), and various devices were employed to prevent their spirits from returning.[16] But there is no convincing evidence that the spirits of executed women were more feared than the spirits of male criminals.

Heretics (and by law also those who engaged in homosexual practices), were condemned to the stake because being a heretic was considered more significant than their gender or social position. The heretics and the homosexuals were regarded as the 'other', not in the internal sense, like women, but as the 'other' who was set outside the pale and lost both social position and rights. They were therefore sentenced to a method of execution normally intended for women only, whereby the evil was not

---

[16] A series of questions drafted in the early eleventh century by Burchard of Worms, for confessors to ask people, included one that asked if the person had stuck a peg into the corpse of a baby that had died unbaptized, or attached one to the body of a woman who had died in childbirth and to that of her stillborn baby. These questions clearly indicate that such things were done to prevent the deceased from returning to haunt the living, as stated explicitly: 'For they said that if they did not do so, the baby might do much harm,' Burchard of Worms, *Decretorum libri viginti. PL* 140, cols 974–975; in later times, a woman who died in childbirth could not be buried in the church (see, for example, *Mirk's Festial. A Collection of Homilies*, ed. T. Erbe, London, 1905, p. 298), because of her uncleanness, since she had not undergone the ritual of thanksgiving and purification that enabled her to rejoin the community. It is not clear if it was also due to fear of her spirit coming back to haunt the living. In Germany as late as the fifteenth century some families demanded to have the ritual done to a woman who died in childbirth before she was buried, and in the eighteenth century it was sometimes recommended that she be buried in an unfrequented corner of the churchyard. See: P. Browe S.J., *Beiträge zur Sexualethik des Mittelalters*, Breslau, 1932, pp. 20–21; S.C. Karant-Nunn, *The Reformation of Ritual*, London–New York, 1997, p. 78. According to the English jurist William Blackstone (1723–1780) a person who committed suicide should be buried with a stake driven through the body, or a stone placed on the face: G.W. Williams, *The Sanctity of Life and the Criminal Law*, New York, 1957, p. 233. Concerning methods to prevent haunting (not only by women and babies), see also: E. Cohen, *The Crossroads of Justice*, pp. 135–136.

only eradicated from the living community, but totally annihi-
lated. Homosexuals were generally regarded as close to women,
and often described as having become women. As John Chrysostom wrote at the end of the fourth century: Through homosexual acts '. . . not only are you made into a woman, but you also
cease to be a man'. And Peter Cantor, writing at the end of the
twelfth century, described homosexuals as those 'who change
themselves from males to females.'[17] Homosexuality as such was
not viewed as a heresy, and heretics were not identified with
homosexuals, but various heretical groups were accused of
violating all norms of sexual morality, including having homosexual relations. (This accusation was levelled especially at the
Cathars who rejected procreation, and were therefore charged
with preferring homosexual relations to relations with women
and marriage.) By these charges and denunciations the heretics
and the homosexuals were sometimes bound into one sinful
group. The concept of homosexuality and the attitude towards it
was expressed mainly in the law, as during the High and Late
Middle Ages it rarely happened that a homosexual was actually
burnt at the stake, whereas with regard to the heretics, the law
and reality took the same form. This method of execution also
prevented the rise of a cult of martyrs' remains among the
sectarians. In this way, as in their manner of interrogation, the
Inquisitors, together with the 'secular arm', crossed the customary
gender boundaries. But while the interrogation of women
brought them nearer to the men – just as in their life the Waldensian women Believers were brought nearer to the men in the sect
and the gender difference was blurred malewards – in the execution of heretics the difference was blurred in the opposite direction, the men being treated in the same way as women usually
were.

The Catholic clerics were disturbed and dismayed by the willingness of heretics to make the supreme sacrifice, namely, to lay
down their lives, to die in their faith and be martyred in the original sense of the word – meaning, to bear witness to the truth of

---

[17] John Chrysostom, *Epistolam ad Romanos*, trans. in J. Boswell, *op. cit.*, p.
361; Peter Cantor, *De vitio sodomitico*, trans., *ibid.*, p. 377.

their faith by dying for it. Original Christian martyrdom had ended in the fourth century. During the High and Late Middle Ages martyrdom, in the original sense, was exceedingly rare, and it is not surprising that during the period in question the term was used in a wide and vague way. Missionaries who had been killed by infidels were called martyrs, even if they had not been put to the test. Some of those who died in the Crusades were regarded as martyrs, and so were people who died in the defence of the Church (e.g. Thomas à Becket). Thomas Aquinas' definition of martyrdom stressed the fulfilment of duty, devotion, resignation and above all the right intent.[18] However, not only the 'Innocents' (i.e. the children who were massacred on Herod's order) were considered martyrs, but also dead children whom the blood libel described as victims of Jewish ritual murder. Some of these were incorporated in the prayer book and their tombs became sites of pilgrimage where miracles were believed to take place. Popular belief also held that victims of injustice and cruelty were martyrs. But the Jews and the heretics had martyrs in the original sense of the word: people who voluntarily went to their death to bear witness to their faith. The record of a 1397 interrogation of a Waldensian from Carmagnola near Turin, a blacksmith by trade whom the record called *Magister*, states: 'He said that Peter the martyr [who was murdered by the Cathars in 1252, and was the only Inquisitor ever to be canonized] had been a sinner and a wicked man who was consiged to hell for persecuting the servants of the Lord, and that the heretics [i.e. the Cathars] and the Waldensians who killed the saint were the servants of the Lord. Also that the death of the Waldensian Jacob Bechus was dearer to God than the death of Peter the martyr.'[19] It is hardly surprising that the Waldensian blacksmith regarded Jacob Bechus

---

[18] Thomas Aquinas, *Summa theologiae* 2a 2ae, q. 124, art. 1,4, ed. and trans. The Fathers of Blackfriars, London, 1960–75, Vol. 42, pp. 42, 44–46, 52; the number of martyrs, both Catholic and Protestant rose again in the sixteenth century: B.S. Gregory, *Salvation at Stake. Christian Martyrdom in Early Modern Europe*, Cambridge, 1999.

[19] In G.G. Merlo, 'Pietro di Verona – S. Pietro martire. Difficoltà e proposte per lo studio di un inquisitore beatificato', in *Culto dei Santi, istituzioni e classi sociali in età preindustriale*, eds S.B. Gajano and L.

as a true martyr but not the Inquisitor Peter, since not every person who suffers and dies for his faith is a martyr, but only one who suffers for the true faith. Those who had promoted the canonization of Peter were no doubt all the more uneasy because the Franciscans and many of the laity refused to acknowledge the martyrdom of the Dominican Inquisitor. (At the same time, the reported reaction of people at the inn to Raymond de la Côte's burning at the stake suggests that at least some of them, though not members of The Poor of Lyons, regarded him as a true martyr).[20] But more than this partial failure, it was the very readiness of heretics to undergo martyrdom that dismayed the Inquisitors.

A letter that Eberwin, the prior of the Premonstratensian monastery of Steinfeld, sent to Bernard of Clairvaux in 1143 or 1144, described a group of heretics who had been arrested in Cologne, two of whom were savaged by the crowd against, he said, the wishes of the clerics. He wrote: 'What is more marvellous, they met and bore the agony of the fire not only with patience but even with joy. At this point, holy father, were I with you, I should like you to explain whence comes to those limbs of the Devil constancy such as is scarcely to be found in men most devoted to the faith of Christ.'[21] The Inquisitor Etienne de Bourbon expressed the same uneasiness in a brief, blunt response to the burning at the stake of one such heretic: his corpse stank,[22] he said. Had his faith been true and pure, it would not have done so. The doctor of theology Stefan Palec, an associate of Jan Hus who turned away from him and became his bitter enemy, formulated a complete dialectical reversal – a formula which echoes Saint Augustine's condemnation as murderers of the Donatists

Sebastiani, Rome, 1984, p. 473; Peter Martyr's *Vita: Acta Sanctorum*, ed. The Bollandist Fathers, Paris, 1863, April III, pp. 694–696.

[20] *Le registre*, Vol. I, p. 169.

[21] *Eberwini Steinfeldensis praepositi ad S. Bernardum epistola*. PL 182, epistola 472, col. 677. Translation: *Heresies of the High Middle Ages*, eds and trans. W.L. Wakefield and A.P. Evans, New York, 1969, p. 129.

[22] Etienne de Bourbon, *Tractatus de diversis materiis praedicabilis*, in *Anecdotes historiques, legendes et apologues tirés du recueil inédit d'Etienne de Bourbon*, ed. A. Lecoy de la Marche, Paris, 1877, p. 310.

who provoked martyrdom: willingness to undergo martyrdom signified heresy. Describing the execution of three young Hussites who had refused to buy the indulgences intended to finance the campaign of Pope John XXIII against the king of Naples, he stated that the Hussite movement had taken a dangerous new turn: its members were now happy to risk their lives for the ideal of a pauperized Church. The 'sweet and bold' death of the three young men was proof of this. Such willingness to undergo martyrdom is a plain sign of heresy, since 'among us there may be hardly one, or not even one, who would risk his life for the faith'.[23] But despite the anxiety that this phenomenon aroused in the Catholic clergy, the logic of their worldview forced the Inquisitors to go on creating martyrs. Those who were sent to the stake were the stubborn heretics who clung to their false religion and refused to recant, and therefore had to be turned over to the 'secular arm' for execution. All the Inquisitors could do was prevent their remains from being venerated by burning them at the stake and even scattering their ashes.

The purpose of the burnings was to extirpate evil so as to protect the Catholic community and the Church's exclusive authority, to punish and to intimidate. In contrast to the self-mortifications undertaken by the ascetics, which were meant as atonement for sins, approaching the Redeemer by imitating his suffering (*imitatio Christi*), and in hope of transcendent experience; in contrast to human suffering in the form of sickness or old age, which was also sometimes described as means of atonement and closeness to Christ; even in contrast to other penalties imposed by the Inquisitors by way of penance – burning at the stake was not a penance and lacked all spiritual meaning. All the other punishments imposed by the courts of the Inquisition, including life imprisonment, were regarded as penance; not so burning at the stake. The flames were supposed to purify the community by exterminating the evil that had infected it, not to

---

23 Quoted in J. Gonnet and A. Molnar, *Les Vaudois au moyen âge*, Turin, 1974, p. 217; regarding St Augustine's attitude: A.J. Droge and J.D. Tabor, *A Noble Death. Suicide and Martyrdom among Christians and Jews in Antiquity*, San Francisco, 1992, Ch. 7.

serve as a means of purification and penance to the person being burnt. And indeed the verdicts of the courts of the Inquisition did not describe the commitment of the condemned person to the 'secular arm' (accompanied by the formal request demanded by canon law to spare the person's life and limbs) as a form of penance. As Jacques Fournier stated formally and dryly in sentencing Huguette and her husband Jean: 'stubborn heretics of the sect of the Waldensians or The Poor of Lyons, who refuse to recant. As such, we turn them over to the secular arm . . .',[24] and dying without recanting or repenting their sins, the heretics were condemned to eternal damnation. In 1230, Philippe de Grève, chancellor of the university of Paris, referred in a sermon to a Waldensian known as 'the Reims baker Echard', who had been burnt at the stake a short while before. He then proceeded to describe the deviations of The Poor of Lyons, depicting them as three ovens of error and evil: an oven of preaching without authority or permission; an oven of disseminating the false doctrine and opposition to the papal indulgences; and an oven of causing a schism in the Church. Towards the end, he reverted to the Reims baker, who had been 'taken from the threefold oven of false doctrine, misleading confession and pernicious congregation, and was handed to the oven of temporal punishment and then to the oven of hell'. Eudes of Chateauroux, who had also served as the chancellor of the university of Paris, said about the heretics: 'They are burnt in the temporal fire for everyone to see the enormity of their sin . . . and in future they will burn in the unquenchable fire of hell.'[25] 'For everyone to see the enormity of their sin', suggests a warning to others. Burning heretics at the stake, like other public executions, was intended as a deterrent. Heretics were sometimes made to watch the burning of a fellow

---

[24] *Liber sententiarum Inquisitionis Tholosanae*, in *Historia Inquisitionis*, ed. Ph. van Limborch, Amsterdam, 1692, p. 291 (147b); another, similarly phrased verdict of Jacques Fournier's: *ibid.*, p. 288 (146).

[25] In Ch.H. Haskins, *Studies in Medieval Culture*, New York, 1929, reprint 1965, Ch. XI, p. 247, Ch. X, p. 237 and note 4; similar statements of Etienne de Bourbon about the heretics consigned to hell: Etienne de Bourbon, *op. cit.*, p. 311.

sectarian. In 1511, the followers of the Lollard William Carder of Tenterden in Kent were forced by the bishop to watch him being burnt at the stake.[26]

Various and disparate cultures have believed that certain men and women had ontologically different sensibilities from the rest of humanity. Thus in India the suttee – the voluntary immolation of a widow on her husband's funeral pyre – was believed to be free from pain. Suttee was the truth that flowed into the woman and made her immune from pain. The spirit triumphed over the body.[27] In early Christian descriptions of martyrdom alongside scenes of death in torment[28] appear also other scenes in which freedom from pain is attributed to the martyrs as in the passion of Pionius the Presbyter: 'Then peacefully and painlessly as though belching he breathed his last.'[29] According to Thomas Aquinas, the joy of contemplating God and thinking of the love of God relieved their suffering.[30] Jacob de Voragine in his 'Golden Legend' went even further. He described in detail the frightful tortures to which martyrs, both men and women, were subjected, yet their corpses gave off a wonderful fragrance – a sign that they had not felt any pain.[31] It is not known to what extent this belief was shared by the Cathars, as it is mentioned only in a single testimony. The castellan's wife, Beatrice Planissol, told the Inquisitor Jacques Fournier about an exchange she had with her husband's squire, who was trying to bring her into the Cathar faith. Speaking of two women who had been burnt at the stake, she said

26 John Foxe, *Acts and Monuments*, London, 1684, Vol. II, pp. 533–534; J.A.F. Thomson, *The Latter Lollards 1414–1510*, Oxford, 1965, pp. 187–188, 234.

27 R. Sunder Rajan, *Real and Imagined Women*, London, 1993, pp. 20–21.

28 *The Acts of the Christian Martyrs*, ed. and trans. H. Musurillo, Oxford, 1972, pp. 131, 139.

29 *Ibid.*, p. 165.

30 Thomas Aquinas, *Summa theologiae*, 3a, q. 15, art. 5, Vol. 49, p. 204.

31 Mentioned in C. Walker Bynum, 'Material Continuity, Personal Survival and the Resurrection of the Body: A Scholastic Discussion in its Medieval and Modern Contexts', in *Fragmentation and Redemption. Essays on Gender and the Human Body in Medieval Religion*, New York, 1991, p. 290.

that they would have done better to recant, and he responded by saying that the Cathar Perfects who were burnt at the stake 'did not feel the fire, which could not cause their bodies any suffering'.[32] There is no evidence that The Poor of Lyons shared this belief, nor is there any evidence that they sought martyrdom. (There is only one piece of evidence for it among the Cathars: a man suspected of Catharism, being interrogated by the court of the Inquisition in Carcassonne, was asked if the Perfect Bernard was likely to return too Toulouse. He said no, unless he returned to seek martyrdom, for he had told him that 'there is no finer death than by fire'.[33]) The fact that the Waldensian Brothers permitted the Believers to swear as the Inquisitors demanded, in order to save themselves and their fellow sectarians, suggests that they did not seek martyrdom. But they did believe that if they were martyred, they would attain the kingdom of heaven, and if put to the test, they were willing to suffer agonies and death as part of their fate in this world, like the prophets, Jesus and the Apostles, to the end of time. Asked if he believed that by being executed he would become a martyr, Raymond de la Côte replied that if he were killed for his faith he would gain God's grace and be a martyr for the Redeemer. He added that anyone who killed him for his faith would ally himself with those who had stoned St Stephen, and innocent blood would be on his head, as the Bible said: 'That upon you may come all the righteous blood shed upon the earth, from the blood of righteous Abel unto the blood of Zacharias son of Barachias, whom ye slew between the temple and the altar' (St Matthew 23:35). Referring to the Catholic position from the opposite side, he said in a later interrogation that a person suffering for a false faith was not sainted, and would be consigned to hell despite his suffering, for only he who suffered for the true faith was a saint.[34] Jacques Fournier put only one question to Huguette on this matter: 'Asked whether she believed and

---

[32] *Le registre*, Vol. I, p. 221.

[33] J.J. Ign von Döllinger, ed., *Beiträge zur Sektengeschichte des Mittelalters*, Munich, 1890, Vol. II, p. 35.

[34] *Le registre*, Vol. I, pp. 50, 72, 87; the Inquisitors' comments on the Brothers' allowing the Believers to swear in order to save themselves

hoped that if she were put to death for defending her errors she would save her soul, she replied that she did believe and hoped this was so.'[35] The question was not put to Agnes, but she knew what to expect if she refused to swear. Ordered to swear, she said that 'in no way would she agree to swear, not even to save her life'.[36]

We have seen that one of the customers at the inn, talking about the executions, said that Jacques Fournier had 'wept and mourned when Raymond refused to recant, because he was a good clergyman'[37] – meaning, he was mourning his failure to save the man's soul.[38] The historical personalities of the Inquisitors fascinated writers and dramatists who produced an extensive literature about the Inquisition in the Middle Ages and in early modern times, a literature which flourished in a variety of genres from the seventeenth century[39] to the last novel of Michel de Castillo, *La tunique de l'infarnie*. They ascribed to them a variety of motives and shaped their characters in accordance with their own psychological interpretation, imagination and literary ability. The historian may not take such liberties, but it is possible to examine other or additional reasons for Jacques Fournier's reaction (just as it is possible to explain his method of interrogation as stemming not only from a great desire to make the accused persons recant).[40] Is it not possible that more than he mourned the fate of Raymond and Agnes in the afterworld, he was frustrated by the failure of his first effort as a newly appointed Inquisitor? After all, an Inquisitor was not only expected to extract information about the suspect's beliefs and fellow-sectarians and to punish him or

and their comrades: David of Augsburg, *op. cit.*, p. 28 (208); Etienne de Bourbon, *op. cit.*, p. 294.

35 See Appendix, p. 148.

36 See Appendix, p. 131.

37 *Le registre*, Vol. I, p. 171.

38 An example of unreserved acceptance of the statements about Jacques Fournier: M. Benad, *Domus und Religion in Montaillou*, Spätmittelalter und Reformation Neue Reihe 1, Tübingen, 1990, pp. 12–13.

39 In this connection, see: E. Peters, *Inquisition*, New York, 1988, Chs 7–8.

40 See Introduction, note 25.

her, but also to make him recant. Sending a heretic to the stake showed the Inquisitor's power, but his object was to bring the heretic back into the fold, not to demonstrate power. Is it not possible that, like other Catholic clerics, he was alarmed by the willingness of Raymond and Agnes to undergo martyrdom, even though ecclesiastical discourse had defined such willingness as a sign of heresy? And was he also perhaps horrified when he witnessed the actual burning at the stake which he had ordered?

A great deal has been written in recent years about the symbolic function and the theatrical aspect of the various methods of execution used in the Late Middle Ages and early modern times. But it should be emphasized that the common spectators, like the jurists and the judges who had handed down the sentences, were aware not only of the symbolic significance of the various forms of execution, but also of the agonies of the condemned. Some of the spectators no doubt also derived a sadistic pleasure from the horrendous sights.[41] The learned ecclesiastical discourse emphasized the primacy of intention, be it just or unjust in the torturer, rather than the victim's subjective pain. But some jurists stated explicitly that the more heinous the crime, the more painful should be the punishment. The author of the work known as *Fleta* wrote about the punishment for a certain crime: '. . . and if found guilty, he should suffer the greatest punishment, intensifying the bodily pain . . .'[42] When the Catholics and Cathars assumed that their respective martyrs did not suffer pain, they were not only expressing belief in their ontologically different sensibilities, unlike those of other human beings – they were also expressing a wish to believe that they were spared the agony (though it conflicted with the belief that voluntary acceptance of suffering is a way to approach the Redeemer, who

[41] See for example: S. Lerere, ' "Represtyd now yower syght": The Culture of Spectatorship in Late Fifteenth Century England', in *Bodies and Disciplines. Intersections of Literature and History in Fifteenth Century England*, eds B.A. Hanawalt and D. Wallace, London, 1996, pp. 29–62; see especially: pp. 30, 36.

[42] '. . . ultimum supplicium sustinebit, cum pene aggravacione corporalis', *Fleta*, Vol. II, Bk 1, c. 21, p. 56.

had willingly undertaken suffering in order to save mankind). The Cathar quoted by Beatrice Planissol did not speak about the end of the Perfects' life on earth, nor about their souls' salvation in the afterworld, but about their immunity from pain. It is possible that Jacques Fournier was not one of those who relished the sight of the agonies suffered by the condemned, but was shaken by the first burning at the stake that he had ordered – a burning not of criminals but, as Pierrette Paravy put it, of 'brother enemies'.[43] Nevertheless, even if he was shaken and therefore wept, it did not prevent him from sending Huguette and Jean to the stake a year later.

As noted before, we do not know if Jacques Fournier delayed sentencing Huguette because she was pregnant, or because he hesitated, seeing that so soon after becoming an Inquisitor he had already sent two Waldensians to the stake, and hoped that the other two would recant. Nor do we know how people reacted to the execution of Huguette and Jean. It is probable that people had become more cautious and their reactions were not reported to Jacques Fournier. As the trial of Raymond's defenders showed, statements in support of a burnt heretic were dangerous. Even mourning for such a person aroused suspicions of belonging to the same sect.[44] And just as we do not know which causes weighed most in Jacques Fournier's sorrow after Raymond and Agnes were burnt, so we do not know what was the decisive motive that made Agnes and Huguette willing to die for their faith. A last-minute recantation was suspicious, but the secular authorities would have been obliged to return the condemned person to the Inquisition, which usually imposed life imprisonment in a narrow cell as a penance. A person who did not die in prison was sometimes released after a few years and received a lighter penance. Were they inspired to accept martyrdom by their faith and the hope of salvation in the next world? Was it loyalty to their fellow Waldensians who had already been burnt at the stake, or were about to

---

43 P. Paravy, *De la chrétienté romaine à la Réforme en Dauphiné*, Rome, 1993, Vol. II, p. 945.
44 About this: *Tractatus de haeresi Pauperum de Lugduno auctore anonymo*, cols 1786–1787.

be burnt, and above all to their loved ones – in Huguette's case to her husband Jean, about whom she had said that she wished to live and die in his faith; in Agnes' case to Raymond, who had been like a son to her? Or was it an outright protest against the dominant Church which collaborated with the secular power in suppressing the true followers of Christ? We have seen that Agnes' heresy was limited to her refusal to swear, so that she exemplified the statement that the Catholic Salvo Burci put in the mouth of The Poor of Lyons: 'Look at them putting people to death for the crime of refusing to swear . . .'[45] But refusing to swear was the way she identified with the sect which forbade swearing and with her fellow sectarians. And even if loyalty to their nearest and dearest was the decisive factor in the two women's voluntary martyrdom, its significance extended beyond their personal and familial circle to the greater circle of a courageous, persecuted sect. It became part of its history.

[45] Salvo Burci, *Liber supra stella*, in J.J. Ign von Döllinger, *op. cit.*, Vol. II, p. 72.

Appendix:[1]
Translation of the Interrogations of Agnes and Huguette

The Confession of Agnes Francou, Widow of Etienne Francou of the Heretical Sect of the Poor of Lyons from the Diocese of Vienne

In the year of Our Lord 1319, on Friday, the feast of Saint Laurence,[2] Agnes, widow of Etienne of Vermelle,[3] of the diocese of Vienne, who was arrested with Raymond de la Côte, also known as Raymond of Saint Foy,[4] being highly suspected of belonging to the Waldensian heretics, or The Poor of Lyons, was summoned to appear before the honourable Father in Christ, the lord Jacques, by grace of God Bishop of Pamiers. The Bishop, who wanted to question her about certain matters concerning the Catholic faith, and chiefly about the Waldensian heresy and additional matters, because of which she was summoned and [about which] she was highly suspected, asked her to swear on a volume of the Books of the Gospels which was extended to her, that she would tell the truth as a principal witness, both about herself and about others, living or dead.

But Agnes refused to obey the Bishop's order and to swear, although he repeated his order several times, and said that on no account would she swear to any matter whatsoever, not even to save her life.

When the lord Bishop asked for what reason she refused to

---

[1] The names of people and places are given in French. The Text: *Le registre*, Vol. I, pp. 123–127; 519–532.
[2] The Feast of Saint Laurence falls on August 10.
[3] Vermelle, in today's Department of Isère.
[4] Saint Foy, in today's Department of Isère.

131

swear, she said it was because about a year before, when she fell ill at Vermelle and received the extreme unction from a certain chaplain who was serving as assistant-chaplain in the local church, whose name she thought was Etienne, after making her confession and receiving the unction, he ordered her never in any circumstances to swear about any matter whatsoever, and never to walk barefoot. She added that Our Lord Jesus did not lie from fear of death, and neither would she lie from fear of death, but would tell the truth about anything she was asked and would abide by her promise never to swear.

When the Bishop asked her if she believed that swearing to a matter of truth was a sin, she replied that it was, because she had been told as much by the said chaplain.

When she was asked if anyone else, other than the said Etienne, had told her not to swear to a matter of truth, she said no.

When she was asked if she had told others that it was forbidden to swear, she said no.

When she was asked if she knew Raymond, in whose company she was arrested in the city of Pamiers, she said yes, and that she had known him for about a year and a half. When she was asked what was his surname, she replied that he was [named Raymond] of Saint Foy, and she had heard from him that he came from the diocese of Geneva, but she did not know from which place in that diocese.

When she was asked where she had first seen Raymond, she replied that she had seen him at Castel-Sarrasin whither he had come directly from Vienne, while she had come through Montpellier, Béziers and Toulouse.

She was asked if after meeting Raymond at Castel-Sarrasin she remained with him the whole time. She said no, and that she left Castel-Sarrasin and went to the town of Beaumont de Lomage. When she was asked how long she stayed in that town, she replied she had stayed there less than one month. When she was asked with whom she had stayed there, she replied that she had stayed with a woman named Huguette of the diocese of Vienne, who had since died. She was asked why she had gone to that town, and replied that it was because of her poverty, and that she had been looking for what she needed [to make a living].

She was asked where she had gone after leaving Beaumont de Lomage. She replied that she went to Toulouse and there met Raymond again. When she was asked if she had gone to Pamiers together with Raymond, she said no, that she had gone there on her own and after a short while Raymond arrived. According to her statement, they remained there for a fairly long time together, but from time to time Raymond left the town and then returned.

When she was asked if she believed that the lord Bishop could absolve her if she swore, she said yes.

When she was asked if she believed that a good and holy man who was not a priest might celebrate mass and absolve sins, she said no.

When she was asked if she believed that there is Purgatory in the next world, she said yes.

When she was asked if she believed that a person who confessed his sins and did penance for them in this world, would do penance for them in Purgatory in the next world [as well], she said yes.

The following year, on the eighteenth of the month of January, the said Agnes was summoned to appear for trial at the Allemans castle before the lord Bishop, in the presence of Brother Gaillard de Pomiès, representing the friar Jean de Beaume, Inquisitor on behalf of the Apostolic See for heretical depravity in the kingdom of France.[5] She was again asked by the lord Bishop to swear to tell the truth about herself and about all the others, the living and the dead, in all that concerned matters of faith, and the volume of the Books of the Gospels was repeatedly extended to her. But Agnes categorically refused to swear and turned her face away from the book, pretending that the reason for her declining to swear was the same reason which was given above.

---

5 Gaillard de Pomiès and Jean de Beaume were Dominicans appointed by the Pope as Inquisitors at the Inquisitorial court in Carcassonne. This was the seat of the bishopric, as well as of the royal adminis-tration of the *sénéchaussée*. Inquisitorial investigation had to be con-ducted in the presence of at least two churchmen in addition to the Inquisitor. The Allemans castle (today's la Tour de Crieu, Ariège) served as the Inquisition's prison.

When she was asked if she believed that to swear to tell the truth was a sin, she replied that it was, because she had promised not to swear from that time forward, as she had already stated, and she believed that if she swore she would be committing a sin.

She was asked if she believed that if the lord Bishop absolved her of her promise not to swear she would indeed be absolved, she said yes. When she was asked if, since she believed she would be absolved if the lord Bishop absolved her of her promise, she would be willing to swear, she replied that on no account would she be willing to swear, not even to save her life.

When she was asked if she believed that to swear to tell the truth was a sin, she said that she did not know, nor did she know what she ought to believe about it. When she was asked if she would be willing to swear, now, standing before the lord Bishop, if he would then release her from prison, she replied that on no account would she swear.

She was asked if any strangers had come to Raymond's house during the time he stayed in Pamiers, and she said yes. She said that sometimes Jeanne, the wife of Arnaud Moulinier, Guillelmette, and the wife of a certain builder who lived nearby, came to vist. They came sometimes to Raymond's house and he strengthened them [in their faith?], and they ate and drank with his sister Jeanne. She said that Raymond's sister had left the place with the cleric André Pascal, about a month before she and Raymond were arrested. She heard them say that they wished to return to the province of Provence, whence they had come with a woman named Jacqueline. She said that André, Jeanne and Jacqueline had come to Pamiers together and left the town together. She stated that there with her lived Jeanne, who often went with Petronille, and who fled with her when Raymond and the others were caught.

When she was asked about Raymond's family name and his origin, she said that he was called Raymond of Saint Foy, and that he was born in Côte Saint-André, in a village in the seigniory of Count Thomas of Savoy.[6]

6 Côte Saint-André, in the Bas Dauphiné, a region which at the time was ruled by the Count of Savoy.

She was asked how long Raymond stayed in the town of Pamiers, and replied that he stayed there from the grape harvest of 1318 until the feast of Saint Laurence in 1319. When she was asked if she had known Raymond for a long time, she replied that she had known him almost from when he was born, because she had been his wet-nurse. She nursed him because his mother died. Raymond's father, who came from Geneva, brought her to him to nurse him at the breast, and she nursed him in that same village of Côte Saint-André.

When she was asked if she had seen Raymond in any other place than Pamiers, she said she had, and said it was in Castel-Sarrasin, where she stayed with him for a few days. From there, she said, she went to Beaumont de Lomage, where she stayed about one month. Then she went to Toulouse and there she met Raymond.

In the same year on the 21st day of January, Agnes was summoned to stand trial at the Allemans castle before the lord Bishop in the presence of Brother Gaillard de Pomiès. Again she was asked by the lord Bishop to swear to tell the truth, and she replied that on no account would she swear to anything whatsoever. She asked the lord Bishop and pleaded with him not to speak to her anymore about the swearing, because in no circumstances would she swear, as she had already said.

In the same year, on the 23rd day of January, Agnes was summoned to stand trial before the lord Bishop at the Allemans castle in the presence of Brother Gaillard de Pomiès. She was again asked by the lord Bishop if she would be willing to swear and she said no. When she was asked if it was a sin to swear, she replied that it is an evil thing to swear by God, by the faith and by what a man believes. When she was asked if she believed that it was a bad sin to swear, she replied that it was evil because it was a sin.

She was asked if she believed that Purgatory exists, and she said yes.

In the year of Our Lord 1320, on the 25th day of April, Agnes was summoned to stand trial before the lord Bishop in the presence of the honourable friar Monsieur Jean de Beaume, an Inquisitor appointed by the Apostolic See for heretical depravity in the kingdom of France. She was once more asked to swear to tell the truth, and it was impressed upon her that she was obliged by law to swear at the trial, and that not swearing constituted a mortal sin. She was told that if she persisted in her stubbornness and refused to swear to tell the truth, as required in trials concerning matters of faith, it would be possible and obligatory to condemn her as one of the heretics. But although they tried to persuade her and several times asked her to swear, she replied that on no account would she swear. Asked why she was not willing to swear, she replied because the Lord had forbidden all oaths.

She was asked if she believed that if she swore to tell the truth she would be committing a mortal sin, and answered that she believed that if she swore to tell the truth she would be committing a mortal sin.

She was asked who had taught her that to swear, even to swear to tell the truth, was opposed to the Lord's commandment, since she, as she herself had said, could not read.[7] She replied that Raymond de la Côte, who was arrested with her, had instructed her on no account to swear, not even to swear to tell the truth.

When she was asked since when she believed that to swear to tell the truth was a mortal sin, she said that she had believed this for about twenty years.

Then Agnes was asked, warned and ordered by the lord Bishop and by the Inquisitor, once, twice and three times, lovingly, to abandon and desist from all the errors and heretical beliefs that she had held and was still holding; to reject the Waldensian heresy and the sect of The Poor of Lyons, to reveal who were the Waldensian Brothers,[8] the accomplices and the Believers, and to return to the faith and the unity of the Church of Rome. When she replied that on no account would she swear, it was stated by

---

7 *Ignoret litteras*, in the original, which here means an absolute inability to read (as distinct from *illitteratus*, which meant someone who was unable to read Latin). It is not recorded that Agnes was asked if she could read – further evidence that not all the questions and answers were recorded.

8 The term used here is *socii*, sometimes used by the Inquisitors to refer to the Waldensian Brothers.

the lord Bishop and the Inquisitor that if she refused to swear and to abandon the above-mentioned errors, it would be proceeded against her as a heretic, according to the canonical sanctions and the law. [This was said] in the presence of Monsieur Germain de Castelnaudary, archdeacon of the church of Pamiers; Brother Gaillard de Pomiès; Brother Arnaud de Carla of the Dominican convent at Pamiers; Brother Jean Esteve of the same order and companion of monsieur the Inquisitor;[9] Barthelemy Adalbert,[10] notary of the Inquisition of Heretical Depravity, and Guillaume Petri Barthe, the notary of the lord Bishop, who at the order of the lord Bishop and the Inquisitor took down and recorded all the above.

Thereafter on Wednesday, the last day of that month of April, Guillaume Petri Barthe, the above-mentioned notary, came in person to the castle of Allemans at the order of the lord Bishop and the Inquisitor to Agnes, to notify her that she must appear before them in person at the door of the church of the Allemans castle to hear the sentence regarding the matters to which she had confessed.[11] Agnes received the notice voluntarily, on the given day, in the presence of Magister Marc Rivel, notary of the *pariage* land,[12] etc. . . . The sentence was published on Thursday, the 1st

---

9 Inquisitors worked in pairs, each of whom was responsible for the other's conduct. The companion was called *socius* (the same term by which the Inquisitors occasionally referred to the Waldensian Brothers).

10 Barthelemy Adalbert, a notary of the Inquisition in Carcassonne, was accused of accepting a bribe. He was dismissed and spent two years in prison, where he fell gravely ill. At the trial, which took place only two years after his arrest, he received a light sentence. See: J.M. Vidal, 'Menet de Robécourt commissaire de l'Inquisition de Carcassonne (1320–1340)', *Le Moyen Age* 16 (1903), p. 436 and note 2.

11 This was the sole authority that Jacques Fournier granted his notaries – to summon the accused and read them the verdict. Unlike some other Inquisitors, he did not allow them to take his place in interrogations. By law, the confession had to be read out (without mentioning the name of the accused who had signed it) before a panel of judges consisting of representatives of the secular priesthood, Mendicants and jurists, who would decide the verdict.

12 *Pariage* (*paragium* in Latin), denoted joint ownership, rule or pos-

day of May, and recorded in the register of sentences concerning the heretical depravity. And I, Renaud Jabaud, a clerk of Toulouse and sworn notary of the Inquisition on behalf of the lord Bishop, set right the above-mentioned confession in faithfulness to the original.[13]

The Confession of Huguette, Wife of Jean of Vienne, a Perfect[14] of the Heretics of the Waldensian Sect or The Poor of Lyons

In the year of Our Lord 1319, on Thursday, the eve of the feast of Saint Laurence, the honourable Father in Christ, Lord Jacques, by grace of God Bishop of Pamiers, in the presence of Brother Gaillard de Pomiès, who had been attached to him by the Lord Inquisitor of Carcassonne, and in the presence of the honourable and eminent Monsieur Pierre de Verdier, archdeacon of Majorca, ordered to bring before him at the Allemans castle Huguette de la Côte, whom he believed to be of the diocese of Lyons. She was the wife of Jean Marinerius, an inhabitant of Arles, and the lord Bishop ordered to confine her in his gaol following informations

session of a territory or property based on a contract. These contracts usually took place between a layman and a Church institution.

13 The accused and the witnesses who appeared before the Inquisitorial courts in southern France generally spoke Occitan, or one of its dialects, or, rarely, in the Gascon language. Translation into Latin was done simultaneously while the clerk heard and recorded the proceedings in a first draft, or during a second draft, if they had previously been recorded in the language spoken by the accused or the witness. In the last stage the record was edited as a final text. The last list of admissions was recorded only in Latin, but it was read out to the accused in his or her own language, to enable them to affirm it or ask for changes to be made.

14 *Heretice perfecte*. As noted in Chapter Four, it is not clear why Huguette was called a *perfecta*, the term sometimes used by the Inquisitors to denote the Sisters (*sorores*), just as they sometimes called them 'Waldensian women' (*mulieres Valdenses*). Huguette was a married woman and a Believer, not a Sister. Perhaps she was so designated to indicate her passionate adherence to the heresy.

about her, on account of which she was highly suspected. When she appeared before him, the lord Bishop wished to question her regarding those informations and ordered her several times to swear to tell the purest truth about all the matters in which he wished to question her as a principal witness, both about herself and about others, living or dead, and a volume of the Gospels was extended to her. But Huguette replied that on no account would she swear, and would not dare to swear, with the pretext that the reason for this was that she was pregnant. Because, she said, once when she was pregnant she swore and miscarried, she feared that if she swore, the same thing would befall her. She said that a certain priest named Jean, who was prior at the church of St Michael de Scala in Arles had forbidden her to swear, and therefore on no account would she be willing to swear.

She was asked what was the name of that cleric who was arrested with her [and if it was] Raymond. She replied that his name was Pierre de la Côte. When she was asked why she had come to the city of Pamiers, she replied that she had come to serve the said Pierre, who was her uncle, her mother's brother, who was sick, and to take care of all his needs. She said that the said Pierre had spent a long time in the papal court,[15] and that she had heard many people say that he was an important churchman. Asked why Pierre had left the papal court, she replied that she had heard from some people, whose name she did not remember, that he had quarrelled with some churchmen and therefore left the papal court and came to this region. When she was asked how long she had stayed with him in Pamiers, she replied about seven weeks, and that she had come to him together with a certain woman named Petronille. She said that she believed in the existence of Purgatory and that the Church helps to release the souls from it.

The following year [1320], on the 21st day of January, Huguette was summoned to appear before the lord Bishop in the presence of Brother Gaillard de Pomiès, a representative of the friar, Brother Jean de Beaume, the Inquisitor for the heretical

---

[15] In the years 1309–1378 the popes resided in Avignon.

depravity in the kingdom of France, appointed by the Apostolic See. The lord Bishop warned her and told her plainly that she must swear by the four Gospels by laying her hand upon them, to tell the whole and pure truth, as a principal witness, both about herself and about others, living or dead, regarding the heresy of the Waldensians or Poor of Lyons, of which she was highly suspected, and about any other heresy that she knew of.

She was asked for her family name and place of origin, and replied that she was the daughter of Jean Roux, who was a baker, that she was born in a village in Côte Saint-André and lived in a village named Boucin, which she thought was in the diocese of Vienne. When her father died, her mother, Petronille, took her to the city of Arles, where she was brought up for four years. Thereafter she stayed for a year in the province of Tarascon, and returned thence to Arles. After some time she married Jean of Vienne, and since then some six years had passed. She stated that at the time of her arrest she was instructed by the people who were there on behalf of the Lord Pope, to say that Raymond de la Côte was named Pierre. She also said that the name of her husband who was arrested with her, who she had said earlier that he was named Jean Marinerius, was Jean of Vienne. She said she called him Marinerius because he had spent a long time at sea. Furthermore, she said that the above-mentioned people were the ones who told her both to say that the said Raymond, whom she called Pierrre, was her uncle, her mother's brother, that he was ill and she had to go to Pamiers to serve him. But all that, she said, had been a lie. She added that what she had said about Raymond, namely, that he had come to Pamiers because he had fallen out with certain churchmen at the papal court and had been an important churchman, she had said on the basis of a mere rumour in Pamiers, and as she had already stated, she could not remember from whom she had heard it. She was asked for what reason she had come to Pamiers, how long she had stayed there, who she had come with and why she went to live with Raymond. She replied that it was her husband who had brought her to Pamiers, because he said that there was a good market there for foodstuffs, and therefore, being a cooper, he would be able to earn well at his trade. She said that they went to live in Raymond's house because they were [from the same place and spoke] the same language.[16] She had gone there with her husband and with Petronille, her husband's sister, who escaped together with Jean, Raymond's servant, when they were arrested. She stated that she and her husband had stayed about six weeks at Raymond's house, and during those six weeks Raymond had been for three weeks away from Pamiers. When he left them he told them that he had to do something at the papal court. When he returned, he told them that he had arranged the marriage of his sister Jeanne,[17] though she was still with him for a few days in Pamiers, as the witness herself saw. When his messenger returned from the papal court, Raymond moved to Narbonne.

She also said that two or three days after she and her husband had come to live with Raymond, Jeanne, Raymond's above-mentioned sister, left Pamiers with Jacqueline, who was of Raymond's family, and with Etienne. She heard people say that Jeanne married a man in a village by name of Villeneuve de Roibes.

In the year of Our Lord 1320, on the 13th of March, Huguette was taken from the gaol in the Allemans castle where she was held, to stand trial before the lord Bishop in the presence of Brother Gaillard de Pomiès, representing the Lord Inquisitor of Carcassonne; Monsieur Germain de Castelnaudary, archdeacon of the church of Pamiers; Brother David, a monk of the monastery of Fontfroide, and friar Arnaud de Carla of the Dominican convent in Pamiers, who had been called hence as witnesses, and in my presence, Guillaume Petri Barthe, the lord Bishop's notary. She was asked by the lord Bishop if she wished to swear to tell the truth in its purest form about herself and about others, living or

---

16 *Eiusdem lingue* – i.e. they came from the same region and spoke the same language.
17 The term used is *maritaverat* (*maritare*) which means both to marry and to provide a dower (*dos* or *dotalicium*), meaning, to guarantee the woman the right to some of the income from her husband's property (usually one-third) for the rest of her life after his death. The reference here is to Raymond's arrangement of a dower for his sister Jeanne.

dead, regarding the heresy of the Waldensians or Poor of Lyons, of which she was highly suspected, and a volume of the Gospels was extended to her. She replied that she would not swear because it was a sin to swear for any reason whatsoever, that even to swear to tell the truth was a sin, because the Lord had commanded not to swear. She was asked why she had sworn in the past and if she believed that she was sinning when she swore at that time. She replied that she had sworn in the past in order to save herself, but already then she believed that it was a sin and hoped to confess that sin and atone for it, and she did not think, she said, that because she had sworn once or twice to tell the truth she would be damned.

She was asked who had taught her this, and where she had first been told that to swear to tell the truth was a sin, and how much time had passed since then. She replied that when she was about twelve, that is, some eighteen years before, since she was now about thirty, when she was living in the house of Bertrand de Tarascon in Arles, near the city gate, a man of the Waldensian sect by name of Gerard instructed her never to swear on any account, because it was a sin and the Lord had forbidden it. When she was asked what was the family name of that Gerard, she replied that she did not know. When she was asked if she believed then that what the same Gerard had said to her was the truth, if she had always believed it and if she still believed it, she replied that she did. She was asked if Gerard was of her family and of what language [region] he was. She replied that he was not of her family, and that he came from the region of Vienne or Burgundy, but it seemed to her more likely that he came from Burgundy, and that he was [then] middle-aged. When she was asked if she had promised him that henceforth she would not swear, she replied that she had told him categorically that she would no longer swear, but did not promise as much. When she was asked who was present [at their exchange], she replied that no-one was present except herself and Gerard. When she was asked if she saw him often, she said yes. She said she had seen him two or three times because he came to see her. Once she gave him food and drink, while he gave her a silver [piece] of Tours. And she promised him that she wanted to join his sect and his faith. She added that she believed he was a good man and that she might be saved by his faith.

She stated that some sixteen years earlier Gerard revealed to her that Jean of Lorraine, their majoral,[18] was in Montpellier. She went from Arles to Montpellier in order to see him and took the opportunity to spend a night's vigil at the church of Saint Mary of the Tablets.[19]

She found Jean of Lorraine in Sannaria street in Montpellier and walked with him to the house of a man named Falco, near Le Peyrou quarter. When she met him in the street she told him that she wished to speak to him and they entered that house and talked there. Among other things, Jean said to her that henceforward she must not swear on any account, as it was a sin to swear for any reason whatsoever.

She said that a Purgatory of sins did not exist save in this world and not in the next, and that those who died unabsolved[20] [of their sins] would go after death either to paradise or to hell. She added that the prayers, alms, masses and all the other things which are done for the deceased were worthless, since there was no Purgatory in the next world. She said it was forbidden to kill any man and forbidden to wound malefactors. She said that Church excommunication was worthless, and that they did not care about it. She said further that since that time until the present she believed all that she had said and believed it still.

She was asked if she had given anything to Jean of Lorraine, or if he gave her anything, and she said no. She stated that the following day Jean of Lorraine sent to her to the Church of Saint Mary of the Tablets, where she was, three [pieces of] silver of Tours, to buy herself stockings. The money was brought her by a servant of Jean of Lorraine, whose name she did not know. When she received the money she bought herself two linen shawls. She added that as she had said before, she had told Jean that she

18 *Major* or *majoralis* – the highest rank in the clerical hierarchy among The Poor of Lyons. Under him was the *presbyter*, and at the bottom of the hierarchy was the deacon (*dyaconus*).
19 *Ecclesia beate Marie de Tabulis.*
20 *Incontinenti* in the Latin original.

wished to join his faith and his sect and to obey him, and that she believed that the things he had said to her were words of truth.

She said that on another occasion, when she had gone to Vauvert and wished to see Jean, she went thence to Montpellier with another woman named Martine of Arles, who lived beside the Church of the Holy Cross. She found Jean and talked to him at the gate of the Franciscan Brothers in Montpellier, but did not discuss with him the above- mentioned errors, and neither gave him anything nor received anything from him.

She stated that she had also seen Jean at St Gilles-du-Gard, at an inn called de Moutone, where she was staying. Since Jean was concerned lest she do something indecent there, he passed through and told her to leave the place and return to Arles. He said nothing then about those same errors, and at his command she returned to Arles.

She also said that she saw him in the garden of the house of Bertrand in Arles, sitting under a fig tree, and she told him to leave the place, as there were many people in that house.

She was asked if she had given anything to Jean and replied she had. She said that she gave him in that garden in Arles half a pound of dates. And Jean gave her in that garden in Arles a linen shawl, and on another occasion he gave her a belt of white linen thread. She went on to say that in the course of five years she saw him frequently and he asked her if she believed well in the things he had told her about, and she told him she did.

She was asked if she had ever confessed her sins to Jean, and she said that she had and often. She was asked if she believed that her sins had been absolved after Jean gave her absolution. She replied that she did believe this, as when she confessed to priests of the Church of Rome. When she was asked if she had heard that he was a priest, or believed that he was a priest, she replied that she had not heard that he was called a priest, and did not believe that he was a priest, because she did not see him celebrating mass, nor had she heard that he celebrated mass. When she was asked if she believed that Jean believed in a good faith and belonged to a good sect, she said yes, and that she believed this still.

She stated that she had seen Gerard, known as the Provençal, who belonged to their sect, and also Jean Cerno. She said that she saw them for the first time on the road leading from Lunel to Montpellier, and later in Montpellier at a certain house near the Franciscans, and she thought that it was the house of Raymond de Roncas of Montpellier. She went with them to that house together with another woman named Jeanne, who was a servant in that house and belonged to their faith and sect. She said that when she had gone to speak with Gerard and Jean she knew that they belonged to the faith and sect of The Poor of Lyons, and that otherwise she would not have gone to them. And that night she remained with those people and heard them discuss the above-mentioned errors. But she had not confessed to them nor given them anything. But they gave her food to eat. She stated that she went to that house six or seven times to see those heretics, knowing that they were heretics.

She was asked if she had ever given anything to those heretics, or if they had given her anything, and replied that she never gave them anything, but Jean Cerno once gave her a scarf of coarse cloth.

She stated that she later saw the heretic Raymond de la Côte in Pamiers, but was not instructed by him.

It was explained to Huguette that the errors she admitted to were opposed to the doctrine maintained and taught by the Church of Rome, and she was asked if she repented of them. She replied that she did not, and that she wished to live and die believing all that she had said, and that she believed that in cleaving to these errors she was following a good faith, and that she wished to persevere in all that she had admitted to.

In that year, on the 16th day of March, Huguette was taken from the gaol in the Allemans castle to stand trial before the lord Bishop in the presence of Brother Gaillard de Pomiès, representing the Lord Inquisitor of Carcassonne; Monsieur Germain de Castelnaudary; Brother David of the Fontfroide monastery and friar Arnaud de Carla of the Dominican Order, who were called upon to serve as witnesses, and in my presence, Guillaume Petri Barthe, the lord Bishop's notary. Then they read out to her in an intelligible form and in the vernacular her confession of the 13th day of March. When asked if what was written in the confession was true, she said yes. She was asked if she wished to recant those errors to which she had admitted, and she said no, since she had not believed and did not now believe that they were errors. Then the lord Bishop explained to her in an intelligible form in the vernacular that the Holy Church of Rome and all of Christ's faithful of God's Church believed and declared that a person may swear to tell the truth when called upon to do so at a trial, especially in matters concerning the faith. He told her that he who refused to swear to tell the truth was committing a sin, and that even in other cases it was permitted to swear. He told her that the Church believed in the existence of Purgatory in the next world in which venial sins are absolved and mortal sins, which have not been atoned for in this life, are punished and atoned for. He told her that the masses, prayers, alms and all the other good deeds that the living do for the dead in Purgatory helped to release their souls from it sooner. He told her that the Church believes that the authorities of the secular power were allowed legitimately and justly, and without sin, to put malefactors to death. He told her that excommunication, imposed by one who is authorized to impose it upon his subjects who remain recalciterant, excluded them from the Kingdom of God and from all the spiritual benefits of the Church. He told her that the Church believed and declared that no-one save a priest might absolve sins that have been confessed to him – all these being in opposition to what she believed and admitted to. When the lord Bishop explained all these tenets of the faith to her, he told her not to continue to believe in the above-mentioned heretical tenets. But she replied that she had believed and still believed in them and that if she said the opposite, she would not be telling the truth, and that she wished to persist in that belief.

She was asked if she had heard from those heretics that there were but three orders in the Church: that of bishop, that of presbyter and that of deacon. She said no, but she was certain that she had heard that Jean of Lorraine was the majoral of their sect, and that he was the wisest of them all.

She was asked if she had heard Jean of Lorraine or anyone else of their sect celebrating mass, and she said no, nor that she had heard about his celebrating mass, and that she herself had not celebrated mass nor heard any person's confession.

She stated that when she had been in Montpellier and first saw Jean of Lorraine she wanted to give him two [pieces of] silver of Tours. But Jean told her that he did not hold nor carry money, and when she looked at his purse she saw that indeed it did not contain money. She stated that when Jean's servant met her and brought her three pieces of silver of Tours, as she had previously admitted, he told her in their conversation that his master neither held nor carried any money.

She said that Jean of Lorraine had died, but that she did not know where, and that she believed that his soul was in paradise.

When she was asked if Jean and the others of their sect regarded themselves as subject to the authority of the Roman Pope, she replied that she had not heard them talk about this, but it seemed to her that they did not regard themselves as subject to his authority, since the Lord Pope was persecuting those who belonged to their sect. When she was asked if she believed herself to be subject to the authority of the Lord Pope, she replied that she believed that she was subject to him in all that concerned faith in God, but not in what concerned other matters. She was asked whether, if the Lord Pope told her that it was permitted to swear to tell the truth in matters of faith, that Purgatory exists, and that the prayers of the Church help those who are in it, that it is permitted to kill malefactors, that Church excommunication was binding and a heavy punishment, and that only a duly ordained priest and no-one else might give absolution, she would believe him and would feel obliged to believe all these things. She said no, because she believed that if the Lord Pope were to say this he would be in error, and she believed that he was more in error in these matters than she was.

She was asked whether, since she confessed, as she admitted she had, to Jean, who she knew was not a priest, it meant that she had believed and still believed that a man who was not a priest could give absolution for sins confessed to him. She replied that only God might absolve sins, while the man to whom one made confession, whether he be a priest or not, might only advise the confessing person what to do and impose a penance. And since

Jean was a wise and honest man, he could advise her and impose a penance upon her as well as any priest.

She was asked if she had heard and believed that Jean, who was not a priest, could have celebrated mass and consecrated the body of Christ. She replied that she had heard it from some of the above-mentioned people (but could not remember from whom), and that she herself believed that if Jean wished, he could have celebrated mass, since he was a majoral, but others were not permitted to do so.

She was asked if she had heard from those heretics that the Church indulgences were worthless. She replied she had heard from some of them (but could not remember from whom) that they were indeed worthless. When she was asked if she herself believed this, she said yes and that she still believed this.

She was asked if she believed that if she were put to death for defending those errors she would be saving her soul. She replied that she believed this and hoped it was so.

She described how she had come from Arles to Pamiers together with Jean Fustier, her husband, and with Petronille, her husband's sister, who escaped. She stated that they had gone from Arles to Belcaire, from thence to Montpellier, from Montpellier to another village near St Tibery, from whence they went the next day to Narbonne, from Narbonne to Carcassonne, from Carcassonne to Mirepoix, and thence to Pamiers. She stated that on their way they stopped only at ordinary inns, and did not see anyone of their sect on their journey. When they reached Pamiers, they went to the house where the heretic Raymond de la Côte resided and resided there with him. She said that apart from Raymond, she herself, her husband Jean and Petronille, there resided also Agnes who was burnt at the stake together with Raymond, Jeanne, Raymond's sister, Jacqueline, who was of Raymond's family, and two other men who were both named Etienne. She added that she believed that they all, other than Petronille, belonged to their sect. A few weeks earlier, she said, Etienne, who was Raymond's nephew, Jean and Jacqueline, had left Pamiers, but she did not know where they had gone.

She stated that she had received a certain notice and went with them to church. And once, she said, on the feast of Saint Anne, she went to the church of St Raymond with Jeanne, the wife of Arnaud Moulinier and Barchinona, the wife of Bernard de Loubens. Now and then, she said, she also went to church with Guillelmette, the wife of Jean Paredes, and with Jeanne, the wife of Pierre Calmellis. She asserted that she had not discussed the above-mentioned errors with them.

Subsequently Huguette was warned and asked, firmly and lovingly, by the lord Bishop and Brother Gaillard to repent of the errors which she admitted she had believed and still believed in, and return to the faith and unity of the holy Church of Rome. They informed her that if she did not abandon those errors she would be condemned by canon law as a non-recanting heretic. They also warned her to tell the complete truth. She replied that she would not recant of those errors and that she wished to cleave to them in life and in death. Nevertheless, the Bishop and Brother Gaillard gave her a respite of eight days to reconsider the matter.

In that year, on the 18th day of March, Huguette was brought from the gaol to stand trial at the Allemans castle before the lord Bishop, in the presence of Brother Gaillard de Pomiès, representing Monsieur the Inquisitor of Carcassonne; the monks Brother Arnaud de Carla and Brother David de Savardi, and in my presence, the above-named notary. Before the set date, Huguette was again asked by the lord Bishop if she wished to recant of the errors to which she had admitted. She replied that she did not wish to recant of the errors which she had admitted that she believed in, because as she had already said, she did not think she was erring by believing in them. She was asked whom did she believe she ought to obey more: Jean of Lorraine or the Lord Pope. She replied that she had considered that she owed obedience to Jean of Lorraine, the majoral of the sect, more than to the Lord Pope. When she was asked who she believed had ordained Jean of Lorraine to hear confessions and celebrate mass, she replied that he was ordained by God and by those who had guided him in that way and appointed him in that sect.

She was asked if according [to their faith] she or any other woman could hear confessions, and she said no.

She was asked if Jean, or others of her sect, had taught her to say the *Credo*, and she answered no.[21] She was asked if she had prayed together with those heretics, and she said no.

She was asked if she had taught anyone the said errors, or talked about them with anyone. She replied that she talked about them with her husband and with Jeanne of Montpellier. When she was asked if she had persuaded Jean to believe in the said errors, she replied that she had done so to the best of her ability, and that she had been very pleased and was still pleased that Jean had believed and still now believed in the said errors.

She was asked if she believed that whoever condemned a heretic to death was committing a sin, and replied that he was. She was asked if she believed that sentencing malefactors to death or life-imprisonment was a sin. She replied that she believed that if she sentenced a man to death or to life-imprisonment she would be committing a sin, and that unless she confessed and did penance for her sin, her soul would have been damned. She also said that whoever killed a Christian in any war whatsoever committed a sin. Furthermore, she said that she did not wish to judge any person, because if she did so she would be breaking the Lord's commandment.

She was asked if she wished to swear that her admissions were true, and replied that she would not swear.

Then they read to her confessions of the previous year, as well as her statement that she did not want to swear because she was afraid she would miscarry, but also because she believed it was a sin to swear to tell the truth. She retracted her statement that the priest who had told her not to swear was named Pierre, because, she said, his name was Jean. She retracted her admission [of belief] in the existence of Purgatory in the next world, and that the help of the Church was valuable in freeing souls from it. She said that since she did not believe that it existed in the next world, she did not believe that it was possible to help a person after death, but only in this life. She said that the meaning of Purgatory

---

21 *Credo* – one of the three central prayers in the Catholic faith, alongside the *Pater noster* and *Ave Maria*. The central prayer of the Waldensians was the *Pater noster*. According to the Inquisitors and also some of the witnesses, they acknowledged only this prayer.

was only the sacrament of penance and atonement for sin, and that prayers can only avail souls in this life. She added that she did not wish for prayers and alms for her soul after she died.

She retracted her statement that the name of the servant of the heretic Raymond, who escaped together with Petronille, her husband's sister, was Jean, and said that his name was Etienne.

But she persisted in the contents of her other confessions. The lord Bishop and Brother Gaillard repeatedly warned her to discard the errors to which she had admitted previously and those she admitted that day, but she refused, and said she wished to cleave to them in her life and her death. She was warned by them numerous times, but would not heed them.

On the appointed day, that is, on the 23rd day of March, Huguette was taken from the gaol to stand trial at the Allemans castle before the lord Bishop, in the presence of Brother Gaillard de Pomiès, representing the lord Inquisitor of Carcassonne; the monks, Germain de Castelnaudary, the archdeacon of Pamiers, Brothers Arnaud de Carla and David, and in my presence, Gauillaume Petri Barthe, as witnesses. The lord Bishop read out to her the following articles of heresy that she had confessed she believed in:

I   She believes that swearing to tell the truth, when one is required to do so in court, and especially on matters of faith is a sin, because the Lord has forbidden to swear.

II   She believes that a Purgatory for sins exists only in this life and not in the next, and that those who die unabsolved go either to paradise or to hell.

III   She believes that the masses, prayers and alms, and all the rest that is done for the dead is worthless, since there is no Purgatory in the next world.

IV   She believes that no man is permitted to kill or injure malefactors.

V   She believes that [Church] excommunication is worthless and she does not care about it.

VI   She believes that when she confessed her sins to Jean of Lorraine, the majoral of their sect, who she did not believe to have been a priest, she was absolved of her sins, just as when she confessed and was absolved by the priests of the Church of Rome.

VII   She believes that Jean of Lorraine and others of her sect are following a good faith, that through this faith she may save her own soul, and that Jean of Lorraine's soul is in Paradise.

VIII   She believes that member of her sect, and she herself, are not subject to the authority of the Lord Pope save in matters concerning belief in God, but not in other matters.

IX   She believes that if the Lord Pope were to tell her that it is permitted to swear to tell the truth in matters of faith, that Purgatory exists [in the next world] and that the prayers of the Church help those who are in it, that Church excommunication is binding and is a heavy punishment, that it is permitted for the secular authority which is in power to execute malefactors, and that only a priest who has been duly ordained according to the rule of the Church of Rome may give absolution for sins, and no-one else – she would not be obliged to believe him, since if the Lord Pope said such things he would have been in error, and that he was now in greater error than she was.

X   She believes that only God can absolve sins, whereas the man to whom a confession is made, whether or not a priest, can only advise the confessing person what to do and impose a penance. She believes that since Jean was a wise man, he could advise her and impose a penance upon her as well as a priest, and could therefore hear confessions.

XI   She believes that although she did not think that Jean was a priest, he was permitted to celebrate mass, if he wished, but others in the sect might not do so.

XII   She believes that the Church indulgences are worthless.

XIII   She believes and hopes that if she is put to death for defending these errors, her soul would be saved.

XIV   She believes that she was obliged to obey Jean of Lorraine in everything, more than the Lord Pope.

XV   She believes that Jean of Lorraine was authorized to hear confessions and celebrate mass by God and by those who had guided him in that way and that faith and appointed him in their sect.

XVI   She believes that whoever puts a heretic to death commits a sin.

XVII   She believes that if she were to sentence a person to death or to life-imprisonment she would be committing a sin, and that unless she confessed it and atoned for it, her soul would be damned.

XVIII   She stated that she would never have judged anyone, because the Lord commanded that no man may judge another.

XIX   She believes that anyone who kills a person in any war whatsoever commits a sin.

XX   She believes that the meaning of the name Purgatory is merely the sacrament of penance, and not some place in the next world where people are sent to complete their atonement for their sins.

XXI   She believes that she is not committing a sin in believing these tenets, because they are a good faith.

They presented and read out to Huguette these articles of heresy in the vernacular. The lord Bishop warned her and firmly entreated her to recant these errors, to return to the unity and faith of the holy Church of Rome, and to abandon these errors and any other heresy which raises its head against the knowledge of God and the holy Church of Rome. She replied that she had persisted and that she wishes to continue to persist in believing these heretical tenets, that on no account would she deny them and would not swear [about her belief in] them, that she would not swear to tell the truth or for any other matter, and that she wished to live and die believing in those tenets. Then the lord Bishop concluded the proceedings in this case, and ordered that the sentence be pronounced.

Later that year, on the 7th day of April, Huguette was brought to trial at the Allemans castle before the lord Bishop, in the presence of Brother Gaillard de Pomiès, deputy for the lord Inquisitor of Carcassonne; Guillaume Audiberti, licentiate in law and bachelor of Canon Law; friars Arnaud de Carla and David, and in my presence, Guillaume Petri Barthe, the notary, as witnesses. They read out to Huguette the tenets of heresy in an intelligible form in the vernacular. And she was once again warned and entreated beyond what was necessary to abandon those errors. She replied that she had persisted and wished to persist in believing in them.

In that year, on the 17th of July, Huguette was brought from the gaol wherein she was held to stand trial at the Allemans castle before the lord Bishop in the presence of Brother Gaillard de Pomiès, deputy for monsieur the Inquisitor of Carcassonne; the friar Arnaud de Carla, of the Dominican convent in Pamiers; monsieur the presbyter, Bertrand Barrau; Bataille de Penna, notary of the lord Bishop, and in my presence, Guillaume Petri Barthe, notary of the lord Bishop, as witnesses. They read out to her in an intelligible form in the vernacular the heretical tenets of the Waldensian sect which she admitted to have believed in and to be believing still. She was warned and asked by the lord Bishop to reject those errors and abandon them, as they were heretical tenets which had been denounced by the holy Church of Rome. She replied that she did not wish to reject either those errors or any others of their sect, and that on no account was she willing to swear. Then she was told that if she refused to reject those errors which had been denounced, she would be subject to the law applying to an impenitent, stubborn heretic. She replied that nevertheless, she would not reject those errors, and that she wished to live and die in the faith in which her husband, Jean Fustier, believed, for she knew that they were of one faith.

Thereafter, in the year of Our Lord 1321, on the 30th day of July, Huguette, daughter of Jean Roux de la Côte and wife of the above-named Jean, was taken from gaol to stand trial in the same hall at the Allemans castle, before the lord Bishop and in the presence of the friars Jean de Beaume and Bernard Gui, Inquisitors of the heretical depravity in France on behalf of the Apostolic See, as witnesses, and in my presence, the above-named notary. The lord Bishop extended to her a volume of the holy Gospels and warned her, demanded of her and asked her to swear upon them to tell the truth about the acts of heresy, and especially about the Waldensian sect, or The Poor of Lyons, both about herself and about all the others, living and dead, about whom she was to testify. She replied that on no account would she swear, and thus finally refused to swear. Then the lord Bishop and the Inquisitor made it clear to her, in unequivocal terms, that anyone who came before a Church judge was required to swear to tell the truth in matters of faith, and if he refused, was condemned according to canon law as a heretic. Nevertheless, Huguette firmly refused to swear. They read out to her, aloud, in total and intelligibly, in the

vernacular, her statements which contained many and diverse
errors and heretical beliefs, which contradict the Catholic faith
and the holy Church of Rome. She was warned, required and
asked repeatedly, once, twice and three times, to recant of her
errors and the heretical beliefs contained in her confessions, to
abandon them under oath and return to the unity of the holy
mother, the Catholic Church of Rome. She replied that she was in
no error, that she did not hold any heretical beliefs, and that she
did not wish to recant or reject anything that was contained in her
statements. She said that she wished to cleave to them in her life
and her death. And although she had denied and disavowed
certain things that were contained in her confessions, she refused
to deny them under oath despite having been warned, required
and asked to do so, again and again.

She was asked if she wished to hear the sentence about her
confessions, and she replied that she wished to hear whatever it
pleased the lord Bishop [to pronounce], the matter being closed
and concluded.

This was said in the presence of monsieur Guillaume Audiberti, canon of Limoges; Brothers Pierre de Annoris and Pierre
Sicre, companion of the said Inquisitor; David and Jean, monks of
the monastery of Fontefroide in the diocese of Narbonne; Guillaume Joulia, Inquisition notary of Toulouse; Menet de Robécourt,[22] notary of monsieur the Inquisitor of Carcassonne, and
Bataille de Penna, notary of the lord Bishop, who obtained this
final ratification and put it in writing.

Thereafter, in the same year, on the 1st day of August, the
notary Bataille de Penna came in person at the order of the lord
Bishop and the Inquisitor, to the Allemans castle and summoned
Huguette, precisely and firmly, to appear the following day,
namely, on the 2nd of August, in the cemetery of St Jean in
Pamiers, to hear from the lord Bishop and the Inquisitor the

---

[22] This notary exceeded his authority and behaved with exceptional
cruelty towards an accused who was innocent, and also took a bribe.
A complaint against him to the pope led to his dismissal. See: J.M.
Vidal, op. cit., pp. 425–449.

sentence about the matters to which she had admitted. Huguette received the announcement that day of her own free will.

She appeared on the appointed day in the cemetery of St Jean the martyr,[23] as she had been instructed by the above-mentioned Bataille, and the lord Bishop and the Inquisitor began reading the sentence as follows: 'Be it known to all etc. . . .' The sentence may be found in the book of sentences.

All the foregoing was set right [in writing] by me, Renaud Jabaud, being faithful to the original.

[23] This cemetery was outside the city walls of Pamiers. The verdict was read out following the Inquisitor's sermon (*sermo generalis*), and was at once followed by burning at the stake.

Bibliography

Primary Sources

Abelard, Peter. *Sermones, PL* 178: 379–610.

———— *The Letter of Heloise on Religious Life and Abelard's First Reply*, ed. J.T. Muckle C.S.B. *Medieval Studies* 17 (1955), pp. 240–281.

———— *Abelard's Rule for Religious Women*, ed. T.P. McLaughlin C.S.B. *Medieval Studies* 18 (1956), pp. 241–292.

Acta sanctorum, eds The Bollandist Fathers. Paris, 1863– .

The Acts of the Christian Martyrs, ed. and trans. H. Musurillo. Oxford, 1972.

Alain of Lille. *De fide catholica, PL* 210: 305–430.

Anonymous of Passau. *Auszuge aus dem Sammelwerk des Passauer Anonymus*, in *Quellen zur Geschichte der Waldenser*, eds A. Patschovsky and K.V. Selge. Göttingen, 1973, pp. 70–103.

Anselm of Alessandria. *Tractatus de hereticis*, in A. Dondaine O.P., ed., 'La hiérarchie cathare en Italie II: Le "Tractatus de hereticis" d'Anselme d'Alexandire O.P.' *Archivum Fratrum Praedicatorum* 20 (1950), pp. 308–324.

Ardizzo of Plaisance. *Litterae episcopi Placentini de Pauperibus de Lugduno*, in A. Dondaine O.P., 'Durand Huesca et la polémique anti-cathare', *Archivum Fratrum Praedicatorum* 29 (1959), Appendix III.

Aubri of Trois-Fontaines. *Chronica Albrici monachi Trium Fontium*, ed. G.H. Pertz. *M.G.H. Scriptores*, Vol. 23, Hanover, 1874, pp. 878–950.

Beiträge zur Sektengeschichte des Mittelalters, ed. J.J. Ign von Döllinger. Munich, 1890, 2 Vols.

Bernard Fontcaude. *Adversus Waldensium sectam, PL* 204: 793–840.

Bernard Gui. *Manuel de l'inquisiteur*, ed. and trans. G. Mollat. Paris, 1964, 2 Vols.

Berthold of Regensburg. *Vollständige Ausgabe seiner deutschen Predigten*, eds F. Pfeiffer and J. Strobl. Vienna, 1862–1880. 2 Vols.

Bullaire de l'inquisition française au XIV siècle, ed. J.M. Vidal. Paris, 1913.

Burchard of Worms. *Decretorum libri viginti, PL* 140: 537–1066.

Cantica, ed. and trans. J.J. Herzog. *Zeitschrift für die historische Theologie* 31 (1861), pp. 486–592.

Chronicon universale anonymi Laudunensis, ed. G. Waitz. *M.G.H. Scriptores*, Vol. 26, Hanover and Berlin, 1931, pp. 442–457.

Le confessioni di fede dei Valdesi Riformati con documenti del dialogo fra 'prima' e 'seconda' Riforma, ed. V. Vinay. Collana della facoltà Valdes di Teologia 12. Turin, 1975.

David of Augsburg. *Tractatus de inquisicione hereticorum*, ed. W. Preger. Munich, 1878.

Decretales Gregorii IX, in *Corpus iuris canonici*, ed. E. Friedberg. Vol. 2. Leipzig, 1879.

Documents pour servir à l'histoire de l'inquisition dans le Languedoc, ed. Mgr. Douais. Paris, 1900. Reprint: 1977. 2 Vols.

Durand Osca. *Liber antiheresis*, in *Die Ersten Waldenser*, ed. K.V. Selge. Vol. 2, Berlin, 1967.

Eberwin of Steinfeld. *Eberwini Steinfeldensis praepositi ad S. Bernardum epistola*, Epist. 472, PL 182: 676–680.

Enchiridion fontium Valdensium, ed. G. Gonnet. Torre Pellice, 1958.

Enguerrand de Monstrelet. *The Chronicles*, trans. Th. Johnes. London, 1809. 8 Vols.

Etienne de Bourbon. *Tractatus de diversis materiis praedicabilis*, in *Anecdotes historiques, légendes et apologues tirés du recueil inédit d'Etienne de Bourbon*, ed. A. Lecoy de la Marche. Paris, 1877.

Evans, F.W. *The American Utopian Adventure. Autobiography of a Shaker*, Glasgow, 1888. Reprint: Philadelphia, 1972.

The Fifty Earliest English Wills in the Court Probate of London, ed. F.J. Furnivall. London, 1882.

Fleta, ed. and trans. H.G. Richardson and G.O. Sayles. London, 1955. 2 Vols.

Fox, George, *A Collection of Many Select and Christian Epistles*. London, 1698.

Foxe, John. *Acts and Monuments*. London, 1684. 2 Vols.

Fueros castellanos de Soria y Alcala de Henares, ed. G. Sanchez. Madrid, 1919.

Gallus of Neuhaus. *Verhorspotokolle der Inquisition des Gallus von Neuhaus (1335 bis ca. 1353/55)*, in *Quellen zur Böhmischen Inquisition im 14. Jahrhundert*, ed. A. Patschovsky. Weimar, 1979.

Geoffroy of Auxerre. *Super Apocalypsim*, in 'le témoignage de Geoffroy d'Auxerre sur la vie cistercienne', ed. J. Leclerq. *Studia Anselmiana* 31 (1953), pp. 174–201.

Heresies of the High Middle Ages, ed. and trans. W.L. Wakefield and A.P. Evans. New York, 1969.

Heresy Trials in the Diocese of Norwich 1428–1431, ed. and trans. N.P. Tanner. Camden Fourth Series 20. London, 1977.

Humbert de Romans. *Sermones*. Venice, 1605.

Innocent III. *Innocentii III romanis pontificis regestrorum sive epistolarum*, PL 214–216.

Joachim of Fiore. *De articulis fidei*, in *Enchiridion fontium Valdensium*, ed. G. Gonnet. Torre Pellice, 1958, pp. 98–100.

Liber sententiarum inquisitionis Thosolanae, in *Historia inquisitionis*, ed. Ph. van Limborch. Amsterdam, 1692.

Le livre Roisin. Coutumier Lillois de la fin du 13e siècle, ed. R. Monier. Paris–Lille, 1932.

Medieval Women's Visionary Literature, ed. and trans. Alvida Petroff. Oxford, 1986.

Mirk's Festial. A Collection of Homilies, ed. T. Erbe. London, 1905.

Mitteilungen aus der Geschichte der evangelischen Kirche des Elsasses, ed. T.W. Röhrich. Vol. I. Paris–Strasbourg, 1855.

Moneta of Cremona. *Adversus Catharos et Valdenses, libri quinque*, ed. T.A. Ricchini. Rome, 1743.

La noble leçon des Vaudois du Piémont, ed. A. de Stephano. Paris, 1909.

Peter Martyr. *Summa contra hereticos*, in T. Käppeli ed., 'Une somme contre les hérétiques de S. Pierre Martyr?' *Archivum Fratrum Praedicatorum* 17 (1947), pp. 330–336.

Pierre of Vaux-de-Cernay. *Historia Albigensis*, eds P. Guébin and E. Lyon. Paris, 1926.

Les premiers statuts de l'ordre de Prémontré, ed. R. van Waefelghem. *Analectes de l'ordre de Prémontré* V8 (1913), pp. 1–74.

A Profession of Faith by Valdes, in A. Dandaine O.P. ed., 'Aux origines du Valdéisme: une profession de foi de Valdès', *Archivum Fratrum Praedicatorum* 16 (1946), pp. 231–232.

Pseudo-Reinerius. *Tractatus*, in M. Nickson ed., 'The "Pseudo-Reinerius" Treatise: The Final Stage of a Thirteenth Century Work on Heresy from the Diocese of Passau', *Archives d'histoire doctrinale et littéraire du moyen âge* 42 (1967), pp. 291–303.

Quellen zur Böhmischen Inquisition im 14. Jahrhundert, ed. A. Patschovsky. Weimar, 1979.

Quellen zur Geschichte der Waldenser, eds A. Patschovsky and K.V. Selge. Göttingen, 1973.

Quellen zur Ketzergeschichte Brandenburgs und Pommerns, ed. D. Kurze. Berlin, 1975.

Rainerius Sacconi. *Summa fratris Raynerii de ordine Fratrum Praedicatorum de Catharis et Pauperibus de Lugduno*, in A. Dondaine O.P. ed., *Un traité néo-manichéen du XIIIe siècle*. Rome, 1939, pp. 64–78.

Le registre criminel du Châtelet de Paris du 6 septembre 1389 au 18 mai 1392, ed. Duplès-Agier. Paris, 1861–1864. 2 Vols.

Le registre criminel de la justice de Saint Martin de Champs à Paris au XIVe siècle, ed. L. Tanon. Paris, 1877.

Le registre de l'inquisition de Jacques Fournier, évêque de Pamiers (1318–1325), ed. J. Duvernoy. Toulouse, 1965. 3 Vols.

Regula secte Waldensium, in Ch. Schmidt ed. *Zeitschrift für historische Theologie* 22 (1852), pp. 239–242.

Regula secte Waldensium, ed. A. Molnar, in 'Les Vaudois et l'unité des frères tchèques', *Bollettino della società di studi Valdesi* 118 (1965), pp. 3–6.

Rescriptum heresiarcharum Lombardiae ad Pauperes de Lugduno, in *Enchiridion fontium Valdensium*, ed. G. Gonnet. Torre Pellice, 1958, pp. 171–183.

Sacrorum conciliorum nova et amplissima collectio, ed. J.D. Mansi. Florence–Venice, 1798. Reprint: Graz, 1961.

Salvo Burci, *Liber supra stella*, in *Beiträge zur Sektengeschichte des Mittelalters*, ed. J.J. Ign von Döllinger. Munich, 1890. Vol. 2, pp. 52–84.

Six Vaudois Poems from the Waldensian Manuscripts in the University Libraries of Cambridge, Dublin and Geneva, ed. and trans. H.J. Chaytor. Cambridge, 1930.

Thomas Aquinas. *Summa theologiae*, ed. and trans. The Fathers of Blackfriars. London, 1960–1975.

Tractatus bonus (pars prima contra hereticos qui Valdensis dicuntur, quorum magistri heresiarche Fratres nuncupantur), in R. Cegna ed., 'La condizione del Valdismo secondo l'inedito "Tractatus bonus contra haereticos" del 1399, attribubile all'inquisitore della Slesia Giovanni di Glewice', in *I Valdesi e l'Europa*, Collana della società di studi Valdesi 9. Torre Pellice, 1982, pp. 39–65.

Tractatus de haeresi Pauperum de Lugduno auctore anonymo. De libro Stephani de Bella-villa accipiuntur ista in *Thesaurus novus anecdotorum*, eds E. Martène and M. Durand. Paris, 1717. Vol. 5, cols. 1777–1794.

De vita et actibus, in *Beiträge zur Sektengeschichte des Mittelalters*, ed. J.J. Ign von Döllinger. Munich, 1890. Vol. 2, pp. 92–97.

Walter Map. *De nugis curialium*, ed. and trans. M.R. James. Revised by C.N.L. Brooke and R.A.B. Mynors. Oxford, 1983.

William of Puylaurens. *Chronica magistri Guillelmi de Podio Laurentii*, ed. and trans. J. Duvernoy. Paris, 1976.

Secondary Sources

Andrews, E.D. *The People Called Shakers. A Search for the Perfect Society*, New York, 1963.

Audisio, G. *Les 'Vaudois', Naissance, vie et mort d'une dissidence (XIIe–XVIe siècles)*. Turin, 1989.

Barnes, Fiertz. 'An Unusual Trial under the Inquisition at Fribourg, Switzerland in 1399', *Speculum* 18 (1943), pp. 340–357.

Bell Groage, S. 'Medieval Women Book Owners: Arbiters of Lay Piety and Ambassadors of Culture', in *Women and Power in the Middle Ages*, eds M. Erler and M. Kowaleski. Athens, Ga., 1988, pp. 188–212.

Bellamy, J.G. *The Law of Treason in England in the Later Middle Ages*. Cambridge, 1970.

Benad, M. *Domus und Religion in Montaillou*, Spätmittelalter und Reformation Neue Reihe 1. Tübingen, 1990.

Bernard, P.P. 'Heresy in Fourteenth Century Austria'. *Medievalia et Humanistica* 10 (1956), pp. 50–65.

Biller, P. ' "Curate infirmos": The Medieval Waldensian Practice of Medicine', in *The Church and Healing*, ed. W.J. Sheils. *Studies in Church History* 19 (1982), pp. 55–77.

———, 'Medieval, Waldensian Abhorrence of Killing pre c. 1400', in *The Church and War*, ed. W.J. Sheils. *Studies in Church History* 20 (1983), pp. 126–146.

———, ' "Multum ieiunantes et se castigantes": Medieval Waldensian Asceticism', in *Monks, Hermits and the Ascetic Tradition*, ed. W.J. Sheils. *Studies in Church History* 22 (1985), pp. 215–228.

———, 'The Oral and the Written: The Case of the Alpine Waldensians', *Bulletin for the Society for Renaissance Studies* 4 (1986), pp. 19–28.

———, ' "Thesaurus Absconditus": The Hidden Treasure of the Waldensians', in *The Church and Wealth*, eds W.J. Sheils and D. Wood. *Studies in Church History* 24 (1987), pp. 139–154.

———, 'Les Vaudois dans les territoires de langue allemande vers la fin du XIVe siècle: le regard d'un inquisiteur', *Heresis* 13–14 (1989), pp. 203–228.

———, 'Medieval Waldensian Construction of the Past', *Proceedings of the Huguenot Society* 25 (1989), pp. 39–54.

———, 'Heresy and Literacy: Earlier History of the Theme', in *Heresy and Literacy 1000–1350*, eds P. Biller and A. Hudson. Cambridge, 1994, pp. 1–18.

———, 'The Preaching of the Waldensian Sisters', in *La prédication sur un mode dissident: laics, femmes hérétiques (XIe–XIVe siècles)*, Actes de la 9e

161

session d'histoire mediévale organisée par le C.N.E.C./R. Nelli, 26–30 août 1996, ed. M.B. Kienzle. Carcassonne. Forthcoming.

————, 'What did Happen to the Waldensian Sisters? The Strasbourg Testimony', in *Mélange Giovanni Gonnet*, ed. F. Giacone. Forthcoming.

Bolton, B. ' "Vitae Patrum": A Further Aspect of the Frauenfrage', in *Medieval Women. Dedicated and Presented to Rosalind M.T. Hill*, ed. D. Baker. *Studies in Church History, Subsidia* 1. Oxford, 1978, pp. 77–85.

Boswell, J. *Christianity. Social Tolerance and Homosexuality*. Chicago–London, 1985.

Boureau, A. *La papesse Jeanne*. Paris, 1988.

————, *Le simple corps du roi*. Paris, 1988.

Boyle, O.P., L.E. 'Montaillou Revisited: *Mentalité* and Methodology', in *Pathways to Medieval Peasants*, ed. J.A. Raftis. Papers in Medieval Studies 2. Toronto, 1981, pp. 119–140.

Brenon, A. 'The Voice of the Good Women: An Essay on the Pastoral and Sacerdotal Role of Women in the Cathar Church', in *Women Preachers and Prophets Through Two Millennia of Christianity*, eds B.M. Kienzle and P.J. Walker. Berkeley, 1998, pp. 114–133.

Brissaud, Y.B. 'L'infanticide à la fin du moyen age: Ses motivations psychologiques et sa repression', *Revue historique de droit français et étranger* 50 (1972), pp. 229–256.

Browe, P., S.J. *Beiträge zur Sexualethik des Mittelalters*. Breslau, 1932.

Cohen, E. 'Symbols of Culpability and the Universal Language of Justice: The Ritual of Public Executions in Late Medival Europe', *History of European Ideas* 11 (1989), pp. 407–416.

————, *The Crossroads of Justice. Law and Culture in Late Medieval France*. Leiden, 1993.

Comba, E. *History of the Waldenses of Italy*, trans. T. Comba. London, 1889.

Dalarum, J. 'The Clerical Gaze', in *A History of Women in the West*, ed. Ch. Klapisch Zuber. London, 1992, 15–42.

Desroche, H. *The American Shakers. From Neo-Christianity to Presocialism*, trans. J.K. Savacool. Amherst, Mass., 1971.

Dondaine, O.P., A. 'Le manuel de l'inquisiteur (1230–1330)', *Archivum Fratrum Praedicatorum* 17 (1947), pp. 85–194.

————, 'Durand de Huesca et la polémique anti-cathare', *Archivum Fratrum Praedicatorum* 29 (1959), pp. 228–276.

————, 'Le registre de l'inquisition de Jacques Fournier à propos d'une edition récente: Examen critique de l'édition donnée par Jean Duvernoy', *Revue d'histoire des religions* 178 (1970), pp. 49–56.

Dossat, Y. *Les crises de l'inquisition toulousaine au XIIIe siècle (1233–1273)*. Bordeaux, 1959.

————, 'Les Vaudois méridionaux d'après les documents de l'inquisition', in *Vaudois languedociens et Pauvres Catholiques, Cahiers de Fanjeaux* 2 (1967), pp. 207–226.

Droge, A.J. and Tabor, J.D. *A Noble Death. Suicide and Martyrdom among Christians and Jews in Antiquity.* San Francisco, 1992.

Dronke, P. *Women Writers of the Middle Ages. A Critical Study of Texts from Perpetua (d. 1230) to Marguerite Porete (d. 1310).* Cambridge, 1985.

Duvernoy, J. 'La noblesse du comté de Foix au début du XIVe siècle', in *Pays de l'Ariège, archéologie – histoire – géographie*, Actes du XVIe congrès de la féderation des sociétés académiques et savantes Languedoc– Pyrenées–Gascogne. Auch, 1961, pp. 123–140.

————, *L'inquisition à Pamiers.* Toulouse, 1966.

————, *Le Catharisme: la religion des Cathares.* Toulouse, 1976.

————, 'À l'époque l'église ne poursuivait pas les Vaudois', in *I Valdesi e l'Europa*, Collana della società di studi Valdesi 9. Torre Pellice, 1982, pp. 27–38.

Espinas, G. *La vie urbaine de Douai au moyen âge.* Paris, 1913.

Finucane, R. *Miracles and Pilgrims. Popular Beliefs in Medieval England.* London, 1977.

Foucault, M. 'Prison Talk', M. Foucault, *Power and Knowledge. Selected Interviews and Other Writings*, ed. C. Gordon, trans. C. Gordon and others. New York, 1980.

Gessler, J. ' "Mulier suspenda": à délit égal peine differente?', *Revue belge de philologie et d'histoire* 18 (1939), pp. 974–988.

Gilmont, J.P. 'Les Vaudois des Alpes: mythes et réalités', *Revue d'histoire ecclésiastique* 83 (1988), pp. 69–89.

Given, J.B. *Society and Homicide in 13th century England.* Stanford, 1977.

————, 'Social Stress, Social Strain and the Inquisitors of Medieval Languedoc', in *Christendom and its discontents. Exclusion, Persecution and Rebellion 1000–1500*, eds S.L. Waugh and P.D. Diehl. Cambridge, 1996, pp. 67–85.

Gonnet, G. 'Waldensia', *Revue d'histoire et de philosophie religieuses* 33 (1953), pp. 204–254.

————, *Le confessioni di fede Valdesi prima della Riforma.* Turin, 1967.

————, 'I primi Valdesi erano veramente eretici?', *Bollettino della società di studi Valdesi* 122 (1968), pp. 7–17.

————, 'La femme dans les mouvements paupéro-évangeliques du bas moyen âge (notamment chez les Vaudois)', *Heresis* 22 (1994), pp. 25–41.

Gonnet, G. and Molnar, A. *Les Vaudois au moyen âge.* Turin, 1974.

Gontier, N. *Délinquance, justice et société dans le Lyonnais médiéval*. Paris, 1993.

Green, M. 'Documenting Medieval Women's Medical Practice', in *Practical Medicine from Salerno to the Black Death*, eds L. Garcia-Ballester and others. Cambridge, 1944, pp. 322–352.

Gregory, B.S. *Salvation at the Stake. Christian Martyrdom in Early Modern Europe*. Cambridge Mass., 1999.

Grundmann, H. *Religiöse Bewegungen im Mittelalter*. Berlin, 1935. Reprint: Hildesheim, 1961.

Hamilton, B. *The Medieval Inquisition*. London, 1981.

Hasenohr, G. 'Religious Reading among the Laity in France in the Fifteenth Century', in *Heresy and Literacy 1000–1350*, eds P. Biller and A. Hudson. Cambridge, 1994, pp. 205–221.

Haskins, Ch.H. *Studies in Medieval Culture*. New York, 1929. Reprint: 1965.

Hentsch, A. *De la littérature didactique du moyen âge s'adressant spécialement aux femmes*. Cahor, 1903. Reprint: Geneva, 1979.

Holdsworth, W.S. *A History of English Law*. London, 1909, 2 Vols.

Kaelber, L. *Schools of Asceticism. Ideology and Organization in Medieval Religious Communities*. University Park, Pa., 1998.

Karant-Nunn, S.C. *The Reformation of Ritual*. London–New York, 1997.

Kieckhefer, R. *Repression of Heresy in Medieval Germany*. Philadelphia, 1979.

Karras, R.M. *Prostitution and Sexuality in Medieval England*. New York–Oxford, 1995.

Kienzle, B.M. 'The Prostitute-Preacher: Patterns of Polemic against Medieval Waldensian Women Preachers', in *Women Preachers and Prophets Through Two Millennia of Christianity*, eds B.M. Kienzle and P.J. Walker. Berkeley, 1998, pp. 99–113.

Koch, G. *Frauenfrage und Ketzertum im Mittelalter*. Berlin, 1962.

Lambert, M. *Medieval Heresy. Popular Movements from the Gregorian Reform to the Reformation*. Oxford, 1992.

Lamdan, R. *A Separate People. Jewish Women in Palestine, Syria and Egypt in the Sixteenth Century*. Tel-Aviv, 1996 (written in Hebrew).

Lea, H.Ch. *A History of the Inquisition of the Middle Ages*. New York, 1906. 3 Vols.

Lemarignier, J.F., Gaudemet, J. and Mollat, G. *Institutions ecclésiastiques*, in *Histoire des institutions françaises au moyen âge*, eds F. Lot and R. Fawtier, Vol. 3. Paris, 1962.

Lerere, S. ' "Represtyd now yower syght": The Culture of Spectatorship in Late Fifteenth Century England', in *Bodies and Disciplines. Intersec-*

tions of Literature in Fifteenth Century England, ed. B.A. Hanawalt and D. Wallace. Minneapolis–London, 1996, pp. 29–62.

Le Roy Ladurie, E. Montaillou. Village occitan de 1294 à 1324. Paris, 1975.

Lorcen, M.Th. Vivre et mourir en Lyonnais à la fin du Moyen Age. Paris 1981.

Manselli, R. 'Bernard Gui face aux Spirituels et aux Apostoliques', in Bernard Gui et son monde. Cahiers de Fanjeaux 16 (1961), pp. 265–278.

McLaughlin, M.M. 'Peter Abelard and the Dignity of Women: Twelfth Century Feminism in Theory and Practice', in Pierre Abelard – Pierre le Venerable, eds R. Louis and J. Jolivet. Colloques Internationaux du CNRS, No. 546, Paris, 1975.

McMurray Gibson, G. 'Blessing from the Sun and Moon', in Bodies and Disciplines: Intersections of Literature and History in 15th Century England, eds B.A. Hanawalt and D. Wallace. Minneapolis–London, 1996, pp. 139–154.

Melcher, M.F. The Shaker Adventure. New York, 1940; Reprint, 1975.

Merlo, G.G. Eretici e inquisitori nella società piemontese del trecento. Turin, 1977.

———, 'Sul Valdismo "colto" tra il XIII e il XIV secolo', in I Valdesi e l'Europa, Collana della società di studi Valdesi 9. Torre Pellice, 1982, pp. 69–98.

———, 'Pietro di Verona – S. Pietro martire: Difficoltà e proposte per lo studio di un inquisitore beatificato', in Culto dei santi, istituzioni e classi sociali in età preindustriale, eds S.B. Gajano and L. Sebastiani. Rome, 1984, pp. 471–488.

———, Eretici e eresi medievali. Bologna, 1989.

———, 'Sulle "Misere donnicciuole" che predicavano', in Identità Valdiesi nella storia e nella storiografia, Valdesi e Valdismi medievali 2. Turin, 1991, pp. 93–112.

Molnar, A. 'Les Vaudois et l'Unité des Frères tchèques', Bollettino della società di studi Valdesi 18 (1965), pp. 3–16.

———, 'Autour des polèmiques anti-vaudoises du début du XVI siècle', in I Valdesi e l'Europa, Collana della società di studi Valdesi 9. Torre Pellice, 1982, pp. 116–136.

Mooney, C.M. Gendered Voices. Medieval Saints and their Interpreters. Philadelphia, 1999.

Moore, R.I. The Formation of a Persecuting Society. Oxford, 1987.

Moorman, J. The Franciscan Order from its Origins to the Year 1517. Oxford, 1968.

Mundy, J. Men and Women at Toulouse in the Age of the Cathars. Toronto, 1990.

Newman, B. *From Virile Woman to Woman Christ. Studies in Medieval Religion and Literature.* Philadelphia, 1995.

Origo, I. *The Merchant of Prato. Francesco di Marco Datini.* Harmondsworth, 1963.

Otis, L.L. *Prostitution in Medieval Society. The History of an Urban Institution in Languedoc.* Chicago, 1985.

Paravy, P. *De la chrétienté romaine à la Réforme en Dauphiné.* Rome, 1993. 2 Vols.

——, 'Waldensians in the Dauphiné (1400–1530): from Dissidence in Texts to Dissidence in Practice', in *Heresy and Literacy 1000–1350*, eds P. Biller and A. Hudson. Cambridge, 1994, pp. 160–175.

Parsons, T. 'On the Concept of Influence', *Public Opinion Quarterly* 27 (1963), pp. 37–62.

Patschovsky, A. 'The Literacy of Waldensianism from Valdes to c. 1400', in *Heresy and Literacy 1000–1350*, eds P. Biller and A. Hudson. Cambridge, 1994, pp. 112–136.

Peters, E. *Inquisition.* New York, 1988.

Praem, A.E. 'Les soeurs dan l'ordre de Prémontré', *Analecta Praemonstratensia* 5 (1929), pp. 5–26.

Reeves, M. *The Influence of Prophecy in the Later Middle Ages.* Oxford, 1969.

Rosaldo, R. 'From the Door of his Tent: The Fieldworker and the Inquisitor', in *Writing Culture. The Poetics and Politics of Ethnography*, eds J. Clifford and G.E. Marcus. Berkeley, 1984, pp. 77–97.

Rouse, M.A. and Rouse, R.H. 'The Schools and the Waldensians: A New Work by Durand of Huesca', in *Christendom and its Discontents. Exclusion, Persecution and Rebellion 1000–1500*, eds S.L. Waugh and P.D. Diehl. Cambridge, 1996, pp. 86–111.

Rubin, M. *Corpus Christi. The Eucharist in Late Medieval Culture.* Cambridge, 1991.

Ruether Radford, R. 'Prophets and Humanists: Types of Religious Feminism in Stuart England', *Journal of Religion* 70 (1990), pp. 1–18.

Scholem, G. *Elements of the Kabbalah and its Symbolism.* Jerusalem, 1976 (Hebrew).

Segl, P. *Ketzer in Österreich. Untersuchungen über Häresie und Inquisition in Herzogtum Österreich im 13 und beginnen den 14 Jahrhundert.* Paderborn, 1984.

Selge, K.V. *Die Ersten Waldenser.* Berlin, 1967. 2 Vols.

Shahar, S. *Childhood in the Middle Ages.* London, 1990.

Stock, B. *The Implications of Literacy. Written Language and Models of Interpretation in the Eleventh and Twelfth Centuries.* Princeton, 1983.

Strohm, P. ' "A Revelle!": Chronicle Evidence and the Rebel Voice', in *Hochon's Arrow*. Princeton, 1992, pp. 33–56.

Sunder Rajan, R. *Real and Imagined Women. Gender, Culture and Post Colonialism*. London–New York, 1993.

Tanon, L. *Histoire de la justice des anciennes églises et communautés monastiques de Paris*. Paris, 1883.

Thickstun, Olofson M. 'This Was a Woman that Taught: Feminist Scriptural Exegesis in the Seventeenth Century', *Studies in Eighteenth Century Culture* 21, eds P.B. Craddock and C.H. Hay. East Lansing, Mich., 1991, pp. 149–158.

Thomson, J.A.F. *The Later Lollards 1414–1520*. Oxford, 1965.

Thouzellier, Ch. *Catharisme et Valdéisme en Languedoc à la fin du XIIe et au début du XIIIe siècles*. Louvain–Paris, 1969.

———, 'Considerations sur les origines du Valdéisme', in *I Valdesi e l'Europa*, Collana de la società di studi Valdesi 9. Torre Pellice, 1982, pp. 3–23.

Treesh, S.K. 'The Waldensian Recourse to Violence', *Church History* 55 (1986), pp. 294–306.

Vauchez, A. *La sainteté en occident au derniers siècles du moyen-âge d'après les procès de canonisation et les documents hagiographiques*. Rome, 1988.

Vicaire, M.H. 'Rencontre à Pamiers: Des courants Vaudois et Dominicains (1207)', in *Vaudois languedociens et Pauvre Catholiques. Cahiers de Fanjeaux* 2 (1967), pp. 165–194.

Vidal, J.M. 'Menet de Robécourt commissaire de l'Inquisition de Carcassonne (1320–1340)', *Le Moyen Age* 16 (1903), pp. 425–449.

———, *Le tribunal de l'inquisition de Pamiers*. Toulouse, 1906.

———, *Histoire des évêques de Pamiers 2. Quatorzième et quinzième siècles (1312–1467)*, Castillon (Ariège), 1932.

Viollet, P. *Le droit du XIIIe siècle dans les coutumiers de Touraine-Anjou*. Paris, 1881.

Walker Bynum, C. *Jesus as Mother. Studies in the Spirituality of the Middle Ages*. Berkeley, 1982.

———, 'The Body of Christ in the Later Middle Ages: A Reply to Leo Steinberg', in *Fragmentation and Redemption. Essays on Gender and the Human Body in Medieval Religion*. New York, 1991, pp. 79–117.

———, 'Material Continuity, Personal Survival and the Resurrection of the Body: A Scholastic Discussion in its Medieval and Modern Contexts', in *Fragmentation and Redemption. Essays on Gender and the Human Body in medieval Religion*. New York, 1991.

Watts, G.B. *The Waldenses in the New World*. Durhan, N.C., 1941.

Weinshtein, D. and Bell, R. *Saints and Society. The Two Worlds of Christendom 1000–1700.* Chicago, 1981.

Wiesner, M. 'Luther and Women: The Death of Two Marys', in *Disciplines of Faith. Studies in Religion, Politics and Patriarchy*, eds Obelkevich, L. Roper and R. Samuel. London, 1987, pp. 295–308.

Williams, G.W. *The Sanctity of Life and the Criminal Law.* New York, 1957.

Wilson, A. 'The Ceremony of Child-Birth and its Interpretation', in *Women as Mothers in Pre-Industrial England, Essays in Memory of Dorothy McLaren*, ed. V. Fields. London, 1990, pp. 68–107.

Wolf, E.R. 'Society and Symbols in Latin Europe and in Islamic Near East: Some Comparisons', *Anthropological Quarterly* 42 (1969), pp. 287–301.

Index

abbesses, role 44, 61, 97, 99
Abelard, Pierre, *Sermo XIII* 43–4
absolution
  by bishop 134
  by Brothers 13, 19
  by God alone 86
  by laity 10
  by majoral 12, 92, 144, 151
  by priest 104, 133, 151–2
  see also confession
Acts of the Christian Martyrs 124 n.28
Adalbert, Barthelemy (notary) 137 &
  n.10
Agnes *see* Francou, Agnes
Alain of Lille, *De fide catholica* 9 n.16,
  18 n.38, 38, 60 n.43
Albi, Council (1254) 81
Alexander III, Pope 2, 39
Allemans castle 67, 133, 135, 137, 138,
  141, 145, 149, 151, 153–5
alms-giving
  as atonement viii, 6
  by Believers 3 n.5, 8, 12, 19–20, 38,
  47
Alsace, and Poor of Lyons 4
Andrews, E.D. 34 n.11
Anonymous of Lyons, *Chronicon
  universale anonymi Laudunensis*
  39–40
Anonymous of Passau
  and administration of sacraments
    9–10, 47–8
  and confession 13–14, 48
  and persecution of Waldensians
    21–2, 22 n.50
  and pregnant women 71
  and role of women 9, 17, 47–8

and social status of Waldensians 5,
  6 n.9
and teaching 17, 58
and veneration of saints 36, 85
  n.48
Anselm of Alessandria, *Tractatus de
  hereticis* 9 n.15, 13 n.24, 47, 48 n.6,
  111
Apostles, Poor of Lyons as heirs to
  6–7, 10, 22
Aquinas, St Thomas, *Summa theologiae*
  120, 124
Ardizzo, bishop of Plaisance 39, 62–3
Arles, and Poor of Lyons 82–4, 86–7,
  140–4, 148
Arles, Council (314) 8 n.14
Arnaud de Carla (Inquisitor) 137,
  141, 145, 149, 151, 153–4
artisans, and support for Poor of
  Lyons 5, 65, 82–3
asceticism 122
  of Brothers 11, 24–5 n.54
  of Shakers 31
Astrac region xi n.12
Aubri of Trois-Fontaines 1 n.2
Audiberti, Guillaume 153, 155
Audisio, G. xi–xii n.13, 23–4 n.52, 37
  n.14, 60, 83 n.44
Augustine of Hippo
  De baptismo contra Donatistas 8 n.14
  and Donatism 121–2
  and sexuality 33
Austatz, Guillaume, trial ix–x
Austria, and Poor of Lyons 4, 10–11
  n.19, 22 n.50, 24–5 n.54, 37, 70,
  106
authority, rejection 11